ON TRIAL FOR MU

Douglas Wynn's interest in criminology and true crime began when his first wife became a magistrate in Grimsby in 1975. He wrote his first book, *Settings for Slaughter*, on his retirement (published 1988) and has since written two further books, *Blind Justice* (1990) and *The Limits of Detection* (1992). He lives in Lincolnshire with his second wife.

ON TRIAL
FOR MURDER

Over 200 of the most dramatic
trials of the 20th century

DOUGLAS WYNN

PAN BOOKS

First published 1996 by Pan Books

This edition published 2003 by Pan Books
an imprint of Pan Macmillan Ltd
Pan Macmillan, 20 New Wharf Road, London N1 9RR
Basingstoke and Oxford
Associated companies throughout the world
www.panmacmillan.com

ISBN 0 330 43748 8

Copyright © Douglas Wynn

The right of Douglas Wynn to be identified as the
author of this work has been asserted by him in accordance with
the Copyright, Designs and Patents Act 1988.

All rights reserved. No part of this publication may be
reproduced, stored in or introduced into a retrieval system, or
transmitted, in any form, or by any means (electronic, mechanical,
photocopying, recording or otherwise) without the prior written
permission of the publisher. Any person who does any unauthorized
act in relation to this publication may be liable to criminal
prosecution and civil claims for damages.

9 8 7 6 5 4 3 2 1

A CIP catalogue record for this book is available from
the British Library.

Printed and bound in Great Britain by
Mackays of Chatham Ltd, Chatham, Kent

This book is sold subject to the condition that it shall not,
by way of trade or otherwise, be lent, re-sold, hired out,
or otherwise circulated without the publisher's prior consent
in any form of binding or cover other than that in which it is
published and without a similar condition including this
condition being imposed on the subsequent purchaser.

ACKNOWLEDGEMENTS

I should like to thank my wife Rosemary for her patience and encouragement, Julian Alexander of Jacintha Alexander Associates for his useful advice and Elizabeth Murray and Marie Elmer for help with the research.

INTRODUCTION

Murder trials are fascinating. The drama of the courtroom, the conflict of the evidence, the clash of the lawyers, the personalities of the witnesses; all these make for stories which are unsurpassed in their interest and excitement. And before 1965, when capital punishment was abolished in this country, the verdict could literally be a matter of life or death to the accused, as it still is in some states of America and other parts of the world.

In this book I have tried to collect together the very best murder trials of the twentieth century. As so many of the older ones are well known I have concentrated on the newer and less familiar ones, while leaving sufficient of the others for those who have not met them before. And where the story of the murder itself is interesting I have included this as well. It would in any case have been brought out in the trial, usually in the presentation of the prosecution case.

Because of the large number of trials involved – there are over two hundred in this book – the space allotted to each is limited. I have therefore made the main stories the newer and less familiar trials and arranged them in alphabetical order of the accused person or persons. The shorter entries I have kept for the older and more familiar cases and related each one to the longer entry it follows. For those who wish to follow up any of the cases or study the trials in more detail I have included a bibliography.

In the Anglo-Saxon system of court procedure, the one used in the United Kingdom, the United States of America and indeed in most of the English-speaking world, there are usually two sets of lawyers, the prosecution team and that representing the accused, the 'defence'. They present their own case and question their own witnesses, but are allowed to cross-examine each other's witnesses. The judge, and occasionally there may be more than one, sits usually with a jury, though in some countries he may sit alone or with assessors. He reviews the case for the jury and advises them on the law, but rarely takes a major part in the trial.

The European system is somewhat different. The presiding judge often does most of the questioning of witnesses, and lawyers who represent the relatives of the victim may also be heard in court in addition to the prosecution and defence counsels. And since the rules of evidence are somewhat looser than in the Anglo-Saxon system it can make for a more spectacular display of histrionics.

In this country the mandatory sentence for murder is life imprisonment. The trial judge fills out a confidential form saying how long he thinks the prisoner should serve. This is passed on to the Lord Chief Justice who adds his recommendations and it then goes to the Home Secretary who makes the final decision. The prisoner is told and since June 1993 can appeal against it, but it isn't made public. Occasionally the trial judge may make public his recommendation, as happened in the Kray case etc, but he is not obliged to do so. On average a convicted murderer serves from twelve to fourteen years.

Early in 1995 it was reported in the newspapers that some fifteen of Britain's worst killers, including Myra Hindley, Donald Neilson, Dennis Nilsen, Archibald Hall, John Duffy and Ronald Barton, have been told by the Home Office that they will have to serve life literally, the so-called 'whole-life tariff'. Ian Brady, who was convicted with Myra Hindley, is not on the list, but he has said repeatedly that he does not want to be released.

In other countries different systems operate and what I have tried to do in the text is to point out anything which differs substantially from the British.

But whatever the sentencing or the trial system, drama is never far away as you'll see in this collection of famous and infamous twentieth-century murder trials.

Dr John Bodkin Adams When Dr Bodkin Adams went for trial at the Old Bailey in March 1957, it was already the legal sensation of the decade. The bombshell had been dropped the previous July when newspaper headlines screamed words like: 'Eastbourne Rich Widow Murder Probe' and 'Six Women in Murder Riddle'. Later there appeared: 'Yard Probe Mass Poisonings' and '400 wills investigated'.

The committal proceedings before magistrates in Eastbourne had taken place in January 1957. Crown Counsel Melford Stevenson QC had described the pattern of the alleged murders. A wealthy patient would be induced to leave the doctor money or gifts in a will, and increasing amounts of morphine, heroin or barbiturates or all three would be prescribed until a last fatal dose was given. He quoted three cases as examples: Edith Alice Morrell, who had died six years before and left the doctor a chest of Georgian silver and a Rolls-Royce, and Mr and Mrs Hullett, who had died the previous year leaving the doctor a cheque for £1,000 and another Rolls-Royce.

At the trial the prosecution was led by no less a figure than the Attorney-General, Sir Reginald Manningham-Buller. The defence was in the hands of a relatively unknown barrister, Geoffrey Lawrence QC, in his first murder trial, and the judge was Lord Justice Patrick Devlin.

Dr Adams was charged only with the murder of Mrs Morrell. Detective Superintendent Herbert Hannam of Scotland Yard gave evidence that Dr Adams had stated on the official form for the cremation of Mrs Morrell that he had no pecuniary interest in the death of the deceased, which was proven not to be true. When questioned about it the doctor said, 'Oh that was not done wickedly. God knows it wasn't.'

The superintendent also reported that the doctor had remarked, 'Easing the passing of a dying person is not all that wicked. She wanted to die – that cannot be murder.' When he was arrested the doctor said, 'I do not think you can prove it was murder – she was dying in any event.'

Dr Douthwaite, a Harley Street specialist, had no doubt at all that Dr Adams's regime of morphine and heroin was deadly, and that it had been given with the full intention of terminating her life.

But the other doctor called by the prosecution was not so certain and during cross-examination by Geoffrey Lawrence revealed that he was reluctant to say that Dr Adams had killed his patient by giving those drugs.

Defence counsel was also able to obtain from Mrs Morrell's solicitor the information that just before she died, in a fit of pique because Dr Adams had gone away on holiday, the irascible old lady had cut him out of her will entirely. He had only received the presents after she had died through her son's generosity.

But Lawrence's real fireworks were released during his cross-examination of the three nurses who had been in round-the-clock attendance on Mrs Morrell. He suddenly produced the nursing record books for the whole of the lady's illness and went through them page by page showing that the entries which the nurses had themselves made departed radically from the testimony they were now giving six years after the events occurred. On one day near her death, for example, when the nurses reported she was semi-conscious, the records showed she ate partridge, celery, pudding and had a brandy and soda.

During the judge's summing up he said that he considered the defence case a strong one. The jury took only three-quarters of an hour to find the doctor not guilty.

But did he get away with it? In Lord Devlin's book on the case, which he published in 1985, he suggests that Dr Bodkin Adams might have been a mercy-killer. A compassionate, but a greedy man, prepared to 'ease the passing' for a price.

Dr Alice Wynekoop was a respected Chicago physician. A sixty-two-year-old widow, she lived with her son and his wife, Rheta. When Rheta was found dead on the doctor's operating table, shot through the breast, Dr Wynekoop confessed to the murder. At her trial in February 1934, she retracted her confession, claiming it had been made under duress. The prosecution theory was that she killed her daughter-in-law for the insurance. In spite of her reputation and age the jury found her guilty and she was sentenced to twenty-five years imprisonment.

Beverly Allitt There were no eye witnesses, no fingerprints and no bloodstains. In fact there was no direct evidence at all linking twenty-four-year-old Nurse Beverly Allitt with the crimes. Yet four young children had been murdered on the children's ward at Grantham Hospital in Lincolnshire, and there had been unsuccessful attempts to kill others.

It began when seven-week-old Liam Taylor was taken to ward four suffering from a bad cold on Thursday 21 February, 1991. He first stopped breathing soon after admission when Allitt was feeding him and had a further respiratory arrest a day later. The emergency team of doctors and nurses brought him back to life each time, but his brain was severely damaged due to periods without oxygen, and he subsequently died in his mother's arms.

In the following thirteen weeks three more children died and another eight suffered respiratory arrest, but survived, mainly it appeared because when they were resuscitated they were taken to the Queens Medical Centre in Nottingham. Evidence of how the children died was difficult to obtain because the medical staff at first did not realize that deliberate attacks were being made on babies. It was later found that some had been injected with massive doses of insulin. Others had abnormally high levels of potassium in their tissues. There were indications that at least one child had had air injected into his veins and another had been squeezed until his small ribs fractured.

The common factor was the presence of Beverly Allitt, the only person alone with the children when the collapses occurred. According to psychiatrist Professor Meadow of Leeds University, she showed the classic symptoms of Munchausen Syndrome by Proxy, where sufferers seek attention by pretending to be ill, and sometimes actually make themselves ill to achieve this end. Some then progress to the stage of making other people ill, the 'by Proxy' condition.

Allitt had struggled through a State Enrolled Nursing course, having to work extra weeks at the end of it because she had taken so much time off due to illness. She had applied for positions as a nurse in every other department at Grantham Hospital and been rejected as unsatisfactory, but obtained a job in the children's ward because they were chronically short of staff. The first attack was three days after she began work as an SEN.

But the psychiatric reports were ruled inadmissible by Mr Justice Latham when the trial opened at Nottingham Crown Court in February 1993. He felt that they could suggest to the jury that she was insane and they might convict her on that basis, instead of on the weight of the other evidence, and this in his opinion would be unfair to her. The prosecution, in the hands of John Goldring QC, thus had to present a quantity of circumstantial evidence to convince the jury.

Charts were produced showing Nurse Allitt's movements. Other nurses testified that she was always present when the arrests occurred and doctors described the condition of the patients and their reasons for saying the crises were manufactured by criminal acts. Some of the children's parents gave evidence of their babies' last few minutes. It was harrowing for all concerned.

James Hunt QC for the defence had to attack the credibility of the medical staff and convince the jury that the breakdowns were all due to natural causes; or that, if there had been any attacks on children on ward four, it wasn't Beverly Allitt who made them.

The sheer weight of evidence told against her. The jury, however, took more than two days to reach their verdicts. Of the eight charges of attempted murder the jury found her guilty of only three, but on the eight counts of grievous bodily harm, against the same eight children, she was found guilty on six. Of the four murder charges she was found guilty on every one.

She was given thirteen life sentences and the judge said: 'There is very little chance of your ever being released.'

When Nurse Genene Jones worked the night shift at a San Antonio, Texas, hospital in 1981 more than twelve babies inexplicably died. She earned the title of 'Death Nurse', but the hospital authorities, unwilling to face reality, simply removed her from the staff. She moved to a private pediatric clinic in Kerrville, Texas, and in September 1982 a fifteen-month-old baby girl died after being injected with a powerful muscle relaxer. Six other children at the clinic, it was shown, had suffered similar attacks. In February 1984, Jones was convicted of murder and sentenced to ninety-nine years in prison.

Herbert Rowse Armstrong The Attorney General was Sir Ernest Pollock KC, a tall military-looking figure. Opposing him for the defence was the more rotund Sir Henry Curtis Bennett KC, with his prominent double chin. The judge was small, almost wizened. Mr Justice Darling was seventy-three and on his last circuit prior to retirement.

On that wintry morning in April 1922 at the Hereford Assizes, the man whose fate they had come together to decide was Herbert Armstrong, a solicitor from the nearby town of Hay. A small man who weighed only seven stones, he liked to be called

'Major' Armstrong. He was charged with poisoning his wife Katherine and attempting to poison a fellow solicitor, Oswald Martin.

Armstrong had been married since 1907. His wife was cultured and played the piano well, but she had a very dominating personality. Her husband could smoke in only one room in the house, was not allowed wine, even when they went out to dinner, and on one occasion she interrupted a tennis match he was playing in to tell him it was time to go home as it was his bath night.

During the First World War, Armstrong, who had been a volunteer and had joined the Territorial Army, reached the rank of major. Although he never served overseas, being involved in various depot duties in England, it broadened his horizons and gave him a taste of a freer life. When the war ended his wife's strict regime must have been even more irksome.

Early in August 1920, Katherine Armstrong began to suffer bilious attacks and severe tremors of the hands, which prevented her playing the piano. She became depressed and anxious and on 22 August the local doctor took her to the Barnwood Private Asylum in Gloucester. There she made considerable improvement and was allowed home again in January 1921. But she then deteriorated rapidly, suffering vomiting and diarrhoea, and died on 22 February.

The major revelled in his new-found freedom, but his business suffered as a consequence. In the autumn of that year he was in dispute with a rival solicitor, Oswald Martin, who was pressing him for the return of a deposit on a property Armstrong was conveyancing but had failed to proceed to completion. The major invited Martin to tea and handed him a scone with the words: 'Excuse fingers'. Soon after he reached home Martin had severe stomach pains, vomiting and diarrhoea. Luckily his father-in-law, John Davies, the local chemist, recognized the symptoms of arsenic poisoning and tests confirmed this. Davies also remembered that Armstrong had bought a substantial quantity of the poison – a quarter of a pound – the previous January, just before his wife died.

Representations were made to the Home Office and eventually Scotland Yard took charge of the case. Major Armstrong was arrested on the last day of 1921 and his wife's body exhumed in the presence of Dr Bernard Spilsbury. John Webster, senior Home Office analyst, afterwards said that the body contained the largest amount of arsenic he had ever found in any case of arsenic poisoning.

When Armstrong was arrested a small packet containing a lethal dose of the poison was found in his pocket.

At the trial, Sir Ernest Pollock claimed that the solicitor had the means, the opportunity – he was often alone with his wife when she was ill in bed and gave her food himself – and the motive to poison his wife.

Sir Henry Curtis Bennett countered with the theory that Mrs Armstrong might have taken the poison herself.

But the major's case received a severe blow when he was asked, during cross-examination by the Attorney General and also, unusually, by the judge himself, to explain why he had bought such a large quantity of arsenic and carried a packet of it around with him. His explanation that it was for killing weeds sounded very unsatisfactory. The ten farmers on the twelve-man jury could not believe he would be buying the poison for this purpose in January and they took less than forty-five minutes to convict him of murder. His appeal was dismissed and he was hanged at Gloucester prison on 31 May 1922.

When Harold Greenwood's wife died on 16 June 1919, having been taken ill after Sunday lunch the previous day, death was certified as being due to heart disease. But Greenwood, a solicitor in Llanelly, was unpopular in the town and when he married again four months after his wife's death the rumours became too insistent to ignore. Mrs Greenwood's body was exhumed and found to contain arsenic. The inquest verdict was that Greenwood had poisoned his wife, and he was sent for trial. The prosecution contended that the poison had been in a bottle of Burgundy drunk at the meal, but when Greenwood's daughter declared that she too had drunk from the bottle, the prosecution case collapsed. Greenwood was acquitted and since the case was widely reported Major Armstrong may have felt he could try the same thing.

John Armstrong   Terence John Armstrong, who was not yet six months old, died on 22 July 1955. His father, John Armstrong, was twenty-five and a sick-berth attendant in the navy, stationed at the Royal Naval Hospital in Gosport. That day he had been home to lunch at the bungalow he and his wife Janet rented in Perth Road, Gosport. He afterwards said that the child, who had been ill for twenty-four hours or so, was impossible to wake and when he got back to work he phoned their family doctor.

The doctor found the child dead. Having no idea why the little boy had died so suddenly he refused to give a death certificate.

'Will there have to be an inquest?' asked Janet Armstrong, who was just nineteen years old.

There was indeed. And a post mortem carried out by Dr Harold Miller, a Portsmouth pathologist, revealed traces of some red material in the child's throat.

Sergeant Bulley, the coroner's officer, interviewed John and Janet Armstrong and learned that there was a *daphne mezereum* bush in the back garden, full of poisonous red berries. The Armstrongs' other child, Pamela, aged three, had been taught to share her sweets with her brother and might easily have given him some berries.

But further examination showed that the red material was not from berry skins, and subsequent analysis of the child's stomach contents by Scotland Yard's forensic laboratory proved that the red material was from Seconal capsules. Four or five had been ingested, easily enough to kill a small child.

The Armstrongs swore they had never had the drug in their home and the police could not find any in the house or in John's locker at the hospital. But it was discovered that in February 1955, five months before the child died, fifty pink Seconal capsules had been stolen from a poison cupboard at the Royal Naval Hospital where Armstrong had been working at the time. Still the pair stuck to their story and there was not enough evidence to charge them with murder.

The Armstrong marriage, however, was in trouble. A year after the death of little Terence, Janet applied to the Gosport magistrates for a separation order and for maintenance on the grounds of her husband's cruelty. It was refused and she left the court bitter and in tears. A policeman approached her and asked, 'Is there anything you'd like to tell the police?'

Janet made a statement saying that there had been Seconal in the bungalow. Her husband had been taking it, but he had told her to get rid of the remaining capsules after the baby had died, and not to mention it to the police. Since she also had access to the poison, both were charged with murder.

Their trial began in the ancient castle of Winchester in December 1956. Sir Reginald Manningham-Buller prosecuted and John was defended by Malcolm Wright QC, while Janet's defence was in the hands of Norman Skelhorn QC.

Each of the Armstrongs accused the other. John admitted having Seconal capsules but said his wife told him she had disposed of them before the baby died. She denied this and claimed that he had had the opportunity to go into the baby's room while she was in the kitchen that lunchtime, and that the baby got worse after he had left.

Mr Justice Pilcher pointed out to the jury that they did not have to give the same verdict for each of the defendants. The jury of nine men and three women took forty-three minutes to find John guilty and to acquit Janet.

He was sentenced to death, but later reprieved and given a life sentence.

A month later, Janet admitted to a Sunday newspaper that at that lunchtime she had given her baby a capsule of Seconal – to make him sleep! She confessed this in the knowledge that no one tried for and acquitted of a crime can be tried for it again.

Graham Backhouse The story that Mr James Black QC, prosecuting counsel, told the jury when the trial opened on Monday 28 January, 1985, at Bristol Crown Court, could well have come from the pages of a crime novel. The ingredients were all there: a picturesque village in the Cotswolds, rumours of sex and seduction, the severed head of a ram stuck on a fencepost with a crudely scrawled message on a scrap of paper: 'You Next!', a car bomb and a callous murder. In addition the accused stood in the dock with a dreadful scar running down his face. Yet the underlying motive was as mundane as it's possible to get – money.

According to Mr Black, Graham Backhouse, erstwhile ladies' hairdresser, had inherited his father's prosperous cattle farm at Horton, near Chipping Sodbury. He had married Margaret ten years before and had two children. But the farmer, who had switched to arable farming, had suffered two bad harvests and was in deep financial trouble, owing £60,000 in bank overdrafts and income tax. He tried writing a sexy novel to make some money but could not find a publisher, so he turned his devious mind to a more practical method of getting out of his financial difficulties.

At the beginning of 1984 Backhouse informed the police that he had received an anonymous letter threatening his life. Then, on 30 March, his herdsman found the severed head of a ram with its baleful message. The farmer told the police, in confidence, that he suspected it was because he was known in the village as a 'ram' and he supposed that a cuckolded husband was seeking revenge.

On 4 April, Backhouse asked his wife to drive into Chipping Sodbury to collect antibiotics for the livestock. Walking outside with her he suggested that she take his car, a Volvo, as her own had a flat battery. Minutes later, just as a school bus was passing the farm, an explosion sent a column of smoke and flames into the sky. Margaret Backhouse was dragged, screaming in agony, out of the wrecked Volvo, suffering serious wounds to her thighs and buttocks from a bomb which had been placed beneath the driver's seat and wired to the ignition. The sturdy construction of the car had undoubtedly saved her life.

The police immediately placed a guard over Mrs Backhouse's hospital bed and also around the farm, to prevent any further attack on the farmer. But Backhouse found so many policemen irritating and asked them to leave.

On 30 April the panic button the police had left him was pressed and squad cars raced to the farm. They found the farmer with fearsome knife wounds to his face and chest and the dead body of a neighbour lying at the bottom of the stairs. Sixty-three-year-old Colyn Bedale-Taylor had a shotgun wound in his chest and was holding a Stanley knife in his hand.

Graham Backhouse said that his neighbour had arrived at 7.30 in the evening. Bedale-Taylor blamed the farmer for the death of his son – who had been killed in a car crash – and after admitting that he had sent the death threats and placed the car bomb had attacked Backhouse with a knife. The farmer broke free, rushed for his shotgun and fired in self-defence.

But that was when it all started to go wrong for the ingenious Mr Backhouse. Mr Geoffrey Robinson, a Home Office forensic expert, said in court that the blood splashes in the kitchen – of which there were many – were of the wrong type. Instead of being pear-shaped as would be consistent with flight, they were round, indicating that Backhouse had stood still and allowed the blood to drip on to the floor.

Home Office pathologist Dr Bill Kennard believed that Backhouse's wounds were self-inflicted. There were also no defence wounds to his hands and in forty years' experience he had never seen a similar situation without defence wounds. In addition, the knife the dead man was loosely holding would have been either dropped or held tightly in a death grasp if he had been holding it when he died. Handwriting experts testified that Backhouse had himself written the death threats.

The final nail in Backhouse's coffin, Mr Black claimed, was that he had raised the life insurance on his wife from £50,000 to £100,000 a month before the bombing. Clearly he had intended to murder his wife and claim the insurance. When this went wrong he had deliberately killed Bedale-Taylor to draw suspicion away from himself.

The jury took five-and-a-half hours to convict him, on a majority decision, and Mr Justice Studdart-Smith sentenced him to two life sentences.

Arthur D. Payne was more successful in blowing up his wife for the insurance. On 27 June 1930, Payne, a lawyer in Amarillo, Texas, walked to work, allowing his wife to use the car. When it exploded, his wife was killed and his nine-year-old son severely injured. A crime reporter from the *Amarillo News* discovered that Payne had a mistress and had taken out a large insurance policy on his wife. The lawyer subsequently confessed and was found guilty, but before he could be electrocuted he blew himself up in his cell.

Marcel Barbeault The tall man who entered the courtroom at the Assize Court at Beauvais, handcuffed to two gendarmes, was obviously overweight. His blue blazer was too small for him and his stomach bulged above his grey trousers. But then he'd been on remand in the prison at Amiens for the past five years and possibly prison food agreed with him. He was accused of five murders and faced the death penalty.

The case began in January 1969, in the small French town

of Nogent-sur-Oise, some thirty miles north of Paris. First, two women were shot and injured by rifle bullets, one fired through the window of her own kitchen. Then the first murder occurred. The body of a forty-nine-year-old cosmetic saleswoman was found near her home. She had been beaten and shot to death with a 0.22 rifle.

In November of the same year a tall man in chestnut-coloured oilskins armed with a rifle broke into a house in Nogent and ordered a middle-aged woman and her daughter outside. There, he tied up and shot the woman in the head. Her daughter managed to escape.

By now the case had become a national scandal, but it was another three years before the 'Killer from the Shadows', as he had come to be called by the newspapers, struck again. In February 1973, the body of a twenty-nine-year-old woman who worked in a local cinema was found, half-naked, with a 0.22 bullet in her neck and dumped near the centre of the town.

Three months later, Eugène Stephan and his girlfriend Mauricette Van Hyfte were found battered and shot to death near his car.

Early the following year twenty-nine-year-old Josette Routier was found in her flat at Nogent. She had been bludgeoned, stripped and shot twice in the temple with bullets from a 0.22 rifle.

Julia Gonçalves was a young woman who originally came from Portugal and lived with her uncle in Nogent. Her near-naked body was found in a park in November 1975. She had been shot in the neck.

In the following January, the last murder occurred. Françoise Jakubowska was struck down on her way to work. She was punched in the chest, beaten about the head, her clothes were removed from chest to knees and she was shot in the temple.

Over the seven years of the crimes the police had few clues to work on. They were convinced that a number of burglaries in the area over the period were committed by the same man. The killer always fired a 0.22 rifle – or a series of 0.22 rifles, for at least three were used in the murders. After the murder of the young couple a 0.22 rifle cartridge was found near a tap in a nearby cemetery. The police surmised that it might have fallen out of the killer's pocket as he washed the blood off his hands. Since the tap was very difficult to find in the dark they guessed that the man must be familiar with the cemetery.

A painstaking check on all who used the cemetery finally turned up the name of Marcel Barbeault, a local man, who was married with two children. A search of his flat revealed a 0.22 rifle, a paratrooper's knife, a cosh and oilskins of the kind seen by one of the witnesses. Barbeault was arrested when it was found that the rifle was the one used to kill Françoise Jakubowska.

Because of the number of victims and the fact that other rifles had been used to kill earlier victims, including one known to have been stolen from a house Barbeault had burgled, he was not brought to trial for five years. On 25 May 1981, his trial began. He was charged with the murders of Eugène Stephan and Mauricette Van Hyfte, Josette Routier, Julia Gonçalves and Françoise Jakubowska, several burglaries and various acts of violence. The trial went on for a fortnight and when it ended Barbeault was found guilty of two murders, three unlawful killings and sixteen burglaries. He received life imprisonment.

His lawyer appealed against the verdict and in March 1982, he was granted a new trial. This took place in November 1983, but it was merely a re-run of the first: the same witnesses, forensic evidence, arguments, and eventually Marcel Barbeault was again sentenced to life imprisonment.

Susan Barber 'Don't you like your steak and kidney pie?' asked Susan Barber. Her husband Michael made a grimace and pushed his plate away.

They were not on very good terms. She was twenty-nine, he

was thirty-four and they had been married for eleven years. Recently Susan had been having an affair with twenty-five-year-old Richard Collins who lived a couple of doors away in Osborne Road, Westcliff-on-Sea. Richard, who was a member of the same darts team as Michael, used to join Susan in bed when her husband, who was a keen fisherman, went off on one of his early morning trips. But two or three days before, on 23 May 1981, the weather had deteriorated suddenly and Michael returned home unexpectedly early. He caught them in the bedroom, thrashed Richard and threw him out, where he was seen dashing up the street with his trousers over his arm. Michael also struck Susan, giving her a perforated eardrum.

The day after the steak-and-kidney meal Michael, who worked in a cigarette factory in Southend, developed a severe headache. Over the next few days the headache got worse and he developed a sore throat. The local doctor prescribed antibiotics and a linctus, but Michael continued to deteriorate rapidly. Soon he was in intensive care in Southend General Hospital, where it was thought he was suffering from a rare disease called Goodpastures Syndrome. Then it became obvious he was suffering from kidney failure and he was transferred to the kidney unit at Hammersmith Hospital in London.

Susan visited Michael at Hammersmith, asking Richard Collins to drive her there; he stayed outside in the car.

A few days later Michael Barber died. His wife received £15,000 in death benefits, plus a refund of pension contributions of £800, and £300 per annum for each of her three children. Soon after Michael's death Richard Collins moved in with Susan.

The death certificate gave the cause as cardiac arrest, renal failure and bilateral pneumonia. A post mortem was conducted and it was decided to send samples of blood and urine to the National Poisons Reference Centre at New Cross Hospital. But apparently the results were negative, and Michael's body was cremated.

Meanwhile Susan was in her element. Richard lasted only six weeks. He was then forcibly persuaded to move out by another member of the darts team, who was soon followed by a succession of pub regulars. There was often jealousy and resentment and the police had to be called in frequently to break up fights as well as noisy drinking parties. Susan is said to have advertised for men friends on citizens' band radio under the call sign 'Nympho'.

Eight months after Michael Barber's death, at a case conference in Hammersmith Hospital, it was found that samples had never been sent to the poisons unit. A frantic search of the hospital finally turned up Michael's lungs, kidney, liver, heart and spleen, preserved under formalin in a bucket. Samples were quickly sent off for analysis and the results showed that they contained the deadly poison paraquat.

The Southend coroner was informed in February and the police began investigations. Susan Barber and Richard Collins were arrested on 5 April 1982.

Their trial took place at Chelmsford Crown Court in November, before Mr Justice Woolf. Mr Derek Spencer QC prosecuted and Susan was defended by Mr Anthony Arlidge QC. Richard Collins was represented by Mr Michael Beckman QC.

Susan went into the witness box and confessed that she had poisoned her husband's steak-and-kidney pie with Gromoxone, a weedkiller she had found in the garden shed, mixing it with the gravy. She administered the weedkiller twice on two successive days, but claimed that she didn't know it would kill him, saying that she only wanted to make him sick. When asked why she hadn't told the doctor when Michael became very ill, and had even denied that they had any poison at home, she claimed that she didn't think his symptoms were due to the poison.

The jury of seven men and five women found Susan guilty of murder and she was sentenced to life imprisonment.

Richard Collins, who was said to be under the spell of his

dominating mistress and not to have known of the poisoning until afterwards, was jailed for two years.

When Mary Creighton and Everett Appelgate were tried in January 1936 in Long Island, USA, for poisoning Appelgate's wife Ada with arsenic, Mary Creighton had already been tried twice for poisoning and acquitted. But this time there was evidence that after the two families began living in the same house, Mary came under the influence of Appelgate who was having sexual intercourse with Mary's fifteen-year-old daughter. Under cross-examination Mary admitted giving Ada milk containing arsenic. Both went to the electric chair in Sing Sing prison in July 1936.

Ronald Barton Fourteen-year-old Keighley Barton left the house where she was living with her mother and her mother's new boyfriend in Forest Gate, London, at about ten o'clock on Saturday 11 August, 1985, to walk her dog on Wanstead Flats, a common about ten minutes away. Her dog came back about an hour and a half later, but Keighley never returned.

A massive search by the police failed to find the missing teenager, but by the end of August, Ronald Barton, Keighley's stepfather, who had recently been thrown out by her mother, was arrested and charged with abducting her. Refused bail, he was kept in Brixton prison and by the October, although the police still hadn't found her body, he was charged with her murder.

The trial was due to begin in February 1986, but his defence counsel, Mr Henry Grunwald QC, asked for it to be postponed. There had been, he told Mr Justice Turner, many sightings of the missing teenager and he pleaded for time to have these investigated. The case was adjourned for eight months, while Barton was remanded in custody.

One of Keighley's teachers came forward to say that she and one of her sons, who had been in the same class as the teenager, had seen the girl in Walthamstow market. Keighley had been accompanied by a woman with red hair. The police took the teacher and her son back to the market several times, but they never saw Keighley again.

When the trial finally began in October 1986, Mr Michael Worsley QC, for the prosecution, pointed out that even though there was no body a conviction for murder was still possible if the evidence was sufficiently strong. He claimed that Barton wanted to get rid of the girl because she was about to make allegations of sexual abuse against him for which he might have been sent to prison, and that he wanted revenge on her mother for throwing him out of the house and taking up with a new lover. Mrs Barton went into the witness box to testify that he had made death threats against the teenager.

A prisoner from Brixton said that Barton had asked him to use his influence to obtain an alibi for the time at which Keighley had disappeared. Another claimed that the accused had confessed to killing his stepdaughter, hiding her body in the boot of his car and putting it through a crusher at a breaker's yard.

Barton furiously denied this story and said that the sex allegations had been concocted by Keighley and her mother.

The teacher and her son reported having seen the young girl, and two more witnesses came forward to say that they also had seen Keighley, one having caught sight of her at Victoria Station.

Defence counsel pointed out that at least twenty people had said they had seen the teenager, who may easily have run away deliberately. And he told the jury that if capital punishment was still in existence and they convicted Barton, he could well be hanged, only to find later that Keighley was safe and well.

This argument obviously weighed heavily with the jury who, after five hours' deliberation, told the judge that they could not reach a unanimous decision. Mr Justice Turner said that he would accept a majority decision, but it was well into the next day before they brought in a verdict by a majority of ten to two – of guilty.

The judge sentenced Ronald Barton to life imprisonment,

with a recommendation that he serve at least twenty-five years. What the jury, quite properly, could not have known was that Barton had a history of sexual abuse against teenage girls. When Keighley was only eight he had been convicted of acts of gross indecency and twice more he was arrested for sex offences against her, but the charges were dropped when she refused to give evidence.

Barton had only just begun his sentence when he asked to see the police officers in charge of the investigation. He told them that he had not put Keighley's body in a car crusher – he had hidden it in the Abney Park cemetery in Stoke Newington. And there, several days later, her bones were found in an overgrown thicket. She had been stabbed to death.

A very similar case involved ten-year-old Mona Tinsley, who disappeared from her home in Newark, Nottinghamshire, in January 1937. Frederick Nodder, a lorry driver who had lodged with her parents, was suspected. Several witnesses had seen her with him on the day she disappeared, but although he admitted going on a bus with her that day, he claimed she had gone on to Sheffield alone. The child had still not been found when he was tried for abduction at Birmingham Assizes in March 1937. He was sentenced to seven years, the judge remarking: 'What you did with that little girl, what became of her, only you know.' The following June her body was found in the River Idle, over twenty miles from Newark. Nodder was tried for murder at Nottingham Assizes in November, found guilty and hanged at Lincoln prison in December 1937.

Martha Beck and Raymond Fernandez

In June 1949, Martha Beck and Raymond Fernandez were tried for murder at the Bronx County courthouse in New York, but this incredible story started a long time before that.

It is usually claimed that a head injury he received when a hatch fell on him when he was a seaman, in December 1945, changed Fernandez's personality. Whether this was so, it is true that soon after coming out of hospital he was jailed for attempted theft and spent a year in prison in Tallahassee, Florida. On being released he began a campaign of theft, fleecing lonely women of their savings. He would meet them through lonely hearts clubs, propose marriage and make off with any money they were foolish enough to transfer to him.

In the spring of 1947 thirty-three-year-old Fernandez met Lucilla Thompson, a middle-aged cook, who was married but separated from her husband. They travelled to Spain for a holiday as man and wife. They had a row one night in their hotel, and the next morning Mrs Thompson was found dead. A doctor diagnosed a heart attack and Fernandez went back to America. There, Fernandez forged a document naming him heir to Mrs Thompson's property and moved into her flat in New York. Later the police discovered that the day before the death he had purchased a bottle of the drug digitalis, which could cause symptoms similar to those of a heart attack.

Soon after this he corresponded with twenty-six-year-old Martha Beck, superintendent of a children's home in Florida, who had her own apartment. She turned out to be twenty stones in weight, with two children and, what was worse, very little money of her own. He rapidly dropped her. But Martha, a strong-willed lady, parked her children with her mother and followed him to New York.

Then began a curious love affair. Raymond continued pursuing women and Martha went along too – as his sister. But it was a scenario for tragedy; several tragedies in fact.

Raymond married Myrtle Young in Cook County, Illinois, in August 1948, and they honeymooned in Chicago, with Martha tagging along. A furious row inevitably broke out between the two women, which ended when Myrtle swallowed barbiturates. The pair had already obtained $4,000 of Myrtle's money, so they promptly put her on a bus for her home in Arkansas. She collapsed on the journey in a state of barbiturate intoxication and died in hospital.

When Myrtle's money had run out Raymond met and married Mrs Janet Fay, a sixty-six-year-old widow from Albany, New York State. He soon persuaded her to part with $3,500, but again problems arose when Martha insisted on sharing her bed while Raymond slept in another room. One night Janet Fay stormed into Raymond's room, saying that his sister would have to go. Martha followed and hit her over the head with a hammer. They bundled the body into a trunk and buried it under the cellar floor of a house they rented in New York City.

The same day that Mrs Fay was murdered Raymond received a letter from a Mrs Delphine Downing, a forty-one-year-old widow with a two-year-old daughter, from Grand Rapids, Michigan. Fernandez and Beck soon moved into her house and, after Downing had been doped with sleeping pills, Fernandez shot her with her late husband's service revolver. Martha drowned the child in the bath and they buried mother and daughter under the cellar floor.

They had just finished when there was a knock at the front door. It was the local police. They had been alerted by the New York police after friends of Mrs Fay had called them in following her disappearance. A search of the Grand Rapids house soon disclosed the grave in the cellar and the murderous pair were arrested.

When Mrs Fay's grave was discovered, the New York authorities asked for extradition so that the two could be tried in that state, which had the death penalty. The murder of the small child in Grand Rapids so horrified the public in Michigan, which did not have the death penalty, that they readily agreed to send the pair to New York

In their trial they both had the same lawyer, Herbert Rosenberg, and Martha's defence was insanity, while Raymond first claimed he had no foreknowledge of the crime, then changed his plea to insanity. After a forty-four-day trial they were found guilty of first-degree murder and sentenced to death.

When Martha had first been arrested, a prison psychiatrist told her that Raymond had syphilis. She wept. 'He never did love me, did he?' she asked. The doctor replied: 'No. He never did.'

Two hours before their executions, on 8 March 1951, Martha sent Raymond a love poem. He scribbled her a note in return. 'I would like to shout my love for you to the world.'

Martha is reported to have said: 'Now that I know he loves me, I can go to my death bursting with joy.'

Henry Clark and Augusta Fullam were a couple who killed for love, in India in 1913. First Augusta gave her husband arsenic, supplied by Clark. Then he hired four native assassins to murder his wife. But the police were soon suspicious and discovered a box of Augusta's letters to Henry which made their intentions clear. As in the Bywaters and Thompson case (see p.310), they provided a significant part of the prosecution evidence. Both were convicted; Clark was executed and Fullam died in prison.

Mary Bell The trial of Mary and Norma Bell, who shared the same name but were not related, opened in December 1968 in Newcastle's Moot Hall. Norma was thirteen and Mary eleven and they were accused of murdering four-year-old Martin Brown and three-year-old Brian Howe.

The contrast between the publicity generated by this and by the recent Bulger case could not be greater. The latter trial was reported in great detail every night on television and in the newspapers, and a televised documentary of the whole story of the abduction and murder and of the interrogation of the culprits by the police was shown after the trial.

In the Bell case the press reported on the case only after the trial was over. Accounts were given on radio and television, but the BBC banned any reporting of the case on the early evening news. Yet in some ways the Bell case was even more horrifying, since it involved the murder of two young children.

On 25 May 1968, the body of Martin Brown was discovered in a derelict house in Newcastle. The post mortem showed that he might have been strangled, but there were no pressure marks on the neck such as an adult would have made. The derelict house was used as a play area by the local children, two of whom were the close friends Norma and Mary Bell who lived next door to each other.

The Bell girls showed an immediate and inordinate interest in the death, badgering the parents of the murdered child to let them see the body. They later admitted to breaking into a local nursery and leaving scribbled notes in which the writers claimed to have murdered Martin Brown.

Two months later Brian Howe was found dead amid concrete blocks on some waste ground known to the local children as the Tin Lizzie. This time there were faint marks on his neck and small puncture wounds on his legs. Nearby lay a broken pair of scissors. The autopsy clearly pointed to the wounds being made by a child.

The police began a series of interviews with local children and it soon became obvious that statements made by Mary Bell and her friend Norma were inconsistent and changed almost every time they were interviewed. In particular Mary knew about the scissors even though the information had not been released by the police.

Eventually Norma accused Mary of strangling Brian and pressing a razor blade into his belly. The body was re-examined and faint marks discovered in the exact places Norma had indicated. Mary then accused Norma of the murder.

At their trial Norma was restless and found it difficult to concentrate. Often in tears, she seemed to be continually looking for sympathy or approval, particularly from her parents, who were allowed to sit just behind her. In contrast the younger Mary was cool and calm and listened intently to all that went on. Indeed, when forensic evidence was given that fibres found on Martin Brown were also discovered on her dress, she changed her story and admitted that she had seen him earlier in the day. Witnesses claimed that Mary had been caught squeezing the throats of several children. One child's mother, alarmed by the marks on her daughter's neck, had called the police.

The verdict came on 17 December. Norma Bell, who was said to be slow for her age at the time of the murders and had plainly been under the influence of the more dominant Mary, was acquitted. Mary was found guilty in both cases, but only of manslaughter, on the grounds of diminished responsibility. The judge, Sir Ralph Cusack, sentenced her to detention for life.

She began her sentence at a girls' remand home, was later sent to an approved school in Lancashire and later still to an open prison. When she was twenty she escaped from prison with another girl, but was recaptured after three days, at a house in Derby.

Steven Truscott was fourteen, only a year older than Norma Bell, when he was arrested and charged, in June 1959, with the rape and murder of a twelve-year-old girl near the town of Goderich, in Canada. After being held in prison with no concessions made to his youth he was tried, in September, as an adult. After the trial, after which serious doubts have been expressed about the evidence, he was found guilty and sentenced to death. The sentence was later commuted to life imprisonment on the intervention of the Canadian prime minister. An appeal against the verdict was rejected in 1960 and Steven, after he was eighteen, served his sentence in prison.

Steven Benson 'But I like to sit in the back,' said Margaret Benson.

'Much more room for you, Mother, in the front, next to the

driver,' said her son Steven. 'Scott can drive and I'll sit in the back with Carol Lynn.'

Steven Benson was bustling about shepherding his mother, sister and younger brother into the small Chevrolet Suburban. He had offered to accompany his mother and sister on a trip to stake out the groundplan of a house Margaret was going to have built nearby.

'Ah, forgotten the tape measure,' said Steven cheerfully. He handed the car keys to Scott through the open driver's window and walked off towards the house, a large bungalow, near Naples, Florida, which was his mother's main home.

It was Tuesday 9 July, 1985.

Carol Lynn felt the heat of the morning in the small car, even though it was only nine o'clock, and opened the passenger door on her side to let in some air.

The action saved her life. The next instant the car was enveloped in an orange fireball. She was hurled out of the vehicle, severely burned, and came to lying on the tarmac drive. She could see Steven staring at her on the other side of the blazing car and called to him for help. He turned and ran into the house.

Margaret and Scott Benson were killed outright. Carol Lynn was in intensive care for three weeks before she could be interviewed. But the police had plenty to go on.

Margaret had been a wealthy widow. Her father, Harry Hitchcock, had been a major figure in the American tobacco industry in Pennsylvania when he retired and gave most of his money to his children. Margaret liked to keep her children close to her and used her money to do it. Scott was actually born to Carol Lynn when the girl was nineteen, but Margaret and her husband raised him as their own and at the time of her death the twenty-two-year-old was being generously supported while he trained as a professional tennis player.

Margaret had also loaned thirty-three-year-old Steven money

to start several businesses making electronic components, but had recently become suspicious that her eldest son might be stealing money from her. The lawyer she called in to investigate afterwards discovered that one of Steven's businesses had swallowed up a quarter of a million dollars of her money in one year alone.

The police found that Steven had purchased two four-inch pipes a few days before the murder, and careful reconstruction of the bomb showed that it had been made from just such a pipe. He had gone to the supply firm in disguise and signed the receipt with a false name, but had left his palm prints on the paper he had signed.

His trial, which opened in July 1986 at Fort Myers, Florida, was a media circus. Television reports of the proceedings displaced the daily soap operas and became known as the 'Benson Chronicles'.

Assistant state's attorney Jerry Brock, for the prosecution, outlined the family history and Margaret's growing suspicions of Steven. The day before she died she had ordered her son to produce the accounts of his companies and he had driven over the next morning from his home in Fort Myers to her house at Naples with the books in his van. He arrived early, offered to go out and get some milk for their breakfast and, saying his van was low on petrol, took the Chevrolet Suburban. But instead of returning in ten minutes he was gone over an hour. He said he had met a friend, but this friend could not subsequently be found.

Carol Lynn, although disfigured by her burns, went into the witness box to describe the last minutes before the horrific explosion.

Steven's counsel Michael McDonnell tried to throw the blame on Scott who was known to be a violent character, but this was unconvincing since Scott himself had died in the blast.

Nevertheless it took the jury eleven hours to bring in a

verdict of guilty against Steven Benson. Judge Hugh Hayes awarded him two life sentences for murder and thirty-seven years for attempted murder and arson.

Marie Besnard   Loudun is a small town in west central France, some thirty-three miles north of Poitiers. Like many small towns occupied during the Second World War, rumours and suspicions were rife. From the days when an unfriendly neighbour or someone to whom one owed money could be got rid of by a quiet word to the German authorities, the possibilities of tale-telling and malicious gossip stretched on well after the war.

In October 1947, Léon Besnard, a wealthy middle-aged man in the town, died after a short illness. The local postmistress suspected foul play. She informed a friend that Léon had told her on his deathbed that he suspected his wife Marie of poisoning him. The friend passed on the suspicion to the police in Poitiers who began an investigation.

Rumours in the town linked Marie with a young German prisoner of war who had worked on one of Léon's farms and there were suspicions about the deaths of a number of Marie's relatives. In all, the police exhumed twelve bodies, including Marie's first husband who had died in 1927, her father and mother, Léon's father and mother and several of his aunts and uncles.

Analysis confirmed that all the bodies contained arsenic in amounts large enough to have caused their deaths.

Marie Besnard was arrested in July 1949, and in February 1952 her trial began in the courthouse at Poitiers.

The trial attracted attention from all over France and an eminent lawyer from Paris, René Hayot, led the defence. He brought in a colleague, Albert Gautrat, who, although he was sixty-four and white-haired, was a star of his profession and a Chevalier of the Legion of Honour.

From the start there was little direct evidence against Marie;

plenty of rumour and gossip and evidence that she had benefited financially in nearly all the deaths, but no evidence that she had ever possessed the poison.

But an impressive array of forensic scientists led by Dr George Béroud, one of the best known toxicologists in southern France, testified to finding substantial quantities of arsenic in the bodies.

Gautrat rose to question the scientist. He produced lists of the samples sent from the graveyard at Loudun to Béroud's laboratory in Marseille, which he distributed to the judges and jury. 'How is it,' he asked the toxicologist, 'that these lists show that there were more samples received in Marseille than were sent from Loudun? Does that mean that the samples might have become mixed up with those from other cases?'

The toxicologist had no answer.

Gautrat went on to show that Béroud's reports claimed that arsenic had been discovered in the hair of one of the bodies, when the person had in fact been bald. And an eye was reported to have been examined although it was in a body which had been buried for eleven years, in which time the eye would have disintegrated.

His final demolition of the scientist came when he invited him to examine the results of some tests done for arsenic and to say – which the man had claimed to be able to do in a letter – which were arsenic and which were not. When Béroud made three mistakes his credibility was destroyed.

Although these were a small number of minor imperfections in a very large number of analyses, they threw doubt on the reliability of the evidence. The court therefore ordered a different set of experts to undertake a completely new toxicological examination.

The second trial of Marie Besnard began in March 1954. There was the same parade of witnesses from Loudun. The post-mistress repeated her allegations, other witnesses claimed to have seen undue familiarity between Marie and the prisoner of war, but again the main evidence was scientific. New experts had examined the bodies and again asserted that they contained substantial quantities of arsenic. One had applied the new technique of radio-chemical analysis to the problem, but he was immediately attacked by Gautrat, who managed to show that because the technique was so new the methods could not be considered completely reliable.

But his main *coup* was to produce a very eminent scientist to suggest that bacteria in the soil of the graveyard could make the arsenic soluble, so that it might be transferred into the bodies from the soil itself. So little was known about this at the time that none of the prosecution experts could say categorically that this could not happen.

Once again the prosecution case was thrown into disarray and one of their experts pleaded for more time to look into this problem. So once again new experts were asked to investigate the toxicological uncertainties and Marie was released on bail.

It took seven years, from 1954 to 1961, before the scientists were ready to proceed again and the third trial opened in November of that year. But again there was no clear evidence that the bodies could or could not have absorbed arsenic from the soil of the Loudun cemetery. And because there was this element of doubt it was perfectly proper that the verdict should be not guilty. Marie Besnard walked free, acquitted of the murders of twelve people.

Daisy De Melker, a South African housewife and a trained nurse, poisoned two of her three husbands with strychnine and her grown-up son with arsenic. When suspicions were raised the police found that Daisy had bought arsenic just before her son died. Exhumation of the bodies showed the unmistakable presence of poison, and subsequent medical examination of the symptoms of their illnesses pointed to the poisons used. She was tried in Johannesburg in October 1932, convicted and hanged.

Kenneth Bianchi and Angelo Buono The deadly duo, Bianchi and Buono, would probably never have been brought to trial at all had it not been for the carelessness of one of them.

The Hillside Stranglings, so called because the victims were dumped naked on the hillsides above Los Angeles, began in October 1977. Over a period of four months twelve bodies were found. They were all young women; two of them were only twelve and fourteen. Some were prostitutes, but some were college girls, and all had been strangled, usually with pieces of cloth. In addition each had been subjected to sexual intercourse by two men.

There were several sightings of the killers. One woman had seen a victim being forced into a car and described one of the men as older than the other with bushy hair. But the police had no clues as to the car or who the men were and panic stalked the city. Then in February 1978, the killings abruptly stopped.

A year later, in the small town of Bellingham, in Washington State, a thousand miles north of Los Angeles, two girls were reported missing. Their bodies were found the next day in the back of a car belonging to one of them. They were fully clothed, but both had been strangled and sexually assaulted.

The last person known to have been with them was a young security guard called Kenneth Bianchi. Although he denied knowing either, forensic evidence linked him with the two girls. While he was being held in custody it was found that he had previously lived in Glendale, a suburb of Los Angeles, and had left there just after the last of the Hillside Stranglings had taken place.

The police in Los Angeles were contacted and they discovered that some jewellery found in his Bellingham home had been stolen from victims of the Hillside killers.

Bianchi was highly cooperative with the police and readily told them about his cousin, Angelo Buono, who owned a house in Glendale, had a car upholstery business, was seventeen years older than Bianchi and had bushy hair. Buono was an unsavoury character. A number of his wives had left him because of his brutality and he was suspected of having forced two young girls into prostitution.

Bianchi claimed to remember nothing of the evening on which the two girls had been killed in Bellingham, or anything about the Hillside Stranglings, but under hypnosis a character called 'Steve' appeared, who was much more aggressive and unpleasant than the charming Kenneth. 'Steve' confessed readily to the Bellingham murders and also to being involved with Buono in all the Los Angeles killings.

The performance split medical opinion down the middle. Several eminent psychiatrists believed that Bianchi was a genuine multiple personality and thus could be classed as insane, while others thought that he was faking it all. There was evidence that he was faking; but was it enough to convince a jury in a murder trial?

If Bianchi was convicted, he would certainly face the death sentence, both in Washington for the Bellingham murders, and in California. He therefore agreed to plead guilty and to give testimony in Los Angeles against Buono in exchange for life imprisonment in a California prison, which are apparently more comfortable than those in Washington, and the possibility of parole.

The Washington authorities agreed as it saved them the expense of a costly trial and Bianchi, after pleading guilty to the two murders, was given life imprisonment by a Washington judge sitting without a jury.

But as soon as he was taken to California he went back on his promise, claiming that he had only pleaded guilty to save his life and that really he was innocent.

This immediately put the Los Angeles district attorney in a tricky situation. The evidence against Buono was not strong and without the cooperation of Bianchi it would be very difficult to get a conviction. In July 1979, therefore, the assistant district attorney, Roger Kelly, proposed in court that all murder charges against Angelo Buono should be dropped.

But Judge George would have none of it. If the Los Angeles district attorney didn't want to prosecute the case, he said, he would refer it to the Attorney General of California. And so, when the trial opened in Los Angeles in November 1981, two deputies from the Attorney General's office, Roger Boren and Michael Nash, led the prosecution.

It was the longest trial in American history, with the prosecution calling over 250 witnesses, including Kenneth Bianchi. There was a small amount of forensic evidence: fibres from two of the victims could have come from Buono's upholstery shop. And there were a number of witnesses. One young girl who had been enticed into a car by Bianchi saved herself by showing them documents which identified her as the daughter of the late filmstar Peter Lorre. They let her go, fearing perhaps that to kill her would invite too much police attention. She readily identified both Buono and Bianchi.

The trial was not concluded until November 1983.

After deliberating for three weeks, the jury found Buono guilty of nine murders but, influenced no doubt by the fact that Bianchi had escaped the death penalty, they would not sentence him to death. Judge George, regretting that he was unable to use the ultimate penalty, gave Buono life without the possibility of parole.

And because Bianchi had violated his plea bargain Judge George sent him back to serve his sentence in the tough Walla Walla prison in Washington.

John Bowden At the end of the trial in January 1982 at the Old Bailey in London, the judge, Mr Justice Mars-Jones, commented: 'Bowden is a man who enjoyed inflicting pain and even killing.'

However, Bowden's parents disagreed, describing their twenty-six-year-old son as a good, kind and gentle person, who only became violent after serving a period of solitary confinement as a punishment for escaping from arrest.

Whichever is true, the facts are that by the time the Londoner was twenty-four he had spent a total of five years in prison for a variety of offences including assault and wounding, carrying an offensive weapon, burglary, robbery and blackmail.

Bowden had two accomplices, David Begley, a meat porter, and Michael Ward, a gravedigger, both alcoholics and drug users like himself. They preyed on the homeless who slept rough in London, beating them up and occasionally robbing them, if the unfortunates had anything worth stealing. But they reached the high point in their careers when they met ex-amateur boxer Donald Ryan.

They lured him to a flat in South London and rendered him incapable by a blow to the head with a machete. Then they dumped him in a bath of boiling water. As if this wasn't enough they carried him into a bedroom and threw him on a bed, then cut off his arms and legs with an electric carving knife, a saw and the machete.

The pathologist reported afterwards that Ryan must have been alive when this was going on.

The final act was to cut off the man's head. According to the others Bowden then held it aloft, laughing and joking about it. The limbs and the trunk were then scattered about on waste ground locally, but Bowden kept the head in a refrigerator for some time as a kind of trophy before dumping it in a dustbin.

Until Ryan's head turned up the police were not absolutely sure who the limbs belonged to, but when they had identified the body they were able to trace his movements back to his meeting with Bowden and his conspirators.

At their trial the evidence from the pathologist and the accompanying photographs was so horrific that the proceedings had to be adjourned because four members of the jury became ill. There was little doubt what the verdicts would be.

John Bowden was convicted of murder and received life, the judge recommending that he should serve a minimum of twenty-five years. Begley and Ward received only fifteen years each because they had given evidence against Bowden.

When Bowden was sentenced he shouted at Mr Justice Mars-Jones: 'You old bastard. I hope you die screaming of cancer!'

William Bradfield and Dr Jay C. Smith   In October 1983 the trial of William Bradfield opened in Harrisburg, Pennsylvania. He was a fifty-year-old teacher at Upper Merion High School, Philadelphia, whose speciality was English, and he was accused of murdering Susan Reinert, a colleague from the same department.

William Bradfield was well known in the school for his many love affairs. Susan Reinert had been one of his conquests. In 1979 she was thirty-three and had two children, Michael, aged ten, and Karen, eleven. Having divorced her husband she had set her cap at Bradfield, telling friends that they were to be married sometime that year and were journeying to England. The previous year her mother had died and left her some money, shares and a valuable ring. She also took out insurance policies totalling $750,000 naming Bradfield as the beneficiary and the inheritor of her estate.

Early on Monday 25 June, 1979, the naked body of Susan Reinert was discovered in the boot of her car, parked near Harrisburg, a two-hour drive from her home in Philadelphia. The autopsy revealed that she had died from a large dose of morphine. On her body were bruises suggesting that she had been held in chains and residues of sticky tape indicated that she had been gagged. But most horrific of all, both her children were missing.

There was little direct evidence linking William Bradfield with Susan Reinert's death. But prosecutor Richard L. Guida pointed out that there was a great deal of circumstantial evidence.

Bradfield had begun a court action to obtain the insurance money. The ring left to Susan had disappeared and she'd told a friend Bradfield had taken it to have the stone reset. Friends of his testified he'd been in possession of a substantial amount of money which he'd tried to keep secret, and he'd actually got one of his friends to help him wipe fingerprints from the notes. A fellow prison inmate where Bradfield had been held said that the teacher had admitted to him he had been present at Susan's death, but said that he hadn't done it himself.

But the crucial point was, as Rick Guida pointed out, that the finding of Susan Reinert's body pointed directly to Bradfield. Extensive searches by the police over a period of four years had failed to find the children's bodies. But for the teacher to inherit the money it was essential that Susan should be found.

It took the jury only seventy-five minutes to find him guilty. He was sentenced to life imprisonment.

The man whom William Bradfield tried to blame for the death of Susan Reinert was Dr Jay C. Smith. He had been the principal of Upper Merion High School, and if William Bradfield might be considered a peculiar character, Dr Smith was positively bizarre.

In August 1977, a man dressed in what appeared to be the uniform of the Brink's security company collected the takings from a Sears, Roebuck store just outside Philadelphia – a bag of cheques and $34,000 in cash – and walked out, just before the real courier arrived.

The following August a couple of teenagers spotted a hooded gunman in a car park who looked as if he was trying to break into a van. They called the police and after a car chase the man was apprehended. It was Dr Jay C. Smith.

Inside his car were four loaded guns, a mask and bolt cutters and two hypodermic syringes, each filled with a powerful tranquillizing drug, which could produce unconsciousness within a minute.

A search of Dr Smith's house revealed a basement where the police discovered a considerable quantity of marijuana and other illegal drugs, a large library of pornographic books, contact magazines, some locks and chains and four gallons of nitric acid.

Another cache contained similar uniforms to those of Brink's security guards and a forged identity card bearing a picture of Dr Smith and the name which had been used by the false courier who robbed the Sears, Roebuck store.

The Susan Reinert murder taskforce, which included the police and the FBI, were convinced that both Bradfield and Smith were concerned in the death of the teacher. But it wasn't until June 1985, six years after the murder, that Smith was finally arrested.

Prosecutor Guida had an even more circumstantial case against him than he had against Bradfield. Scrapings from the carpet in the principal's basement showed a number of hairs which might have come from Susan Reinert and fibres found on the body could have come from a rug in the same place, but the evidence was not conclusive.

Dr Smith had written a number of letters from prison to his wife and his brother stressing that they must clear up the basement and the inside of his car but this, though suspicious, was not hard evidence. Two convicts testified – one an ex-cop serving a sentence for burglary and perjury – that Smith had admitted killing Susan Reinert. But plainly the jury did not regard their evidence as very reliable.

But Rick Guida's masterstroke was to call a succession of witnesses from Karen Reinert's class. Police had found part of a small green pin under one of the front seats in Dr Smith's blue Capri. It proved to be part of a lapel badge from the Philadelphia Museum of Art. In early June 1979, a few weeks before the murder, Karen's class had been on a school trip to the museum.

Several of her classmates gave evidence that they had seen Karen with such a pin. Elizabeth Brook, who used to live next door to the Reinerts, said that on the day they disappeared she had seen Karen wearing it.

The jury were visibly affected by the children's evidence and after brooding overnight brought in a verdict of guilty. The same jury also sentenced Dr Smith to death. The children's bodies have never been found.

Ian Brady and Myra Hindley It has been called the trial of the century. Certainly the world's press were there in force, and not only reporters. Many writers were present who would later produce books on the case. For this was a story which shocked everybody.

The trial opened in April 1966 at Chester Assizes in the ancient castle. For the first time since the trial of Dr Bodkin Adams (see p. 1) in 1957 the Attorney General, Sir Frederick Elwyn Jones, prosecuted. He was assisted by Mr William Mars-Jones, who later became a judge and presided over the trial of John Bowden (see p. 33).

Ian Brady, the prosecution reported, had been born in Glasgow. While still a baby he had been placed in the care of foster parents, but went to live with his mother in Manchester when he was sixteen. In February 1959, at the age of twenty-one, he obtained a position as a stock clerk at Millwards Merchandise Ltd, a small chemical distributing firm in Gorton, a suburb of Manchester.

Two years later, Myra Hindley, a nineteen-year-old typist, joined the firm. She too had been fostered. After her sister Maureen was born, when she was four, she had been sent to live with her grandmother.

Unlike Brady, Hindley had never been in trouble with the law. What the jury did not know when they heard Brady's story was that from the age of thirteen, up until he joined Millwards, he had had a string of convictions, mostly for housebreaking and theft.

From the beginning Hindley was attracted to Brady, but he

seems to have ignored her for nearly a year, until just before Christmas 1961, when they had their first date. Brady had been collecting books on Nazism and the history and practice of torture for some time and Hindley joined eagerly in his studies. Together the pair would eventually indulge in some of the foulest activities in the history of crime.

It was early on the morning of 7 October 1965 that the police received a telephone call from a terrified David Smith, who babbled that he and his wife Maureen were in fear of their lives. He said that the previous evening he had been woken by Myra Hindley, his sister-in-law, arriving at their flat. She had asked him to walk her back to where she lived with Ian Brady and her granny, a few streets away. The two couples had been going around for some time and were very friendly.

Smith, who was only seventeen, obliged and was then asked by Myra to come in as Brady wanted to give him some miniature bottles of wine. He was taken into the living-room of the small council house to witness Brady battering a youth to death with a hatchet. It was plainly a ruse to involve Smith in the murder of the young man, Edward Evans, a homosexual Brady and Hindley had picked up at Manchester station some time previously. But it badly misfired.

The police arrived at Hindley's home, discovered the body of Evans and eventually a left-luggage ticket from Manchester station in the spine of a prayer book. This led them to two suitcases containing books, plans for robbing a bank, pornographic photographs involving Brady and Hindley and the pair and a young girl and some sound tape recordings. These contained the voices of a twelve-year-old girl, Lesley Anne Downey, and of Brady and Hindley. Played in court it horrified all who heard it and reduced many to tears. There were also some photographs taken on Saddleworth Moors, near Manchester, one of which showed Hindley crouching and looking down at the ground.

This was afterwards discovered to be the grave of a twelve-year-old boy, John Kilbride, who two years before had gone missing from a market near his home in Ashton-under-Lyne, near Manchester. The grave of Lesley Anne Downey was also found in the same general area.

Ian Brady was tried for the murders of Edward Evans, Lesley Anne Downey and John Kilbride. Myra Hindley was charged with the same murders and also with harbouring Brady knowing he had murdered Kilbride. Although they both tried to throw all the blame on to Smith there was a wealth of circumstantial evidence against both of them and – if you believed Smith – direct evidence as well.

The all-male jury found Brady guilty of the three murders, Hindley not guilty of the murder of John Kilbride, but guilty on the other charges, and Mr Justice Fenton Atkinson passed concurrent life sentences on them for all the murders.

The police were convinced that these were not the only deaths which could be attributed to the evil couple, and in 1987 both confessed to a further two murders. Sixteen-year-old Pauline Reade had disappeared on her way to a dance in Gorton on 12 July 1963, and twelve-year-old Keith Bennett left his home one night in June 1964, not very far from where Brady had lived with his parents, and never returned. Hindley and Brady assisted in the search of Saddleworth Moors for the two graves. Pauline Reade's was eventually found, but the whereabouts of the final resting place of Keith Bennett remains a mystery.

Karl Gustav Hulten, an American private on the run from the army and with a stolen pistol, met Elizabeth Marina Jones, unemployed striptease artiste of eighteen, in a London café in October 1944. They cruised around for two days in an army truck attacking and robbing the occasional defenceless woman. On the third day they shot and killed a private-hire taxi-driver, took his takings and the car. The car was soon traced and Hulten arrested. The US government agreed that he should be tried in a British court and in January 1945, he and Jones were tried together. They were both convicted of murder. Hulten was hanged, but Jones was reprieved and served life imprisonment.

Theodore (Ted) Bundy When Ted Bundy first walked into court in Salt Lake City, Utah, in February 1976, most people thought that the police had the wrong man. The perfect picture of the all-American boy, he was tall, clean-cut and handsome, and a law student at the University of Utah. Bundy had poise and self-confidence, was articulate, and observers thought he would walk out of court a free man.

He had been arrested the previous August for driving his Volkswagen without lights and trying to escape when the police ordered him to stop. Inside the car the police found a steel bar, a pair of handcuffs, a knitted balaclava and a mask made from ladies' stockings. Bundy was identified by a young woman called Carol DaRonch as the man who had tried to abduct her one night the previous November. He was also seen in a school car park the same night, when a young girl, Debbie Kent, disappeared.

In fact Debbie had been the fourth girl to disappear in the Salt Lake City area in the previous five weeks.

Most of the evidence the police had against Bundy came from Carol DaRonch. Blood on her coat, which came from her attacker when she scratched him, matched his. Strands of her hair were found in Bundy's car and she picked him out at an identification parade. It was enough. He was tried by a judge sitting without a jury, which the accused can ask for in some US States (*see* the case of John Floyd, p. 110); found guilty he was sentenced to serve from one to fifteen years in jail.

Bundy was also the leading suspect in the other abductions in Salt Lake City. Two of the girls were subsequently found naked, sexually assaulted, strangled and their faces so badly beaten that their families had difficulty recognizing them.

Seattle, in Washington State, lies 750 miles to the north-

west of Salt Lake City. Between January and July 1974, when
Bundy was at university there, a number of assaults on young
girls occurred and eight vanished altogether. The last two were
Janice Ott and Denise Naslund who disappeared from Sammam-
ish Park Lake on 14 July. Human bones identified as belonging
to the two girls were found months later, two miles from the
lake.

Descriptions of a man seen accosting girls at the lake that
day fitted Bundy – but he was only one of nearly four thousand
suspects in the cases.

Early in 1975 and subsequent to the abductions in Salt Lake
City, Caryn Campbell, a young nurse on holiday with her fiancé
at the Wildwood Inn, Snowmass Village, Colorado, also disappeared. She was found a few days later, naked, lying face down
in the snow. She had been raped and had died from head wounds
inflicted probably with a steel bar. Although Bundy denied ever
being in Colorado, credit card receipts for petrol put him only a
few miles from Snowmass Village at the time of the murder.

In January 1977 Bundy was moved to a prison in Aspen,
Colorado, and appeared in court in June charged with the murder
of Caryn Campbell. Since he acted as his own defence counsel
he was allowed into court unmanacled and one lunchtime escaped
by jumping from a courthouse window. He was recaptured within
a few days, but in December of that year, after adroitly apply-
ing a series of delaying tactics in court, he escaped from Garfield
County jail.

A couple of weeks later in Tallahassee, northern Florida,
several female students were attacked in a sorority house. One,
Margaret Bowman, was strangled to death and sexually assaulted.
Another, Lisa Levy, suffered severe injuries to her anus and
vagina, a bite mark on her buttock and was beaten about the
head with a baseball bat. She died on the way to hospital. On 9
February of that year, Kimberly Leach, a twelve-year-old schoolgirl, left her classroom to fetch a purse and didn't return. Her

body was discovered in April. Injuries to the pelvic region suggested a sexual assault.

In the early hours of 15 February, in Pensacola, near the border with Alabama, a policeman saw a Volkswagen being driven erratically. Over the radio he learned that it had been stolen. He stopped it and after a fight arrested the driver. It was Bundy.

Once again he acted as his own counsel and again succeeded in having the trial put back, from October 1978 to June 1979, and the venue changed to Miami, as he claimed the Tallahassee jurors would be prejudiced against him. At one point he took advice from a local defence team. They advised a plea bargain: plead guilty to the murders of Margaret Bowman, Lisa Levy and Kim Leach in exchange for a guarantee that he would not receive the death sentence.

But the self-confident Bundy rejected their advice and pleaded not guilty. An impression of his teeth, however, fitted the bite mark on Lisa Levy's buttock and several people had seen him leave the sorority house. A stocking mask he'd dropped in the room of one of the attacked girls was identical to one found in the stolen car.

On 23 July 1979, the jury found him guilty and he was sentenced to electrocution. But it was not until 24 January 1989 that Bundy entered the execution chamber. Time for the brutal and sadistic sex killer who may have killed over forty girls had finally run out.

C

Kathleen Calhaem Mr George Carman QC, the defence counsel, called it a trial 'so bizarre and macabre it makes Dallas sound like a children's bedtime story'. The character of fifty-seven-year-old Kathleen Calhaem contributed substantially to the incredible nature of the story.

A domineering personality, she was a business woman who owned a filling-station, a fish-and-chip shop and a gift shop in the small town of Cheddar, near Weston-super-Mare. Forceful and hard-working she seemed to have no other interests in life except her businesses and collecting antiques until, during the late 1960s, she met Kenneth Pigot.

A handsome, white-haired man, he was chief partner in a firm of solicitors in Wedmore, five miles south of Cheddar. At first their relationship was purely professional, but by the early 1970s it was ripening, at least on her part, into love.

Pigot, separated from his wife, was living near Bridgwater and Calhaem used to get up early and drive to a convenient lay-by where she would leave her car and walk or cycle to near where Pigot lived. He would pick her up in the road and drive to where she had left her car. This went on, two or three times a week, for several years. Usually they just talked. Very occasionally there might be kisses, but it rarely went any further than that. Calhaem undoubtedly wanted a closer relationship, but there was a fly in the ointment: Kenneth Pigot had another lady friend.

She was Shirley Rendell, the wife of a fellow solicitor, and they were having a much more torrid affair. Secret afternoon meetings in secluded spots in the Somerset countryside were interspersed with assignations when her husband was at church on Sundays.

Pigot came to wish that he had not started his relationship with Kathleen Calhaem, but she was extremely persistent. Used to getting what she wanted she was prepared to go to great lengths to obtain it.

In October 1982, she hired twenty-nine-year-old Julian Zajac, a steel worker from Avonmouth and a part-time private detective, who advertised in the Yellow Pages. At first she wanted Pigot followed, but when Zajac reported the solicitor meeting another woman, Calhaem began to hint that she would like something to happen to the woman.

Zajac told her it would cost £5,000 and on 14 February 1983, having previously collected the money from Calhaem's house, he stole a car and drove to the bungalow in Yatton where Shirley Rendell lived with her husband. He attacked her in the hall, raining blows on her head with a hammer and stabbing her to death with a knife. Afterwards he destroyed his bloodstained clothing and other evidence in a furnace where he worked.

It was the perfect murder. But Zajac couldn't resist boasting about it to his workmates and the information soon reached the police. He was arrested and brought to trial at Birmingham Crown Court in September 1983. He pleaded guilty, but made a statement throwing most of the blame on to Kathleen Calhaem, and even the prosecuting counsel, Mr Roger Titheridge QC, claimed that she had instigated the murder.

Julian Zajac was sentenced to life imprisonment and soon after, Calhaem was arrested. Her trial took place at Winchester Crown Court in January 1984. Zajac was the main witness for the crown and testified that she was an evil woman who exerted a malignant influence over him. He also said that the killing was accidental. He had not gone to the bungalow with that intention.

It must have sounded incredible to the jury. But then Calhaem had no real defence either. She didn't give evidence herself and her only witness was a convicted murderer who had been in prison with Zajac and claimed that the private detective told him he was going to give false evidence against Calhaem. The jury didn't believe any of them and took only four hours to bring in a unanimous verdict of guilty.

Kathleen Calhaem was sentenced to life imprisonment.

Marie Tarnovska was not so desperately in love as Kathleen Calhaem. She merely wanted to get rid of superfluous lovers. By 1910 she had three. One, Count Paul Kamarovski, she persuaded to insure himself for £20,000. Another, Dr Nicholas Naumoff, she inflamed with the story that the count had repeatedly ravished her against her will and stolen her jewels. The third, a lawyer called Donat Prilukoff, was to call the police at the appropriate time. Naumoff rushed off to Venice where Kamarovski was on holiday, closely followed by Marie and Prilukoff. The besotted doctor duly shot the count and was promptly arrested by the police. He confessed all and the police soon had the whole story. All three were arrested and tried in Venice in March 1910. Marie Tarnovska received eight years imprisonment, Prilukoff ten years and Naumoff only two.

John Cannan   When Shirley Banks did not return after a shopping trip in Bristol, driving her Mini Clubman, on the evening of Wednesday 8 October, 1987, her worried husband of only a month went to the police. They were even more worried. The previous day a man had wrenched open the passenger door of a car waiting at traffic lights in the centre of Bristol and threatened the woman inside with a gun. She began kicking and screaming and the man ran off. Was this an abortive attempt at an abduction which succeeded the following day with Shirley Banks?

An immediate search was mounted for the missing bride and her yellow Mini, but there was no sign of her.

Three weeks later, in Leamington Spa, a tall dark-haired man tried to rob a shop. He threatened the assistant with a gun, but she resisted and he hit her over the head with it and rushed out emptyhanded. She quickly gave the alarm and the police ringed the area with cars. They stopped a black BMW and interviewed the driver, a tall dark man called John Cannan.

When detectives searched the BMW they found a replica revolver, a sharp fishknife and a pair of handcuffs. Cannan said that he was a car salesman; this was curious equipment for a businessman. And the police discovered that he had a long record of robbery with violence and rape. In fact he had been released only the previous year after serving five years for a particularly vicious crime in which he had entered a shop, robbed the woman owner, then taken her into the back room where he raped her in front of her mother, whom he tied to a chair.

A further search of Cannan's car revealed keys belonging to a flat in the Leigh Woods area of Bristol, which he had rented, and in the garage of the flat they found Shirley Banks's Mini, now painted blue.

In November 1987, Cannan was charged with kidnapping Shirley and stealing her car, assault and attempted robbery on the assistant in the Leamington shop, and the attempted abduction of the girl in Bristol.

The following month he was charged with the murder of Shirley Banks. It looked as if this was going to be one of those 'no body' cases, but on Easter Sunday 1988, a woman out looking for mosses near Bridgwater found a naked body. It was badly decomposed, but dental records identified it as Shirley Banks.

John Cannan's trial opened in April 1989, at Exeter Crown Court. But the first thing the jury heard was a description of a rape committed in Reading almost a year before Shirley was abducted. Cannan had threatened with a knife a woman he found alone in a car and raped her twice on the back seat. He was arrested soon after, but DNA samples tested at the time showed a one-in-two-thousand chance that he was not the rapist. The Crown Prosecution Service considered this was not conclusive enough and he was released. But samples taken when he was rearrested after the Leamington job and tested with an improved technique showed it was now 260-million-to-one that he was not the rapist. The jury duly found him guilty of the Reading rape.

In the Shirley Banks trial a fingerprint found in the Leigh Woods flat was shown to belong to the young bride. And a woman came forward to say she had seen a man attacking someone in a wood in the Bristol suburbs on the day following Shirley's kidnap. She could not see the victim, who was lying on the ground, but she could see that the man was hitting her with a stone. The man was Cannan.

He was found guilty of the kidnap and murder of Shirley Banks and received three life sentences with a recommendation that he should never be released.

Similarities in the crimes pointed to possible connections with the unsolved disappearance of Suzy Lamplugh, who worked at an estate agent's office and vanished after arranging to meet a client to look over a property in Fulham. Cannan had been released from Wormwood Scrubs prison, after serving a sentence for rape, only three days before she disappeared. A likeness of a man seen with Suzy on the same day looks very much like the car salesman. And he was thought to have previously used the ploy of posing as a house buyer. Although interviewed by detectives Cannan has always denied being involved, but many people, including Suzy Lamplugh's mother, believe he was the killer.

On 22 December 1921, Irene Wilkins was lured to Bournemouth by a telegram offering a job. She was found the next day battered to death in a field outside the town. Tyre tracks nearby led the police to Thomas Allaway, who, when asked to write the word 'Bournemouth', did so missing out the 'e', just as it had been in the telegram sent to Irene Wilkins. He was convicted at Winchester in July 1922, and hanged.

When a taxi-driver was found shot in a London street in May 1923, a gold-mounted walking stick was discovered nearby. This led the police to Eddie Vivian, a convicted criminal. He claimed that his walking stick had been borrowed by another crook, Alexander 'Scottie' Mason, who had earlier obtained a revolver and expressed a desire to rob a cab-driver. Mason, tried at the Old Bailey in July 1923, said that it was Vivian who had shot the taxi-driver, but he was found guilty and sentenced to death. The sentence was later commuted to life imprisonment.

Alice Lynne (Lindy) Chamberlain When her seven-year-old son said that he was hungry, Lindy Chamberlain, who was in her early thirties, took him over to join her husband at the barbecue area of the campsite. They were near Ayers Rock, a huge redstone hill rising a quarter of a mile up out of the central Australian desert. It was an August night in 1980.

Her husband, thirty-six-year-old Michael, a minister in the Seventh Day Adventist Church, suddenly asked: 'Is that Bubby crying?'

Lindy went back to the tent, which she had left unzipped, to see the rear end of a dingo, an Australian wild dog, disappearing into the darkness. Inside the cot blankets were strewn about, but there was no sign of nine-week-old baby daughter Azaria.

'My God, the dingo's got my baby!' shrieked Lindy.

Three hundred volunteers immediately searched the area and the slopes of the rock by torchlight, and again the next day, but the baby was not found. A week later, some three miles from the campsite, a tourist found some baby clothes near a dingo lair. There was a bloodstained jumpsuit, napkin, singlet and bootees, but no sign of the matinée jacket the child had been wearing in her cot.

The first inquest took place in December and was televised because of the intense interest the case had aroused. The coroner concluded that the baby was attacked by a dingo.

Public opinion was evenly divided. Some people found it

incredible that a live baby would be carried off by a dingo and were amazed that the Chamberlains appeared to take it all so philosophically. Others were more sympathetic. Nevertheless the Northern Territory police began a new investigation. The second inquest opened in December 1981; by this time there was forensic evidence against the dingo theory and the inquest ended with Lindy Chamberlain being committed on a charge of murder and Michael as being an accessory after the fact.

Their trial began in Darwin in September 1982. Prosecuting counsel, Mr Ian Barker QC, attempted to prove that little Azaria died of a cut throat while being held in her mother's arms in the front passenger seat of their car. His case depended almost exclusively on forensic evidence.

A forensic biologist told how she had found bloodstains from a baby inside a camera case and the car and on a pair of nail scissors. The child's clothing had been sent to the noted British forensic scientist Professor James Cameron and he concluded that the bloodstains on the jumpsuit indicated the child had been upright at the time of the assault. Holes in the suit thought to have been made by dingo's teeth he suggested had been made with scissors. He also noted the absence of animal saliva and hair on the material. And his examination of the suit by ultra-violet light revealed a handprint in blood; too large for a baby, but too small for a man – a woman's handprint.

The defence called experts who disagreed that there were bloodstains attributable to a baby in the car. A dental authority said the holes in the suit could have been made by an animal. And the defence scientists could find no trace of a handprint in blood.

There was also the absence of motive. There seemed to be no reason why Lindy Chamberlain would want to kill her baby and her doctor pointed out that she was not suffering from post-natal depression.

Although Mr Justice Muirhead cautioned the jury to treat

the forensic evidence with care, their verdict was unanimous – guilty for both.

Lindy Chamberlain was sentenced to hard labour for life, but Michael received a suspended sentence of eighteen months.

A federal court rejected Lindy Chamberlain's appeal in April 1983 and the following February the High Court of Australia also dismissed an appeal.

But reaction against the verdict was growing. A family described how eight weeks before the disappearance of baby Azaria, a dingo at Ayers Rock had dragged their child out of the car. And the chief ranger of the Ayers Rock area wrote to a newspaper saying he was convinced that a dingo would attack a child. A number of scientists also protested at the conclusions drawn from the forensic biologist's evidence.

In February 1986, a tattered baby's jacket was found close to the spot where young Azaria had disappeared. Soon after this Lindy Chamberlain was released from prison. In 1987, following an inquiry into the case by Mr Justice Morling, Lindy Chamberlain was pardoned.

When the body of eight-year-old Helen Priestly was found inside a sack in a hallway of the Aberdeen tenement where she lived, on 21 April 1934, a neighbour was suspected. Mrs Jeannie Donald was known to dislike the child, who had died of asphyxiation, though there were signs the girl had been injured to simulate rape. There was a web of forensic evidence against Mrs Donald and her fate was sealed when a loaf of bread was found in her flat which her daughter did not recognize and which was of the type young Helen had been sent out to buy. She was found guilty and sentenced to death, which was later commuted to life imprisonment.

Andrei Chikatilo   The first victim in an incredible and long undetected spree of violence was nine-year-old Lena Zakotnova. Andrei Chikatilo, an unlikely serial killer, was an intelligent man with a degree in Russian philology and literature and a school-teacher in the town of Shakhti in south-western USSR.

Lena Zakotnova was killed on 22 December 1978. Her body was found two days later, but there were no clues as to who had killed her. The police eventually picked up a man who had already been convicted of killing a child and served a long jail sentence and who lived nearby. He was tried and although there was almost no evidence against him convicted and eventually executed in 1984.

The killing of little Lena Zakotnova by Andrei Chikatilo began a reign of terror which was to last for nearly twelve years, mainly in the Rostov region of Russia, although he committed some murders in other parts of the Soviet Union. During that time he is thought to have slaughtered fifty-five women and children. Although he admitted all of them – even telling the police about atrocities which they hadn't attributed to him and some which they didn't even know about as the bodies had not been discovered – there was enough evidence to charge him with only fifty-three murders.

Mostly he picked up his victims at railway or bus stations, on trains, at bus stops or occasionally in the street, took them into convenient woods usually near railway lines and killed them.

In September 1984 after having been observed by Inspector Zanasovski for several hours trying to pick up women, he was detained in Rostov's central market. He was questioned in connection with several murders, in particular the murder of a ten-year-old boy some months before. But a sample of his blood did not match a sample of sperm found on the murdered boy's clothes. No one then realized that in very rare cases a man's blood group does not match his sperm. Chikatilo was released.

Six years later the deployment of by now enormous police resources to catch the Forest Path Killer, as he was known, paid off. All railway stations in the region were watched, a procedure requiring huge numbers of men. Chikatilo was spotted coming out of a nearby wood. His name was taken routinely, although it wasn't realized then that he had been committing another murder. But when one of the senior policemen noticed that Chikatilo had already been questioned years before, he was arrested.

He eventually confessed to all the crimes, but his trial, which took place in April 1992 in Rostov, was by no means an open and shut case. It took two days to read out all the indictments, and when the revolting details of the murders were heard in court some of the parents of the defiled children collapsed and had to receive medical attention. Emotions against Chikatilo ran high and he had to be confined in a glass cage to prevent incensed relatives getting at him.

Even though he had confessed to the murders and told the whole of his story to psychiatrists before the trial, he refused to cooperate in court. He interrupted the proceedings frequently by shouting and arguing. He took his clothes off twice and made obscene gestures and remarks to the judge. But after six months the marathon dragged to its inevitable conclusion. Andrei Chikatilo was found guilty of fifty-two murders and judged to be sane and responsible for his actions. He was sentenced to death.

After several appeals had failed, including one to President Boris Yeltsin, Chikatilo was shot in Novocherkassk prison, near Rostov, on 14 February 1994.

Peter Kürten was known as the 'Monster of Düsseldorf'. He too was excited by blood and in 1929 embarked on a series of savage attacks on young women and children, by stabbing, strangulation and blows to the head. He did not kill all his victims and one young lady, whom he had met at the railway station and taken home to his lodgings, he allowed to go after making sure she did not know his address. She wrote to a friend telling of her experience, but incorrectly addressed the letter, which was eventually opened by the post office and passed on to the police. The girl was able to remember how to get to Kürten's house. He was tried in April 1931 for nine murders, convicted and sentenced to death. He was guillotined in Cologne in July 1931 after expressing the hope that he would be able to hear his blood rushing out when his head was cut off.

John Reginald Christie and Timothy Evans   When Timothy Evans was tried for the murder of his baby daughter at the Old Bailey in January 1950, he was twenty-six. He and his wife Beryl, who was nineteen, had moved into the top flat at 10 Rillington Place, Notting Hill, two years before. They soon had one child, Geraldine, and by the summer of 1949 Beryl was again pregnant. She didn't want another child and considered an abortion, something not so easy to obtain in those days. Evans was a Roman Catholic and much against the idea, but he was an easily influenced young man and he was quickly overruled. Beryl arranged for it to be done by the tenant who lived in the ground-floor flat, John Christie, a small, balding, middle-aged man who had been a special constable and claimed to know about medical matters.

One day early in November Evans came home from work to be told by Christie that the operation had been a failure and Beryl had died. He persuaded Evans not to go to the police, said that he would help him by getting rid of the body and he and his wife would find someone to look after little Geraldine.

The distraught Evans, after going to Wales to stay with his aunt and uncle, eventually went to the police.

10 Rillington Place was searched and the bodies of Beryl and fourteen-month-old Geraldine were found in an outside washhouse. They had been strangled. Evans, who was educationally very backward, and according to some authorities mentally deficient, was kept in police custody for three and a half days without being allowed to see a solicitor, a procedure which was then quite possible. After making a number of patently untrue

statements, apparently to protect Christie, he was eventually persuaded to confess to the murder of his wife and baby.

He repudiated this confession at the trial and accused Christie of being responsible. But the ex-policeman, who was one of the main witnesses for the prosecution, denied having done an abortion. He claimed to have been ill in bed with fibrositis – making it impossible for him to move a body – on the day Beryl died. Evans was a poor witness. His hesitant manner and the fact that he had given so many different versions made it easy for the prosecutor, Mr Christmas Humphreys, to show him as unreliable. The judge, Mr Justice Lewis, summed up against him. The jury took only forty minutes to bring in a guilty verdict and Evans was hanged on 9 March 1950.

Three years later almost to the day, a new occupant of the top flat, who had been given permission to use the ground-floor kitchen, Christie having moved out, decided to decorate. He peeled off some wallpaper to discover a papered-over alcove containing the nearly naked bodies of three young women. They had all been strangled.

The police found another body under the floorboards in the front room. It was Christie's wife and she too had been strangled. Two skeletons were discovered buried in the back garden, which pathological reports confirmed were of young women buried ten years before, while the ex-policeman was living at number ten.

When Christie was picked up a few days later he readily admitted killing all the women including Beryl Evans, who he said was depressed and wanted to commit suicide, so he gave her a whiff of gas and strangled her.

All the other women, except for his wife, he said were prostitutes he had invited back to the house when his wife was away. He induced them to sample his 'inhaler', a jar with a metal lid containing perfumed water with tubes coming out of it. Unbeknown to them one of the tubes was connected to the coal gas supply. When they became drowsy he strangled them and had sexual intercourse either just before or just after death.

But he strenuously denied killing the baby, and it is not difficult to see why. His account of how he killed the other women was so bizarre he might get away with a defence of insanity, but the killing of a baby would surely antagonize a jury.

John Reginald Christie's trial began in June 1953, in the same room he had given evidence in at the Evans trial. His counsel, Mr Derek Curtis-Bennett, indeed relied on the defence of insanity. He produced Dr Jack Hobson, senior psychiatrist at Middlesex Hospital, to claim that Christie was insane under the M'Naughten Rules, which state that a man is not guilty if he did not know what he was doing was wrong. But this was strongly contested by the prosecution scientific witnesses, who said that Christie was abnormal but not suffering from any form of hysteria.

The jury took eighty-two minutes to find him guilty and he was sentenced to death.

Then began a clamour to have Evans declared innocent. The Recorder of Portsmouth, Mr John Henderson, was asked to conduct an enquiry and he interviewed Christie in the death cell. The report, put together in three weeks and presented only two days before Christie was hanged at Pentonville, stated that the evidence was overwhelming that Evans had killed his baby daughter – and his wife as well!

The movement to rehabilitate Evans nevertheless continued with books being written by Michael Eddowes (*The Man on Your Conscience*, 1955) and Ludovic Kennedy (*Ten Rillington Place*, 1961) which demolished the case against Evans, and the struggle was continued by some Labour MPs in parliament. In October 1966, Evans was posthumously granted a free pardon.

Wilbert Coffin   The trial of Wilbert Coffin opened in July 1954, in the town of Percé, in the remote Gaspé region of south-eastern Quebec, Canada.

The prosecution case was at best circumstantial. Three men had come up from Pennsylvania in June of the previous year to hunt bear: Eugene Lindsey, his son Richard and Richard's friend Fred Claar. They were eventually reported missing and the police authorities in the town of Gaspé began a search on 5 July.

Wilbert Coffin, a thirty-nine-year-old prospector, said that he had seen the three men on 10 July. He had come across a truck by the side of a road near an abandoned mining camp on the St John River. According to him they explained that the petrol pump on their vehicle had failed and asked him to take Richard into Gaspé – a matter of some sixty miles – to replace it.

Coffin agreed and on the way back the young lad gave the prospector a combination knife which his cousin, who was with the United States Air Force in Japan, had given him. When they returned, Coffin said that another two Americans were there with a jeep which had a yellow plywood box covering the back.

He then left to drive to Montreal to see his common-law wife and when he returned to the area on 12 July found the hunters' truck empty and no sign of the Lindsey party.

Eugene Lindsey's body was found on 15 July, but it was too badly decomposed and eaten by bears to say how he had died. On 23 July the bodies of the two young men were found nearly two miles away. This time it was obvious that at least one of them, Richard Lindsey, had been shot through the heart.

Eugene Lindsey's wallet had been found empty near his body and the police established that it must have contained somewhere in the region of $650. They also discovered that Wilbert Coffin had been spending money freely on his way to Montreal, drinking in various bars, and they could account for nearly all the money – if Coffin had indeed stolen it.

They also searched his wife's house and found a valise, a pair of binoculars and a new petrol pump, all of which were proved to have come from the Lindseys' truck.

At the trial the prosecution produced a witness who said he

had seen Coffin coming into town on 12 July, driving a borrowed truck with the end of a rifle poking out of the back. The prospector had been recently convicted of poaching and was banned from possessing a rifle.

They also found two Americans who had a yellow jeep, but they had left the area before the Lindsey party arrived.

Although Coffin was interrogated for sixteen days he never wavered from his original story and proudly told his father at the end of it: 'They're not man enough to break me.' The prosecution claimed that this was simply an admission of his guilt.

It took fifteen days for the prosecution case to be presented and for two of those days Coffin's lawyer, Mr Raymond Maher, was not even present in court. He apologized to the court, claiming that he had been interviewing witnesses and would be calling a substantial number for the defence, but when the time came for him to present the defence case, he merely said: 'The defence rests.'

His final speech was extremely low-key, whereas the prosecution had two counsel and both made long and energetic speeches, one telling the jury that the eyes of America were on them and exhorting them to set an example for their district, province and for the whole of the country. The jury took it to heart and in half an hour brought in a verdict of guilty. Wilbert Coffin was sentenced to death.

Raymond Maher dropped out of the case and two new lawyers, François Gravel and Arthur Maloney, took over. They made vigorous efforts on Coffin's behalf, for although the prosecution may have proved that he was a thief they surely never proved he shot anyone. The lawyers re-interviewed the witness who claimed to have seen the rifle. Now he had second thoughts and said he couldn't be sure. They even found witnesses who had seen two Americans and a yellow jeep in the Gaspé region in June and the Americans had actually asked after the Lindsey party.

In all they made seven appeals. But in the last one the Supreme Court of Canada by a majority of five to two ruled that the trial had been fair. In view of the split decision, however, François Gravel went before the Minister of Justice and the cabinet to argue that the death sentence should be commuted to life imprisonment. This too was rejected and Wilbert Coffin was hanged on 10 February 1956, one of the most controversial hangings in Canadian history.

John Norman Collins The police were frustrated. The 'co-ed killer' as they called him had just slipped through their fingers again. This was the seventh time in a two-year period that a young girl had been abducted and brutally murdered in the area around the two towns of Ann Arbor and Ypsilanti.

This one was an eighteen-year-old student at Eastern Michigan University in Ypsilanti. Karen Beineman had disappeared on 23 July 1969, and her naked body had been found four days later in a wooded gully north-west of Ann Arbor. She had been raped, strangled, stabbed repeatedly and her panties stuffed into her vagina.

There were indications that the killer had often kept the bodies in abandoned farmhouses and barns. He seemed to be fascinated with the bodies of the girls he had murdered, a not uncommon trait among serial killers. To try and take advantage of this behaviour, Sheriff Harvey kept the finding of Karen Beineman's body out of the papers in the hope that the murderer would return to it. He substituted a tailor's dummy and the police kept watch for several nights. One night one of the officers saw a young man approaching, but because it was raining hard he couldn't see him properly and his radio wouldn't work either. The man disappeared before the watchers could get to him.

But the killer's luck had finally changed.

Karen had been on her way back from a wig shop when she disappeared. She had told the shop owner, Joan Goshe, that she had been given a lift by a young man she didn't know on a powerful motorcycle and he was now waiting outside. Mrs Goshe watched as they drove away and was able to give a good description of the driver. A young campus policeman thought it sounded like a student he had known, John Norman Collins.

Collins had already been interviewed, having been seen with one of the other victims late on the night she disappeared, but had been subsequently eliminated from the enquiry. He was also the nephew of an Ypsilanti policeman, Corporal David Leik.

When Leik heard that Collins was now the number one suspect in the Michigan murders he recalled that when he and his family had returned from holiday not long before, his wife had pointed out to him some recent paint marks on the floor of the basement. Since Collins had been looking after the house in their absence Leik called in the lab men.

The fresh paint drops covered what looked like blood, but turned out only to be red varnish; while they were there, however, one of the technicians noticed some hair clippings by the side of a washing machine.

'My wife cuts the children's hair down here,' explained Leik.

Collins's trial opened in June 1970, in the Washtenaw County Court building in Ann Arbor. William F. Delhey, the prosecutor, decided only to proceed with the murder of Karen Beineman.

The wig-shop owner and an assistant from the Chocolate House shop next door both identified Collins as the young man waiting outside on the motorcycle. But the defence, led by Neil Fink, pointed out that they were viewing through shop windows and could easily have been mistaken.

The defence case was blown apart, however, when Walter Holz, a chemist from the Department of Health, took the stand. He testified that the hairs found on the floor of the basement in Corporal Leik's house were identical to hairs found on Karen's panties.

On 19 August, Collins was unanimously declared guilty of the murder of Karen Beineman and sentenced to life imprisonment.

Raymond Cook, Eric Jones and Kim Newell One might almost have called them 'The Three Stooges' and laughed at their exploits, except that what they were up to was a deadly business. For the two men who went on trial at Oxford Assizes on 5 April 1967 were charged with murder and the charge against Kim Newell was accessory before the fact.

This doesn't mean that the prosecution thought she played a minor rôle; Mr Brian Gibbens, who led for the Crown, pointed out that she 'did counsel, procure and hire the two men to commit the murder'.

Kim Newell was a very pretty twenty-three-year-old whose photographs, according to the policemen who interviewed her, did not come anywhere near doing justice to her beauty. After some time as a children's nurse, she met Raymond Cook in 1966 at the Borocourt Mental Hospital, near Reading, where they were both working as trainee nurses. He was thirty-seven, a tall, balding draftsman who had been made redundant from the Handley Page Aircraft Company in 1963.

They were soon lovers and Cook became besotted with Kim, cashing a £700 insurance policy to spend the money on her. He hadn't a lot of his own, but his wife June, who was a teacher, had. She owned property and insurance stocks and her bank balance was over £11,000.

Raymond Cook left his wife to live with the younger Kim, who soon became pregnant. This did not unduly worry the girl for she had her own abortionist. Eric Jones, a middle-aged man who lived in Wrexham, North Wales, ran a profitable sideline in abortion. According to Superintendent Ian Forbes, one of Scotland Yard's top murder specialists, who was in charge of the case, Jones was a boaster who liked to claim that he had gangster connections. He had known Kim for some years; indeed he had been responsible for her first pregnancy and abortion when she was seventeen.

What stung the plotters into action was the fact that June Cook cut her husband out of her will; soon the three were considering ways of getting rid of Mrs Cook. In furtherance of this Raymond went back to his wife claiming that he had given up Kim. June Cook promptly reinstated him in her will and on the evening of 2 March 1967, they went out for a celebratory meal at the George Hotel in Pangbourne.

A few hours later Mrs Cook was in Battle Hospital, Reading. She had massive head injuries from which she soon died, caused, her husband said, when she crashed their red Mini into a tree along a twisting lane in Rummerhedge Wood, near the village of Peppard. But the police were suspicious, as the Mini was hardly damaged and Raymond had suffered only a bruised knee.

He was arrested a fortnight later and soon after this Mrs Janet Adams, Kim Newell's sister, went to the police.

She gave evidence at the trial that Kim had told her that Cook had persuaded his wife to drive home through the wood, passing the place where Jones was waiting with his blue Cortina. Jones had waved and Cook persuaded his rather reluctant wife to stop, whereupon Jones asked for a lift. As he got into the back he battered Mrs Cook with a car jack. He then attempted to run the car into a tree, but could not get up enough speed, so that the car only gently hit the tree. During this manoeuvre he managed to knock June Cook out of the car. While she was lying on the ground another car stopped.

This motorist, a fireman driving a friend home, was able to describe in court how the man standing over the prone woman muttered something about getting some towels, went back to his own car and drove off. And that was the last they saw of him.

All this time Raymond was pretending to be unconscious in the passenger seat of the Mini.

On the fourth day of the trial Eric Jones changed his plea to guilty and was sentenced to life imprisonment by Mr Justice Stable. Jones then gave evidence for the Crown, describing how Newell had asked him to help smash the car, to get rid of Mrs Cook, and had pointed out the tree to crash the car into.

Cook's story was that he didn't want his wife killed, merely taken out of the way while he obtained a divorce. But this wouldn't have helped him since he could not then inherit.

Kim Newell put all the blame on Cook, saying that he was the prime mover and that she did not want to marry him and didn't mind if he did go back to his wife.

But the jury had no difficulty in finding both Cook and Newell guilty. They were sentenced to life imprisonment.

Reginald Ivor Hinks was another young man who murdered for an inheritance. A petty criminal, in 1933 he married Constance Pullen who lived with her wealthy eighty-five-year-old father in Bath. Hinks put the old man's head in the gas oven and the coal gas killed him. He tried to explain a bruise on the back of the victim's head by saying that he must have caught it when he was pulled out of the oven. But experts at the trial pointed out that the bruise must have been formed before death. Hinks was found guilty and hanged in May 1934.

David Cooper, Michael McMahon and Patrick Murphy   Reginald Stevens locked up his post office in High Town Road, Luton, promptly at six o'clock on the evening of Wednesday 10 September, 1969, and walked round the corner to the car park in Welbeck Road. As he was getting into his car he was confronted by three men. One had a sawn-off shotgun. They demanded the keys of the post office, in the safe of which there was a large amount of money. Stevens refused to give up the keys and during the subsequent struggle was shot in the stomach. He died very quickly.

A green van was seen racing out of the car park soon after

with a man struggling to get in the back. The van was next seen in the station car park, where four men got out. One was an older, grey-haired man and another a younger man with a brown holdall which he threw over a fence onto an embankment. These two climbed into a Vauxhall car and a bystander noted its number. The other two, younger men, got into a red sports car.

The Vauxhall was traced to fifty-three-year-old Alfred Mathews, who had grey hair. Mathews had a number of convictions, including one for robbing a post office. But he had disappeared.

In the meantime Detective Chief Superintendent Kenneth Drury of Scotland Yard's Flying Squad, who was in charge of the murder investigation, became interested in three men: David Cooper, who had a red Mercedes sports car and knew Mathews; Patrick Murphy, who had been arrested and charged with one post office robbery, and Michael McMahon, who was suspected of another. All were small-time thieves from the East End of London.

About a month later Mathews was picked up by the police and in December 1969, he, Cooper, McMahon and Murphy faced murder charges at the committal proceedings in Luton. Drury had recommended to the Director of Public Prosecutions that the charge against Mathews should be dropped and no evidence was offered against him. The three others were committed for trial.

Cooper, McMahon and Murphy were then offered a deal; plead guilty and the charges would be reduced to manslaughter. They all refused and their trial began at the Old Bailey in February 1970.

The prosecution, led by Mr Victor Durand QC, had virtually no forensic evidence at all against the three. The brown holdall had contained the shotgun, which had been traced to Michael Good, another East End man, but it could not be linked with any of the men in the dock. Cooper's sports car could not be positively identified as the one in which two of the robbers were seen to drive off.

In fact the prosecution relied almost entirely on Mathews's evidence. He claimed to have been tricked into driving his Vauxhall to Luton by the three men, but said that he'd been sitting in the car watching the post office when the murder took place and that they had subsequently driven up in the van.

Cooper, McMahon and Murphy had alibis, but as these were provided largely by relatives, they were obviously considered unsafe by the jury, who took only two-and-a-half hours to convict each man of murder. They were all sentenced to life, with the recommendation that they serve at least twenty years.

In 1971 they were refused leave to make a full appeal. But in the following year, after a campaign by Patrick Murphy's father, Terence Edwards, a sewing-machine mechanic, came forward to say that he had seen Murphy in London at 4.30 on the day of the murder and thus he couldn't have been in Luton. In the light of this evidence Murphy's conviction was quashed in November 1973, but he remained in jail as in the meantime he had been convicted of another post office robbery.

At the time of the police investigation Michael Good's wife had claimed that she had previously given the shotgun to her brother, Terence Langston, but he had denied this. In 1972, however, he admitted that he had lent the gun to Alfred Mathews, and in a BBC television programme on 25 October of that year, Mathews's brother said that Alfred had told a string of lies at the trial.

Early in 1972, Drury, who had since been promoted to Commander, was reported in the *Sunday People* as having taken a holiday in Cyprus with a pornographer and operator of strip-clubs in Soho, who had several convictions. Drury was suspended from duty and resigned from the police force. In July 1977 he was sentenced to eight years imprisonment for corruption.

Soon after the murder the Postmaster-General, John Stonehouse, had offered a reward of £5,000 for information leading to the capture of those responsible and Mathews, on Drury's recommendation, had received nearly half of it.

Throughout the 1970s pressure from public opinion to get the case re-opened mounted. It went back to the appeal court five times, but in each case the law lords refused to change their minds, even when publicly criticized by Lord Devlin, a former law lord. In 1980 many people, including Lord Devlin, Tom Sargant, secretary of the organization Justice, and many MPs, were working behind the scenes. And in that year Ludovic Kennedy published a book on the case. Its title, *Wicked Beyond Belief*, was a quote from the trial judge, Mr Justice Cusack, who said that Mathews would have been 'wicked beyond belief' to have made up the participation of the others, thus presumably inviting the jury to think that this was not a possibility.

In July 1980 Cooper and McMahon were suddenly released by Home Secretary William Whitelaw. He told the House of Commons that there was a widely felt sense of unease about the case, which he shared. But although their sentences were remitted they were not declared innocent; a situation which is an injustice in itself.

Dr Carl Coppolino   Dr Carl Coppolino was indicted by a Monmouth County grand jury in New Jersey on 21 July 1966 for the murder of William Farber. Four days later, a Sarasota County grand jury in Florida indicted him for the murder of his late wife, Dr Carmela Coppolino.

Dr Coppolino was living in Sarasota at the time with his second wife Mary, whom he had married only seven weeks after his first wife died, but he was extradited to New Jersey to stand trial there first.

Bill Farber was a retired army colonel. In 1962, he and his wife Marge, who was forty-eight, lived in Middletown, New Jersey. She became friendly with a neighbour, Carmela Coppolino, a medical doctor working as a consultant to a pharmaceutical firm. Near the end of January 1963, Marge told Carmela that she wanted to give up smoking and the doctor suggested she see her husband Carl.

Dr Carl Coppolino had been an anaesthetist at Riverview Hospital, New Jersey, but after a series of heart attacks at a very young age, he resigned aged thirty, and lived on a disability pension. He was an expert in hypnosis and had written a book on its use in anaesthesiology. He began to give Marge Farber hypnosis treatment and soon they were having a love affair.

Bill Farber died on 30 July, Carmela signing the death certificate as coronary thrombosis, and later that year Marge and Carl bought adjoining building sites in Sarasota. Carl moved his family to Florida in April 1965, but Marge didn't arrive until the August. By that time Carl had met a thirty-eight-year-old divorced woman called Mary Gibson. Carmela was found dead on 28 August. The cause of death was given as coronary occlusion by a local doctor and there was no autopsy or suspicion about the death.

After Carl married Mary Gibson, Marge went to the police and accused him of killing his wife by injecting a drug into her, and also of murdering her husband.

The story Marge told the jury at the trial which opened in December 1965 in the Monmouth County courthouse, New Jersey, was extraordinary. She claimed to have been under some sort of hypnotic spell ever since she had met Carl. In June he had given her a drug, succinylcholine chloride, used by anaesthetists to paralyse muscles during surgery, and showed her how to inject it. She claimed that she began to inject her husband with it, but could not bring herself to finish and called in Carl. He completed the injection and afterwards, when Bill seemed to be taking a long time to die, smothered him with a pillow.

Her testimony was damaged somewhat in cross-examination by defending counsel, F. Lee Bailey, who had recently successfully defended Dr Sam Sheppard in another wife murder case (*see* p. 289). Marge had denied in the witness box that Carl had withdrawn from the case on the very day her husband had died because she refused to send him to hospital. Bailey showed her a release form she had signed which showed exactly that.

He brought hypnosis experts to testify that a person could not be caused to commit a criminal act if they didn't want to and that a hypnotic trance could not be made to last for weeks or months.

Prosecution witness Dr Milton Helpern, the famous New York pathologist, said that when he examined the body of Bill Farber after exhumation he found a fractured cricoid cartilage, a classic indication of strangulation. But Bailey was able to show that the injury could well have been caused by the spades of the workmen during disinterment.

The jury were out for only four-and-a-half hours before coming to a verdict of not guilty. Dr Carl Coppolino and his wife Mary heaved a sigh of relief. This had been the difficult trial; the next one in Florida should be a foregone conclusion.

But it wasn't. It opened in April 1967 in Naples, and Bailey, again defending Coppolino, began by making what might have been a bad mistake. He obtained agreement from Judge Lynn N. Silvertooth that no reference should be made to the previous trial. Thus when Marge Farber went on the stand to give her version of events, her admitted involvement in her own husband's death was not mentioned. She came across as a concerned citizen and Bailey's attempt to portray her as a vindictive woman was much less effective.

Dr Helpern had discovered a puncture mark on Carmela's buttock which could have been caused by an injection. Although much of the medical evidence was confusing, there was some indication of succinylcholine in the tissues around the puncture. And it was shown that Carl had ordered six bottles of the drug five weeks before Carmela died.

The all-male jury, after deliberating for five hours on a Thursday evening, retired for the night and in the morning returned a verdict of guilty of second-degree murder, which in Florida meant murder without premeditation. This curious verdict may have been the jury's device to avoid the death penalty. But the judge gave Dr Carl Coppolino the maximum sentence possible – life.

In the end Marge had her revenge.

Dean Corll, Wayne Henley and David Brooks The police arrived at 2020 Lamar Drive, Pasadena, a southern suburb of Houston, Texas, in response to a frantic telephone call. It was eight in the morning of Wednesday 8 August, 1973. They found three dishevelled-looking teenagers, two boys and a girl, sitting outside a small bungalow. Inside was a naked man lying in the hall. He had bullet wounds in the head, back and shoulder. Dean Corll was dead and one of the teenagers, Wayne Henley, who had made the telephone call, described how he had come to kill him.

The night before, Dean Corll, who was thirty-three and an electrician by trade who managed his mother's sweet factory in Houston, had invited eighteen-year-old Henley and his teenaged friend Timothy Kerley to a paint-sniffing party. They left Corll's bungalow around midnight, but returned later with Rhonda Williams, who had just run away from home. Corll was annoyed with the boys for bringing the girl. 'You've spoilt everything!' he said.

Later he calmed down and they all sat round sniffing the fumes from a paper bag into which acrylic paint had been sprayed. They soon passed out. Henley came to in daylight to find he had been tied up. The other two teenagers had also been trussed and Kerley had been stripped. Corll was very angry and, waving a 0.22 pistol about, threatened to kill them all. 'But first I'm gonna have my fun.'

Henley, however, who had known Corll for some years, managed to talk him into releasing him and offered to help in killing the other two. Corll said that he was going to rape Kerley first, and began undressing. He suggested Henley should rape Williams and gave him a knife to cut off her clothes. The teenager began doing this, but when Corll put down the gun he grabbed it. As the older man advanced on him he shot him several times until he collapsed in the hall.

The teenagers were taken to Pasadena police headquarters for questioning. Tim Kerley said that while they had been waiting outside the bungalow for the police to arrive Henley had told him that if he hadn't been his friend he could have got $1,500 for him.

The police who had been searching the bungalow found two large pieces of plywood with handcuffs at two corners and ropes fixed to the other two corners. Clearly they were used for securing victims. They also found a seventeen-inch dildo which hinted at sadistic sexual practices.

Questioned about these, Henley said that Corll liked little boys and had sometimes paid him to procure them for him. He also said that Corll had once told him that he had killed boys and buried them in a boatshed. He took the police there and they began digging. Body after body was recovered. They were all teenagers, naked, wrapped in plastic sheets, and had been either strangled or shot to death.

By this time the world's press had got word and the site soon became crowded with newspaper and television people. By and large the press were deeply critical of the Houston police. How could numbers of young boys – most appeared to be between twelve and eighteen – simply disappear, reporters asked, and the police do so little to find them?

The publicity brought another youth forward. Eighteen-year-old David Brooks had first met Corll when he was twelve and the man had paid him for oral sex. He subsequently became

Corll's lover and helped him to procure other young boys. Between them Brooks and Henley pointed out to the police two more sites where bodies were buried. One was north of Houston, at Lake Sam Rayburn, where Corll's family had a weekend cottage, the other on the coast at High Island Beach.

The body count eventually rose to twenty-seven – at the time a record for mass murder in America. The murders had been committed over three years and it soon became obvious that Henley and Brooks had done more than simply procure the boys for the monster Corll; they had actively participated in at least some of the killings.

In June 1974 they were tried in San Antonio, Texas, for murder.

Henley was defended by Charles Melder and Brooks by Ted Musick. Both attorneys put forward insanity pleas, which were rejected by the jury. David Brooks, however, was convicted on only one count of murder and was sentenced to life imprisonment. Wayne Henley was convicted on nine counts, which didn't include the shooting of Dean Corll, and was sentenced to six consecutive ninety-nine-year life imprisonment sentences, making a total of 594 years in prison.

He told the police there were more bodies buried, but after a time they gave up looking. 'I don't know if we found all the bodies or not,' Lieutenant Porter of the Houston police is reported to have said. 'What difference does it make?'

Dean Corll may have held the record for mass homosexual murder in America for a time, but he was equalled by Fritz Haarman in Germany. Haarman lived most of his life in Hanover. He had a history of thieving and in 1918 became a meat smuggler on the black market. He used to meet refugee trains and invite young boys back to his room, where they were killed, the clothes sold and the 'meat' distributed on the black market. Tried in Hanover in December 1924, he confessed to twenty-seven murders, but was thought to have killed many more boys than this. He was sentenced to death by decapitation.

Alice Crimmins Alice Crimmins phoned her estranged husband Eddie around breakfast time on 14 July 1965 to say that her two children, her four-year-old daughter, known as 'Missy', and five-year-old Eddie Junior, were missing from the apartment. He phoned the police and when they reached the ground-floor flat in Queens, New York, they found the window of the children's room open; but a chest of drawers underneath the window had a covering of dust which would have shown tracks if the children had gone out that way.

Alice's story was that she had fed the children at 7.30 in the evening, on manicotti and string beans – though she later said that the food was veal cutlets – and at midnight took young Eddie to the toilet; Missy said she didn't want to go. She never saw the children after that.

The girl's body was discovered a day later on a vacant lot near her home. Eddie Junior was found five days later near an expressway, about a mile from Alice's apartment. Because of the hot weather his body was so badly decomposed that it was very difficult to say how he had died. It was decided to charge Alice only with the death of Missy.

At the trial, which began in May 1968, Dr Milton Helpern, the New York pathologist, reported that the autopsy had shown the stomach to be full of beans and manicotti, practically undigested, which meant that death must have occurred no later than two hours after the meal. If this was true it meant that Alice was lying.

Joe Rorech, one of her boyfriends, testified that Alice had said she would rather see the children dead than let Eddie have custody of them. And, when she and Joe were spending a night together at a motel, she had broken down and confessed to killing Missy.

At this Alice jumped to her feet screaming abuse at him and caused an uproar in court. The judge had to ask the defence attorney to restrain his client. But she erupted again when Mrs Earomirski gave her evidence.

This middle-aged lady lived opposite the Crimmins's flat and at two o'clock on the morning the children disappeared she saw a man and a woman in the street, the man carrying a bundle, the woman leading a child by the hand. The man threw the bundle into the back of a car; the woman said, 'My God, don't do that to her,' and the man replied: 'Now you're sorry?' Mrs Earomirski identified Alice as the woman.

The accused went into the witness box and denied everything. She came under severe cross-examination from prosecution attorney Tony Lombardino who emphasized her flagrant affairs with many men and her neglect of her children, but she maintained her version throughout.

The defence, somewhat predictably, was that the prosecution witnesses were against her because of her morals.

At two o'clock in the morning the jury brought in a verdict of guilty of manslaughter and the sentence was that she should serve not less than five years and not more than twenty. But she stayed in prison for only twenty-four days in the next three years.

A new defence counsel, Herbert Lyons, won an appeal on the grounds that three of the jury had made an unauthorized visit to the street outside Mrs Earomirski's apartment. A new trial was ordered.

This time the prosecution decided to have Alice indicted for both deaths and the second trial began in March 1971. The medical evidence now included the autopsy on young Eddie. Joe Rorech's evidence was again greeted with a tirade of abuse from the accused. This time he said that Alice had identified the man who helped her that night. She called him Vinnie 'Carrabella'. The police had actually found a convict – he was serving a sentence for dope peddling – called Vincent Colabella, who boasted to another convict that he had driven Alice's car that night, but he refused to testify.

The jury went out in mid-afternoon, but it wasn't until six o'clock the next day that they brought in a verdict. Guilty of murder, for Eddie, and guilty of manslaughter for Missy. The sentence was life for murder and five to twenty years for the manslaughter.

But this incredible story was not yet finished. In 1973 the murder verdict was reversed by the Supreme Court of Brooklyn, a new trial on the manslaughter charge was recommended and Alice was released from prison. After further appeals in 1975 the manslaughter conviction was upheld and Alice was returned to prison. She was granted parole in 1977.

Craig Crimmins 'What I hope to show . . .' said defence attorney Lawrence Hochheiser – known as one of the toughest lawyers in New York City – 'what I hope you will understand, is that a miscarriage such as we are going to see presented during this trial is not done by evil men who seek to frame someone who is entirely innocent of a murder, in order to further their own ends. Not at all. What you are going to see is these police-men were all well-meaning men . . .'

On 23 July 1980, at about 9.45 in the evening, Helen Mintiks, a brilliant young violinist at the Metropolitan Opera House, disappeared during the interval of a performance of the Berlin Ballet Company, starring Rudolf Nureyev. Her body was found eleven hours later at the bottom of a ventilator shaft. She had been bound and gagged and her clothes had been cut from her body with scissors. She had not been raped.

Investigations revealed a used sanitary towel at the bottom of the stairs leading to the lowest basement in the labyrinth of the building and a woman's shoe up on the air-conditioner fan roof. A careful search of the area turned up a palm print on one of the large pipes leading across the roof.

The print was soon matched with that of a stage hand, Craig Crimmins, a twenty-one-year-old stage carpenter, and after two long interviews he eventually confessed to the murder.

The police surmised that he had followed the violinist along a corridor when she left the orchestra pit during the interval. She was seen getting into a lift with a man by a dancer at about the time she disappeared. Then, according to Crimmins, when they were alone in the lift he said something rude to her and she slapped his face. He threatened her with a hammer, took her out of the lift and down the stairs to the bottom basement, where he forced her to undress. After attempting an unsuccessful rape, he eventually ejaculated by rubbing himself against her. Then he allowed her to get dressed and took her up on the roof where he tied her up near one of the huge air-conditioner fans. He took away her shoes and cut off her clothes so that, according to him, she would be too embarrassed to escape. But when he left he could hear her trying to get free, so he went back and kicked her into one of the narrow ventilator shafts, where she fell three storeys, about thirty feet, and was killed.

The trial in April 1981 was finely balanced. The dancer, under hypnosis, had been able to give a good description of the man, and a photofit picture looked remarkably like Crimmins, but she could not pick him out of a line-up. The palm print on the pipe could have been made long before the murder. Crimmins repudiated his earlier confession at the trial and claimed to have been asleep backstage at the time of the murder. The prosecution brought witnesses to say that he was not where he insisted he was, but absenteeism, drunkenness and drug-taking were rife among the backstage staff and the witnesses were not all that reliable.

It all came down to his confession and whether the jury believed it. Hochheiser hammered away at the two policemen who had been responsible for obtaining it, accusing them of exerting psychological pressure on the young man, but could not shake them. A videotape record of the confession made to an assistant district attorney backed up their assertions that Crimmins was not unduly influenced.

The jury, after deliberating for nine hours, found the defendant guilty of felony murder, i.e. of causing death while committing a felony. He was sentenced on 2 September 1981 to twenty years to life.

He was placed in the prison infirmary at Riker's Island while awaiting sentence, and shared a room with Mark Chapman, the man who murdered John Lennon. Crimmins referred to Chapman as a nutcase and the two quarrelled and had to be separated.

Young Eileen 'Gay' Gibson, an actress, disappeared from the liner *Durban Castle* on a return trip to England from South Africa in October 1947. A nightwatchman remembered he'd seen thirty-one-year-old ship's steward, James Camb, in the girl's cabin the night she disappeared. Camb, tried for murder in March 1948 at Winchester Assizes, claimed that Gibson had invited him to her cabin. During intercourse she'd had a fit and died and in a panic he'd pushed her body through the porthole. Although the case against him was not strong his calm demeanour under pressure in the witness box and the fact that he'd not called for help went against him. He was found guilty, sentenced to death, but reprieved.

Jeffrey Dahmer   The trial of Jeffrey L. Dahmer began in January 1992 in the old Safety Building in downtown Milwaukee, which is on Lake Michigan just north of Chicago. He was accused of fifteen homicides and he pleaded guilty but insane. The jury simply had to decide if Dahmer was sane or not.

The first witness was Detective Kennedy of the Milwaukee police department who read out Dahmer's 178-page confession.

It began by recounting events in 1978, when he was only eighteen. His parents were going through an acrimonious divorce. He was lonely and alone in the house at West Bath Road, Bath Township, Ohio, since his father had already left and his mother and younger brother were away visiting relatives. He went out in the car and picked up a young man hitch-hiking home from a rock concert. They went back to Dahmer's house and drank beer and talked. When the youth said he was going to leave Dahmer tried to persuade him to stay and when he found he couldn't, struck him on the head with a dumb-bell and strangled him. He dismembered the body and eventually got rid of the pieces in the waste disposal. Dahmer never even knew the young man's name.

Nothing further happened for another ten years. By that time Dahmer was living with his grandmother in West Allis, a suburb of Milwaukee, and working at the Ambrosia Chocolate Company in the city. He used to hang round gay bars and had served a year's probation for exposing himself to two twelve-year-old boys. Six days after the end of his probation he picked up twenty-four-year-old Stephen Tuomi in a gay bar. They went to a hotel for sex and the next morning Dahmer apparently awoke to find he had strangled the young man. He went out and bought a large suitcase, put the body in it and took it by taxi to his grandmother's home where he had a basement apartment. There he again dismembered the body and disposed of it in the garbage.

During the next four years he killed another fifteen boys and young men, eleven blacks, one Laotian, one Hispanic and two whites. The Laotian boy, fourteen-year-old Konorak Sinthasomphone, was persuaded to go back to Dahmer's apartment – he now had a place of his own on the seedier side of the city – to pose for sexual photographs. There he was given drugged coffee and when he was unconscious, stripped and raped. Dahmer then went out to buy beer and returning was horrified to see the naked boy, who had somehow escaped, in the street pleading with some girls to help him. Dahmer tried to grab the boy and the girls called the police. He explained to the three officers who came that it was just a lovers' quarrel and they rather surprisingly believed him, allowing him to take the still semi-conscious boy back to his flat. After a quick look round the living-room the police left and Dahmer promptly strangled Konorak, cut up the body and took polaroid photographs of the dismembered corpse.

When the three officers returned to the police station they joked about the homosexual quarrel they had just settled, not realizing that a tape recorder had been turned on. When Dahmer was finally arrested and confessed, the significance of the incident was appreciated and when someone leaked the tape to radio and television the police were accused of racial bias.

But Dahmer's luck had to run out sometime and a few weeks later a young black man approached a police car in Milwaukee with a pair of handcuffs hanging from one wrist. He pleaded for them to release him and said that a madman had abducted him. He had gone to a white man's home, he said, and the man had tried to drug him, had struggled with him and threatened to cut out his heart and eat it. He had eventually made his escape.

The young man led the police to an apartment block occupied almost exclusively by blacks, to a flat where a young white man opened the door. He was calm and polite, but when asked for the key to the handcuffs became abusive and violent and had to be arrested.

This time the police took more than just a quick look round. In the freezer they found plastic bags containing pieces of meat, one of which looked remarkably like a human heart. Three human heads were also in plastic bags. A filing cabinet contained a number of human skulls with holes drilled in them; one was painted grey. In several boxes they found human bones together with a number of hands and a male genital organ. A large plastic barrel in the bedroom contained the remains of three male torsos. There were also a large number of photographs of dismembered corpses.

Dahmer was taken to the police station where he made confessions to all his murders, even telling how he had cooked and eaten some parts of the bodies he had cut up.

The confessions, however, were only part of the trial. Three eminent psychiatrists were called by the defence and they all said that Dahmer was suffering mental illness such that he was not responsible for his actions. The prosecution called two, who said that Dahmer undoubtedly was suffering from a psychiatric disorder, but that it didn't prevent him knowing right from wrong. Judge Lawrence Gram then produced two more, perhaps feeling that the jury could not really trust any of the others, and though they disagreed as to motive they each were of the opinion that Dahmer was legally sane when he committed the murders.

Not surprisingly the jury verdicts were guilty on all fifteen counts. Jeffrey Dahmer was sentenced to fifteen terms of life imprisonment, since the state of Wisconsin has no death penalty. It meant he could never be released.

On 28 November 1994, Dahmer was battered to death with a broomhandle by a fellow convict in the Columbia Correctional Institute, Portage, Wisconsin.

Plainfield, Wisconsin, a small town in a farming area, is only some hundred miles to the north-west of Milwaukee. In November 1957, an incident occurred there with eerie similarities to the Dahmer case.

Edward Gein, a middle-aged farmer living alone, was suspected of being involved in the disappearance of middle-aged Bernice Worden and the police searched his farmhouse. They found the headless and eviscerated body of the woman hanging from the ceiling. They also found parts of fifteen other female bodies. Bracelets had been made of human skin, which had also been used to cover a tom-tom. A skull had been converted into a soup bowl and Gein had worn human skin as a waistcoat. But when the farmer confessed, which he did quite readily, it turned out that he had only actually murdered two women, Bernice Worden and another Plainfield resident, Mary-Hogan, in 1954. The other body parts he had obtained by digging up newly made graves.

At the preliminary trial hearing Gein's attorney entered a plea of insanity and the judge committed him to the Central State Hospital for the Criminally Insane for psychological tests. In January 1958, three psychologists claimed that he was not mentally competent to stand trial and Judge Bunde committed him indefinitely to the state mental hospital, where he died in 1984.

The case inspired several books; the film *Psycho* was based on one of them, as was *The Texas Chainsaw Massacre*.

Ronald DeFeo   'Someone shot my father and mother!' Twenty-three-year-old Ronald DeFeo Jr rushed into a bar in the Long Island coastal town of Amityville on the evening of 13 November 1974 with this hysterical shout.

When the police arrived at the house on Ocean Avenue they found the bodies of Ronald DeFeo Sr and his wife Louise in their bedroom. In a nearby bedroom were twelve-year-old Mark and seven-year-old John and in two other bedrooms teenagers Dawn and Allison. All the victims had been shot and post-mortem examination revealed that the murder weapon was a 0.35 Marlin rifle.

In a search of the house the police found an empty box which, according to the label on the outside, had contained a 0.35 Marlin rifle. It was in Ronald DeFeo Jr's room, and talks with the young man's friends showed that he was a gun buff and had been trying to buy a silencer for his rifle the week before.

At first Ronald suggested that his family had been associated with the Mafia and that the killings were the work of a hitman, but he soon confessed to the murders and told the police where he had got rid of his bloodstained clothes, the discharged cartridges, which he had carefully gone round the house picking up, and the rifle, which he had since thrown into the dock at Amityville.

When he came to trial in October 1975, his defence was insanity. To bolster this he started a fire in his cell at Riverhead County jail, destroyed his mail and threatened suicide. A defence psychiatrist testified that he thought Ronald was insane and had not known what he was doing when he murdered his family. But the prosecution brought their own medical man, who said that the young man was not psychotic.

Ronald's family had come from the tough neighbourhood of Brooklyn, New York. He was undoubtedly a misfit, but was indulged by his father, who kept him well supplied with money while he ran through a succession of jobs. The young man regularly took drugs and had a history of petty crime. He undoubtedly hated his family and admitted in the witness box that he shot them all, but claimed that it was the fault of his sister Dawn, who gave him the gun and murdered some of the children herself before he shot her.

But Ronald DeFeo Jr was found guilty on all six charges of

second-degree murder and received twenty-five years to life on each, although they were all to be concurrent.

The house on Ocean Avenue was sold and the new owners lived in it for less than a month before claiming that it was haunted. A book was written about their experiences, *The Amityville Horror*, which was made into a very successful film. The present occupiers, however, say there is no evil presence in the house.

Sidney Fox murdered his sixty-three-year-old mother in a hotel room at Margate by strangling her and setting fire to the chair in which she sat. Suspicions were aroused because he hurriedly claimed the life insurance. When asked at the trial why, having discovered his mother's chair was alight, he closed the door before running for help, he said that he didn't want the smoke to spread to the rest of the hotel. He was found guilty and hanged at Maidstone prison in April 1930.

Dr Geza de Kaplany   It was Dr de Kaplany himself who called the police on a hot night in August 1962, in San Jose, California. Officers went to the flat in Ranchero Way. Outside were several residents who had been roused by the loud music coming from apartment 30, and by the screaming.

The door was opened by the thirty-six-year-old doctor, an anaesthetist at the local Doctors' Hospital. He was wearing only Bermuda shorts and rubber gloves. He indicated the bedroom.

There the police officers were greeted with a sight they would remember for the rest of their lives. On the floor between the twin beds was what had once been the beautiful Hajna, the wife of only five weeks of Dr de Kaplany. She was naked and her legs and arms had been secured with surgical tape and electrical flex.

The upper half of her body was covered in a yellow substance and she was screaming loudly. She was quickly transferred to hospital where it was discovered that she had nitric acid burns to her face, breasts and genital area and she had been mutilated with a knife.

The police found a note in the bedroom, written on the back of a prescription form, in Hungarian. It read:

> If you want to live
> 1. Do not shout
> 2. Do what I tell you
> If not you will die

De Kaplany told the police, 'I know she was unfaithful for a fact. She only married me for my station in life. I did not want to kill her. I only wanted to take away her beauty.'

Although she was not expected to last the night Hajna in fact lived for another thirty-three days, most of the time in terrible agony, and died on 30 September. De Kaplany was charged with first-degree murder.

The trial began in January 1963. His defence attorney, E. F. De Vilbiss, wanted him to plead guilty so that he could concentrate his efforts on an insanity defence. But the doctor refused because first-degree murder, in California law, implies an intention to kill.

On the second day of the trial, when the surgeon from the county hospital was describing Hajna de Kaplany's horrific injuries, the prosecution produced in illustration a large photograph of the body taken after death. De Kaplany at once jumped up and lunged across the courtroom shouting: 'No! No! What have you done to her?'

That same night he sent for his attorney and changed his plea.

'I am a doctor,' he said. 'I loved her. If I did this . . . I must have done this . . . Then I am guilty.'

The defence concentrated on the insanity defence, bringing out de Kaplany's traumatic childhood, with his stern and distant mother and father in Hungary in the Second World War, during which he lost three brothers.

But the prosecution showed that de Kaplany had followed

his wife to San Francisco when she went to visit her mother, thinking she was going to visit a lover, the day before the attack. He saw there a family friend who told him that his wife was continuing to see a married man with whom she had had an affair the previous year. The doctor went to a lawyer who told him that a divorce might take some time. 'I cannot wait a long time,' he replied. 'I could not control myself for a long time.' He then bought bottles of acid, surgical tape and flex.

On the night of the murder they went to bed, but de Kaplany, thinking of her supposed lover, found himself impotent and in his own words 'just blew up'. The prosecution claimed that this showed a jealous rage and not insanity.

The jury agreed and brought in a verdict of guilty. But when it came to deciding the sentence they seemed to side with the defence psychiatrist who proposed that de Kaplany was legally sane but mentally ill, and instead of the death sentence their recommendation was for life imprisonment.

He served twelve years and was then deported, since he was not an American citizen. He went to Taiwan and worked in a missionary hospital.

John George Haigh was another murderer who used acid. This time it was sulphuric acid and he used it to destroy the bodies of his victims. He was discovered because of his association with Mrs Durand-Deacon, who disappeared in London in February 1949, and he admitted eight other murders. His assertion that he drank the blood of his victims might have been an invention, since his defence at the trial in July 1949 was insanity. But he was convicted of murder and executed in August 1949.

Count Marie Alfred Fouquereaux de Marigny   The body of multimillionaire Sir Harry Oakes was found lying on the bed in his palatial beach-side mansion, Westbourne, on the island of New Providence in the Bahamas, in the early morning of 8 July

1943. He had been severely beaten about the head, doused with petrol and set on fire. Someone had sprinkled white feathers from a ripped pillow over the blackened corpse.

The murder caused a sensation in the islands and the governor, the Duke of Windsor, imposed a forty-eight-hour news blackout. He had been a personal friend of the murdered man and he went over the heads of the detectives in the Bahamas' own criminal investigation department and called in two American policemen from Miami, Captain James Barker and Captain Edward Melchen – he asked for them by name – to conduct the investigation.

To many people Count de Marigny was the obvious suspect. He had married Sir Harry's eighteen-year-old daughter Nancy against her parents' wishes and there was bad feeling between the two men. He had also angered Sir Harry by refusing to go to a cocktail party with the Duke of Windsor, and he was thus unpopular with most of the white population of the islands.

Alfred de Marigny did not have a good reputation concerning women. At thirty-three he had been married twice and was rumoured to have had many affairs. On the night of the murder, with his wife Nancy away in America, he and a friend took two young RAF wives out to dinner and subsequently he escorted the young women back to their cottage, afterwards driving home. His route would have taken him past Sir Harry's residence during the time – 1.30 a.m. to 5.30 a.m. – when it was estimated the millionaire had died.

Within thirty-six hours of the murder Alfred de Marigny had been arrested. However, Nancy brought in a well-known American private detective, Raymond Schindler, to help clear her husband's name. Schindler found policemen busy scrubbing the walls of the murder room, and when he asked why, was told they were removing fingerprints which did not match those of the accused.

He also found that the American policemen had failed to

find the two nightwatchmen who should have been on duty the night of the murder and who had subsequently disappeared. No proper search had been made either for the murder weapon or the automatic which the millionaire always kept under his pillow. There were also many unexplained footprints on the stairs which looked as if several people had been up and down them during the night.

Count de Marigny's trial began in October 1943 in the Supreme Court and things looked decidedly bad for the accused when Captain Barker produced a print of de Marigny's left little finger, taken from the Chinese screen near Sir Harry's bed. Under cross-examination by the Honourable Godfrey Higgs, however, Barker could not remember where exactly on the screen it had been. And contrary to British police practice at the time it had not been photographed on the screen or the screen produced with it on.

The count had actually been interviewed at Westbourne on the day of the fingerprint examination of the murder room and had been taken to the room during the interview, but the police claimed that had been in the afternoon, after the fingerprint examination had been completed. Higgs, however, produced two witnesses who had been at Westbourne in the morning and had seen de Marigny there then. At this stage the police witnesses all confessed they had been mistaken. It was beginning to look as if the fingerprint evidence against the count had been manufactured.

Certainly the prosecution case had collapsed; the jury were out for two hours before bringing in a verdict of not guilty. But it was only a majority verdict, at nine to three, and they added a curious rider. They recommended that de Marigny should be deported. The Chief Justice, Sir Oscar Daly, said that he had no jurisdiction in such a matter, but would pass on the recommendation to the proper authorities.

Alfred de Marigny was duly deported.

The murderer of Sir Harry Oakes was never found, although the work of Thomas Schindler suggests that the Mafia, who were trying to obtain a gambling licence in the Bahamas at the time, might have been behind it.

Peter Demeter   On 18 July 1973, ex-model Christine Demeter was found with her head in a huge pool of blood on the garage floor of her luxury home near Toronto, Canada. Her husband Peter, a wealthy property developer, was the obvious suspect. Although he had a perfect alibi – he was taking some house guests shopping while his wife was being bludgeoned – he could well have hired someone to do it.

Peter had recently taken out an insurance policy for a million dollars on Christine's life. Police investigations soon revealed that he had previously taken up with an old girlfriend, an Austrian beauty called Marina Hundt. He didn't seem unduly upset by his wife's death and there were persistent rumours that he had been plotting to kill her.

Most of these came from a young Hungarian refugee, Csaba Szilagyi, who had known Demeter for sixteen or seventeen years. Both had come from Hungary; Peter had paid for Csaba's passage to Canada and had allowed him to live in his home rent-free for over a year. But now the young Hungarian seemed anxious to blacken Demeter's character, describing how he and the businessman had discussed various ways of getting rid of Christine. After being contacted by the police he even went so far as to wear a concealed microphone to record conversations he had with Peter after the funeral.

On 17 August 1973 Demeter was arrested and charged with the murder of his wife. He finally went to trial on 23 September 1974, in London, Ontario, after lengthy pre-trial hearings to determine the validity of the tapes. But two weeks before the trial began a curious incident occurred.

A policeman in Toronto spotted a Chevrolet making an

illegal left turn. He followed in the police car, but the Chevrolet refused to stop. Indeed, after becoming trapped in a one-way street, the driver got out and began shooting at the police. A gun battle developed and the gunman was eventually killed. He turned out to be an escaped convict called Laszlo Eper, who had been serving a sentence for shooting a police officer. In his room was a piece of paper with Peter Demeter's name on it.

The judge, the Honourable Justice Campbell Grant, allowed Szilagyi's taped conversations as evidence, but though in them Peter Demeter repeatedly hinted that he wanted someone to kill his wife, he said nothing really definite. And Mr Joe Pomerant, one of the defence lawyers, subjected Csaba Szilagyi to such a severe cross-examination that he was largely discredited as a witness.

Prosecuting counsel, Mr John Greenwood, then produced another witness, Freddie Stark, an old Hungarian associate of Demeter's who had worked for him as a plumber. Stark said that the businessman had kept on at him to find someone to kill Christine, and eventually he found a gambler known as Cutlip Kacsa or 'The Duck'. He was to meet Mrs Demeter in one of Peter's properties and push her down the stairs. She would be carrying a rolled-up blueprint which Demeter had given her and which unbeknown to her carried the money for the hit in it. But The Duck lost his nerve at the last minute, grabbed the blueprint with the money, and fled.

The police had actually found the rolled up blueprint at Kacsa's girlfriend's house, but the would-be assailant had left for Hungary. And while extradition proceedings were going on he mysteriously died.

But the sensation of the trial was yet to come. The police had always suspected that Laszlo Eper might have been the man Peter Demeter had hired to kill his wife, and when a close associate of Eper's, Joe Dinardo, a huge man and an ex-boxer, fell into their hands after he tried to burn down a garage, they were delighted. Dinardo's evidence, however, was so explosive that John Greenwood refused to bring it in himself, but presented it to the defence.

Before the jury were allowed to hear it, however, the evidence had to be brought before the judge to see if it was admissible.

Dinardo said that Eper had indeed approached him with a proposal for killing a person for $10,000. The proposal, however, had come from Christine Demeter and she had wanted Eper to kill Peter! The ex-boxer claimed that he would have nothing to do with it. But one day Eper came to him in a panic. His clothes were saturated with blood and he said that after an argument about the money he had killed Christine.

Greenwood immediately claimed that the evidence was inadmissible because it was hearsay – literally what one hears, but does not know to be true. And Judge Grant, after hearing submissions from the defence, agreed.

The jury thus never heard Dinardo's evidence and on 5 December, after just three hours, they brought in a verdict of guilty of murder against Peter Demeter. Asked if there was anything he would like to say, Demeter, in a broken voice, absolved the jury from all blame, saying that on the basis of what they were allowed to hear they could not have reached any other decision.

Demeter was sentenced to life imprisonment. Two appeals, one to the Ontario Court of Appeal, and another to the Supreme Court of Canada, were turned down. And though there will be those who think that in this case justice was turned upside down, others might think it was poetic justice.

Wayne Lonergan was the young estranged husband of a brewery heiress who was found bludgeoned and strangled in her New York apartment on 24 October 1943. Although he had recently joined the Royal Canadian Air Force, he was known to have been in New York on that date. Tried in March 1944, his so-called confession had not been signed by him and it could not be shown that he had visited the murder scene or handled the candlestick used to kill his wife. Nevertheless he was found guilty of second-degree murder and sentenced to thirty years to life.

Evelyn Dick The trials of Evelyn Dick made her the most notorious woman in Canada. She lived in Hamilton, Ontario, and by the summer of 1945 was a beautiful woman of twenty-five. She was also highly promiscuous, having had a number of affairs with prosperous men in the town, and having acquired in consequence an illegitimate daughter. Financially she did well out of the men, and had a high standard of living, but she craved a stable relationship.

She met John Dick in the autumn of 1945. He was a forty-year-old Polish emigrant and a driver for the Hamilton Street Railway. Evelyn's father, Donald MacLean, was a janitor for the same firm. John told her that he had a part share in a cannery and they were married on 4 October. But Evelyn discovered that he had been lying about his financial prospects and two hours after the ceremony she deserted him, going home to her mother.

Soon after this she was seen about with a hefty young steel-worker called Bill Bohozuk. John Dick did not prove easy to get rid of, however, and when Evelyn, her daughter and her mother moved into a large house on Carrick Avenue he insisted on moving in with them.

Evelyn's mother had separated from her husband, who lived at a house on Rosslyn Street; Evelyn remained close to both of them.

Early in March 1946 John Dick disappeared, and on the 16th of that month some boys found a headless torso on a wooded hillside a few miles from Hamilton. It had gunshot wounds and was soon identified as the missing driver.

Evelyn was interviewed and over the next few weeks made eleven different statements to the police, many of them without her lawyer being present. These were to prove significant in the trials which followed. In her final statement she said that Bohozuk had shot John Dick in the head while they were riding in a car she had borrowed. She also said that her father, who hated Dick, had lent the steelworker the gun and had cremated the murdered man's head and limbs in his own furnace at Rosslyn Street.

But a search of Evelyn's home at Carrick Street turned up fragments of bone and teeth in ashes concealed in a hamper in the cellar. And, most bizarre of all, in a suitcase in the attic the decomposing corpse of a baby was found with a cord around its neck. Evelyn admitted the child was hers, but said that Bohozuk had killed it.

She was tried in October 1946, in Hamilton, for the murder of her husband. The judge, Mr Justice Barlow, refused most of the defence submissions and summed up heavily against her. She was found guilty and sentenced to death. An appeal was lodged on her behalf by a new lawyer, Mr John J. Robinette of Toronto, on the grounds of many errors in the first trial. One of these was that the police had not properly cautioned Evelyn before she made her statements. The appeal was upheld and a fresh trial was ordered.

At the new trial the confessions were ruled inadmissible, but the prosecution brought in a witness who had not appeared in the first. He claimed to have seen Evelyn in a car with a body in the back. His credibility was dented in cross-examination by Robinette with questions like: why had he not come forward before? and the revelation that he had a criminal record. On 6 March 1947, Evelyn was acquitted of murder.

There was very little evidence against Bohozuk. Evelyn refused to give testimony against him or her father. The steelworker was acquitted. Donald MacLean was given five years for being an accessory after the fact.

Evelyn Dick's acquittal was very unpopular, but she was soon on trial for the murder of her child. This time she was found guilty of manslaughter. The sentence at the time in Canada for a mother convicted of the death of her baby was not usually very severe, but Evelyn received life imprisonment.

Elvira Dolores Barney was twenty-seven and a wealthy socialite when she was tried for murder at the Old Bailey in July 1932. She claimed that she obtained a revolver to commit suicide, and when her lover tried to prevent her he was shot accidentally. A gunsmith said the trigger pull was heavy, making it unlikely the gun had gone off by accident, but Patrick Hastings, the brilliant defence counsel, calmly pointed the gun at the court ceiling and repeatedly pulled the trigger. Afterwards he revealed that it nearly broke his finger, but Mrs Barney was acquitted.

Diane Downs   When the tearful Diane Downs brought her three children to the Willamette-McKenzie Hospital in Springfield, Oregon, on the night of 19 May 1983, seven-year-old Cheryl was already dead and Christie, eight, and Danny, three, were barely alive. Diane said that she had been driving the children when a man flagged her down and attempted to steal the car at gunpoint. When she resisted he shot all three children, and her in the left arm.

At the scene of the crime the police could find no cartridge cases. There was no gunshot residue either on the outside of the car, and Diane's wound was minor compared to the children's, who had each been shot through the body. The police considered also that she didn't act like a woman whose children had just been shot. She was not distraught and seemed concerned only with her own injury. They were deeply suspicious of her story.

A possible witness was young Christie, but she had suffered a stroke and was seriously ill in hospital. To ensure her safety she was made a ward of court and Diane allowed to visit only in the presence of a social worker. Diane bitterly resented this and publicly accused the police of not searching for the man who had attacked them. She petitioned the juvenile court for visitation rights, but was refused.

She then persuaded her divorced ex-husband – the children's father – to let her see them secretly on one of his visits, which were not supervised; during the visit she tried to persuade Christie not to talk to the doctors about what had happened. Found to be in contempt of court she was sentenced to thirty days in jail, but this was suspended when it was learned that she was pregnant.

Diane had a new boyfriend, and though she basked in the publicity she refused to say who it was because he was married. The prosecution at her trial suggested that a similar situation had occurred before her children's deaths. A previous lover had been married. She had considered her children an encumbrance to her love affair and had decided to get rid of them, shooting them while they were in the car and giving herself a minor injury to support her story.

Her trial began in May 1984. She was accused of the murder of her daughter Cheryl and the attempted murders of Christie and Danny. Diane said in her evidence that her upbringing had been harsh and brutal, her father having assaulted her over a period of four years, and she had learned not to show her feelings. This was why she had appeared so callous after the shootings.

But Fred Hugi the prosecuting attorney called police witnesses to show that on the night of the attacks they had found a gun at Diane's home, and experts testified that rifling on the bullets fired from this weapon were identical to that on bullets taken from the wounded children. Diane and her attorney replied to this by accusing the police of planting the bullets in her house.

However, Hugi called Christie Downs, and the small nervous child told in a quavering voice how she had seen her mother shoot her sister and brother and then turn the gun on Christie herself. She underwent forty-five minutes of cross-examination, but remained firm in her story.

Even so it took the jury three days to make up their minds. Some of them apparently simply couldn't believe that a mother would kill her own children. But eventually the verdict was guilty. Diane Downs was sentenced to life imprisonment.

Christie made an almost perfect recovery, young Danny remains paralysed from the chest down. Both were adopted by Fred Hugi and his wife.

John Francis Duffy It was 2 December 1985, and in the magistrates court at West Hendon a small red-haired man of twenty-seven was appearing to have his bail renewed. John Duffy, of Irish parentage, had attacked his estranged wife and her boyfriend a few weeks before and had been charged with assault and malicious wounding. He was out on bail awaiting trial.

Into the back of the courtroom came a twenty-year-old woman led by a police officer. She had recently been attacked and raped in Copthal Park, North London, and the detective, who had previously been involved in investigating Duffy for the rape of his estranged wife, wondered if the little man was responsible for both. But the young woman could not identify Duffy.

The Irishman recognized her, however, for he had indeed been the man who raped her, and he suddenly realized the danger of his being picked out by a victim. This almost certainly launched him on his career of murder.

On 29 December, nineteen-year-old Alison Day disappeared near Hackney Wick Station in East London. Her body was found seventeen days later in a canal. Her hands had been tied behind her back and she had been strangled with a strip of her skirt, used as a tourniquet with a piece of twig. It was impossible to tell if she had been raped.

The police were nevertheless convinced that the attack fitted the pattern of the railway rapist, although he had not killed before. The series of outrages had begun in June 1982, with a rape by two men at West Hampstead Station, and since then there had been twenty-five repetitions, though latterly they seemed to be by one man only. They were all near railway stations and it was obvious that this was how the rapist escaped. It had sparked off a massive computer-based police hunt, called Operation Hart, involving four separate forces, the Metropolitan, Surrey, Hertfordshire and the Railway Police. In all there were over 5,000 suspects, of whom Duffy was one because of the alleged rape of his wife.

17 April 1986 was a Thursday and on that day fifteen-year-old Dutch schoolgirl Maartje Tamboezer went missing while riding her cycle near Horsley Station, Surrey. Her body was found the next morning. She had been tied like Alison Day, raped, and strangled with a tourniquet made from a piece of her skirt and tightened with a twig. Her body had also been set on fire, presumably to get rid of evidence.

The guard and passengers on a train leaving Horsley at about the time Maartje disappeared noticed a small man getting on, and one woman gave a good description of the man, who sat opposite her. She said he had staring eyes. The police also obtained some useful clues. Semen on the girl's clothes indicated that the rapist had blood group A, and the victim's hands had been tied with a distinctive type of brown string, called Somyarn.

Mrs Anne Lock, twenty-nine, a secretary working for London Weekend Television, disappeared from Brookmans Park Station in Hertfordshire on 17 May. Nine weeks later her body was discovered near the railway line. Like the other two she had been tied up. She had been raped and a sock stuffed in her mouth. But the body was not in good enough condition to tell exactly how she died.

By this time Duffy had been questioned by the police, but he refused to give a blood sample, as was his right, and eventually put himself out of reach in a mental hospital where he said he was suffering from loss of memory. However, he was soon released and kept under close observation by the police.

At this stage the Surrey police consulted a behavioural scientist, Professor David Canter of the University of Surrey. Using an American concept known as 'psychological offender profiling' he provided a psychological portrait of the killer, listing seventeen points, nearly all of which fitted Duffy to a T. Late in November Duffy was arrested.

The trial, which lasted six weeks, began in January 1988. During the proceedings the judge, Mr Justice Farquharson, directed the jury to find Duffy not guilty of the murder of Mrs Anne Lock because of insufficient evidence.

But several women were able to identify Duffy as the man who had raped them. A search of his mother's house turned up a large ball of string of the Somyarn type, and thirteen fibres found attached to Alison Day's clothes when she was taken from the canal were a perfect match for fibres on a pullover of Duffy's.

His defence was one of amnesia; he simply couldn't remember. This didn't impress the jury of six men and six women who found him guilty of two murders and five rapes. He was given seven life sentences with a recommendation that he serve at least thirty years. Early in 1995 the Home Office announced that he would never be released.

The other man who was involved with Duffy in the early rapes has never been apprehended.

E

Sergeant Frederick Emmett-Dunne The trial took place in June 1955, in Steel House, Düsseldorf, the pre-war headquarters of the German Iron and Steel Corporation. But it was a British military court martial, because the accused, Sergeant Emmett-Dunne, was an Irish citizen – born in a Dublin workhouse and abandoned by his unmarried parents he was given the name of his mother followed by the name of his father – and a British civil court had no jurisdiction over him.

The case began two years earlier at Duisburg, fifteen miles from Düsseldorf. Late on the evening of Saturday 30 November, 1953, Maria, the German wife of Sergeant Reginald Watters, phoned the sergeants' mess at Glamorgan Barracks from her married quarters to say that her husband had not come home. Sergeant Emmett-Dunne suggested to the orderly officer that Watters might be in No 2 Barrack Block, where he had a friend.

They found the sergeant, who was only five-feet-one in height, in the foyer, hanging from a rope which was tied to the banister rail. His feet were no more than six inches from the floor and an overturned fire bucket was nearby. They cut the man down, but he was already dead.

A young army pathologist performed a post mortem and reported that the injuries were consistent with strangulation. The verdict of the court of enquiry was that Watters had hanged himself.

He was buried in Germany, and his wife moved to Leeds to stay with Watters's sister, but seven months later Maria married handsome, broad-shouldered, six-feet-two Emmett-Dunne. This news came as a shock to Sergeant Frank Walters of the Rhine Army Special Investigation Branch, the army CID, who had known Watters and Emmett-Dunne and remembered the rumours at the camp at the time of Watters's death. He persuaded the SIB to begin an investigation and subsequently Home Office pathologist Dr F. E. Camps went to Germany. Watters's body was exhumed and a second autopsy performed. Early in March 1955, Sergeant Emmett-Dunne was charged with murder.

The court martial consisted of seven officers under the presidency of Brigadier D. L. Betts. The judge-advocate was Mr Charles Cahn and the prosecution was led by a civilian barrister, Mr Mervyn Griffith-Jones, assisted by two officers of the army legal service. The defence was in the hands of Mr Derek Curtis-Bennett.

Mr Griffith-Jones brought a succession of German women witnesses to show that at the sergeants' mess Emmett-Dunne always sat at Maria's table and danced with her, that he often rang her up at her home, and they went out together when her husband was away on duty. One reported that he had told her he was in love with a married woman. Sergeant Brown, who had shared a room with Emmett-Dunne, said that some weeks before Watters's death Emmett-Dunne had remarked that there was a member of the mess who would commit suicide if his wife didn't behave herself.

Dr Camps told the court that after his examination of the exhumed body at the Cologne Military Hospital, he came to the conclusion that death had resulted from a heavy blow to the Adam's apple and the body had then been hung to make it look like suicide. A physical training instructor said that he had taught Emmett-Dunne unarmed combat when he was under training, in particular the 'flying wedge' blow, delivered with the edge of the hand hard across the Adam's apple. It was known as the 'silent kill' and used to dispose of enemy sentries.

The prosecution star witness was Private Ronald Emmett,

the sergeant's younger half-brother. He was in the same camp as Emmett-Dunne and on the night Watters died received a message to meet his brother in the car park. Emmett-Dunne told him that he had accidentally killed a man and asked for his help. Together they strung up the body of Sergeant Watters. Ronald Emmett said nothing about it to anyone, thinking it was an accident, until he heard that Emmett-Dunne had married Maria; then he went to the police.

The defence, under the direction of cheerful, roly-poly Derek Curtis-Bennett, was that it was indeed an accident. Emmett-Dunne went into the witness box to deny any involvement with Maria until he met her by chance one day in Leeds after Watters's death. He claimed that Watters was suspicious of him and Maria, and on the night he died was in a suicidal mood and Emmett-Dunne offered to drive him home. In the car Watters suddenly produced a gun and threatened to shoot Emmett-Dunne who, fearing for his life, lashed out and caught the smaller man in the throat. He panicked on finding Watters dead, and tried to make it look like a suicide.

Curtis-Bennett even staged a reconstruction with Emmett-Dunne and a small man to represent Watters in a BMW car similar to Emmett-Dunne's. Officers and lawyers clustered round as the sergeant demonstrated what he said happened in the vehicle.

But he didn't convince the seven army officers, who took seventy-six minutes to find him guilty of murder, with no recommendation for mercy. He was sentenced to death, but it was not carried out because the murder was committed in Germany. That country did not have the death penalty, and the arrangement was that occupying forces were bound by the same rule. Emmett-Dunne received life imprisonment.

It has been suggested by Rupert Furneaux in his book *Famous Criminal Cases 3* that a jury of twelve ordinary citizens might well have agreed that the blow was accidental, but seven officers, who had been through a war and might have had experience of combat, would not accept that such a precise thrust could be anything but deliberate.

Kenneth Erskine 'Erskine', said Mr James Crespi QC when he opened the prosecution case at the Old Bailey trial in April 1987, 'is a killer who likes killing.'

One of the first witnesses was Mr Frederick Prentice, who was seventy-three and lived in an old people's home in Clapham, South London. He described a night in late June 1986 when he heard footsteps in the passage outside his room. He saw a shadow on the glass door. It slowly opened. A slim young man with very short Afro-Caribbean hair and coffee-coloured skin came in. Mr Prentice didn't know him and he was frightened. He shouted for the man to go away, but the intruder only put his finger to his lips to indicate silence, then leaped across the room and jumped on top of the frail old man.

He sat astride Frederick with his knees on his arms, and his hands gripped the old man's throat. As he steadily applied pressure he muttered the word 'kill'. But Mr Prentice did not give up without a struggle; he shouted and screamed and jerked about. The pressure on his neck was increasing, then it eased off, then it came again. The old man realized that his attacker was playing with him, torturing him, before finishing him off. He tried to yell louder, but his strength was failing.

Suddenly his attacker hauled him out of bed and smashed him against the wall. He slid down onto the floor. The intruder must have assumed he was dead, for with that he left.

Although Mr Prentice did not know it at the time, he was the only survivor of the man who came to be known as the 'Stockwell Strangler'.

The attacks had begun when Nancy Emms, a seventy-eight-year-old spinster, was found strangled and sexually assaulted in her bed in West Hill Road, Wandsworth, on 9 April that year.

Two months later a couple of elderly men, one eighty-four, the other ninety-four, were found dead in their beds, in next-door rooms, at an old people's home in Stockwell. They had been strangled on the same night and one had been sexually assaulted. The following day a sixty-seven-year-old woman was found strangled in bed at her flat in Stockwell.

The next month brought three more murders; two elderly men and an eighty-year-old woman, all of whom were found strangled in bed; all had been sexually assaulted.

In all, twenty-three-year-old Kenneth Erskine, who had an English mother and an Antiguan father, was charged with seven murders. In five cases, two women and three men, according to Mr Crespi, the sexual assaults took the form of buggery, but it was not possible to say if they took place before or after death.

Although he left only one witness to his murderous night-time escapades, there were some other clues. A palm print was found on a bathroom widow, a thumb print on a plant pot at the residence of one victim and a palm print on a garden gate and the wall of another. A sole print he left in the home where the two old men were killed matched a print on the roof of the home where Mr Prentice was attacked. And Mr Prentice was able to pick out Erskine at an identification parade.

It was very much a circumstantial case against him as he made no confession and refused to give evidence in court. The police were able to produce tapes, which were played in court, of interviews they had had with him. In these he spoke of a whispering woman's voice which came to him out of walls and doors and tried to control him. He admitted that he burgled the homes of the victims – indeed his prints were on file because he had a history of burglary – but he denied killing anyone and claimed that someone must have gone into the rooms after he had left and killed the old people.

Mr Justice Rose, summing up, commented on the fact that psychologists had reported that Erskine had a mental age of eleven and a very poor memory. But, he said, this did not prevent him giving testimony in court and it didn't mean he was not responsible for his actions. He told the jury that the only thing they had to decide was: did he do these things?

The jury thought that he had and convicted him of murder in all seven cases. Mr Justice Rose said: 'I have no doubt that the horrific nature and number of your crimes requires that I should recommend a minimum sentence . . . In all the charges . . . I shall recommend to the Secretary of State that you serve a minimum of forty years.' It was the longest sentence of its kind ever imposed by a judge in England.

F

Madame Marguerite Fahmy It was a newspaper sensation; murder among the wealthy at one of London's most prestigious hotels, an undercurrent of sexual perversion and a heroine described as 'The Tragic Princess'.

In truth, Madame Fahmy had been a prostitute, albeit a high-class one, who had raised herself from humble beginnings in Paris to a position where she could attract wealthy men.

She shot her well-heeled husband of only six months three times in the head, afterwards admitting that she had done it. This was in 1923 and, only a few months before, Edith Thompson had been hanged for merely inciting her lover to kill her husband (*see* p. 310). In France Mme Fahmy might have been able to claim that it was a crime of passion and been leniently treated, but this was no defence in a British court. A coroner's jury found her guilty of murder. Yet at her trial at the Old Bailey in September 1923 she was acquitted, of murder and even of manslaughter.

So how did she manage it? The answer is Sir Edward Marshall Hall, the most famous criminal lawyer of his age.

He began by attacking the character of the dead man, who called himself Prince Ali Kamel Fahmy, though he never was a prince. He was the son of a wealthy Egyptian industrialist and first met Marguerite when he was attached to the Egyptian embassy in Paris. They were married in December 1922 in Egypt.

Marshall Hall spent four hours cross-examining Said Enani, Fahmy's secretary and constant companion, getting him to admit that the Egyptian had had his wife followed, and treated her with persistent cruelty, including striking her on the chin so that he dislocated her jaw. He also brought out the fact that Fahmy had gone back on his original promise that if Marguerite adopted the Moslem religion she would still have the right to divorce him, through a civil contract.

The secretary refuted the suggestion that Fahmy was a man of unnatural sexual appetites, though it was patently obvious that he was. This was apparently the reason for their last, fatal quarrel, though it never came out in an explicit way at the trial. Mme Fahmy was suffering from a large thrombosed pile and a fissure of the anus, following anal intercourse with her husband, the only sort he seemed to like, in early June. She needed an operation and wanted to have it in Paris, whereas he wanted her to have it in London.

On 9 July the couple were staying at the Savoy Hotel and had spent most of the day quarrelling. Mme Fahmy told hotel staff that her husband was going to kill her within the next twenty-four hours. In the early hours of the next morning, while a summer storm raged outside, a hotel porter came across the couple shouting at each other in the corridor outside their room and asked them to go inside. A few moments later three shots rang out and Fahmy was found slumped in the doorway, bleeding from wounds in the head.

Mme Fahmy said, in French, 'What shall I do? I have shot my husband. I lost my head.' But Marshall Hall insisted that the last phrase should be translated: 'I was frightened out of my wits.' Mme Fahmy agreed.

He also persuaded the famous gun expert, Robert Churchill, to admit that if one shot was fired from the 0.32 Browning pistol another was automatically loaded and was ready to be fired, and that a novice might suppose that if one shot was fired, out of the window for example, the gun would then be empty. This was his 'accidental firing' defence.

The other defence was self-defence. Marshall Hall extracted the testimony from yet another prosecution witness – the doctor who had been called at the time of the shooting – that a scratch he'd seen on the back of Mme Fahmy's neck was consistent with a hand clutching her throat.

Mme Fahmy's evidence had to be given through an interpreter. She claimed that her husband had sworn to kill her and that she was in fear of her life. She said that she had never fired a pistol until that night and when Fahmy advanced, threatening to kill her, it had gone off accidentally.

But the famous advocate's final speech was the real clincher. He painted a picture of Fahmy as a raving, lustful beast, attacking his wife because she would not agree to his disgusting demands. In a blatant piece of racist invective he pointed out that Fahmy was an oriental, and if you stripped off the external civilization you discovered the real primitive whose treatment of women did not fit the way Western women consider they should be treated by their husbands.

It went down well with the jury, and was warmly applauded by many newspapers. Mme Fahmy was acquitted and released. When she was asked: 'Will you be inheriting your husband's fortune?' she replied, 'Of course. He's dead, isn't he?'

But she didn't. After a six-year battle the Cairo court ruled that since she had shot her husband she had no right to his fortune.

Madame Henriette Caillaux, the wife of the French Finance Minister, in March 1914 put five bullets into Gaston Calmette, the editor of *Le Figaro*, who had been publishing attacks on her husband. She went on trial for murder in July 1914 on the eve of the First World War. Her husband, however, produced evidence that Calmette had been in the pay of the Germans, and she was acquitted amid scenes of national fervour.

Mark Fein 'Gentlemen of the jury,' said Defence Attorney William Kleinman, 'have you ever seen such a depraved, diabolic-

ally clever, diabolically vicious, evil, scheming creature as Gloria?'
And he was merely talking about a prosecution witness!

But he had good reason. The fact that his client was in the
dock at all was almost entirely due to a thirty-seven-year-old lady
known as Gloria Kendal, Mrs Margaret Foster, Mrs Carmela
Lazarus (that was actually her name) and some twenty other
aliases. And the story she told in the witness box must have been
one of the most incredible ever heard in a courtroom.

The case began on Thursday 10 October, 1963, in New
York, when forty-year-old Rubin Markowitz disappeared. His
body was recovered four weeks later from the junction of the
Hudson and Harlem Rivers. He had been shot four times with
a 0.22 calibre weapon. His movements on the day he disappeared
were not easy to trace because Markowitz was a part-time book-
maker and at that time the New York penal code stated that a
bookmaking operation handling more than $5,000 on any given
day was a felony punishable by a five-year prison sentence.

That afternoon Markowitz was known to have been due to
meet Mark Fein, a thirty-two-year-old millionaire industrialist
and a heavy gambler, who owed him $7,200. Fein admitted he
had met the bookie, but claimed he had paid his debt and left
him alive.

The laborious business of checking answering-service records
of the bookie and a notebook containing codenames of his customers eventually led the police to apartment 5B at 406 East
63rd Street and to the tall, voluptuous redhead with the little-
girl voice, Gloria Kendal.

She had worked as a high-class prostitute nearly all her adult
life and also supplied girls. She claimed to be a friend of Fein's,
although he denied it. It was proved he paid the monthly rent
of her apartment.

About 5.30 p.m. on the day of the murder, Gloria said that
Mark Fein phoned her at another apartment and asked her to
come to East 63rd Street. When she arrived she saw a large

steamer trunk in the living-room which Fein told her contained the body of Markowitz. He said they had been talking and someone had come in and shot the bookie. Fein implored Gloria to help him get rid of the body. Accordingly she phoned a couple of friends to come over while she and Fein went out and hired a station waggon. Then she and her friends took the trunk in the station waggon and dumped it in the river. In a later statement she said that Fein admitted shooting Markowitz himself.

The trial began in October 1964. The defence attorney naturally went into Gloria's background, showing that both her husbands had been convicted criminals and she herself had been in prison. The relatives of one of her husbands, he suggested, had been involved in robbing bookies.

Mark Fein did not help himself. It was proved that he had lied to the police and he didn't go into the witness box. Though there was no compulsion on him to do so, juries often suspected that a defendant who did not, must have something to hide. The all-male jury had to decide whether to believe the prosecution's version of the murder, bolstered by Gloria's story and that of her friends, who might have been nearly as suspect as she was, but went into the witness box; or to trust the defence strategy, which was essentially to deny everything and claim that Mark Fein had been framed.

The jury deliberated from Monday 23 November to the early hours of the following Thursday, before bringing in a verdict of guilty of second-degree murder against the defendant.

Less than three weeks after her husband's conviction Mrs Fein put the defence into the hands of Louis Nizer, one of the most famous courtroom lawyers in America, who immediately began appeals for a new trial. They were eventually denied by the court of appeals and the judge's sentence allowed to stand.

The sentence was minimum term thirty years, maximum life, the maximum which could be imposed for the crime of second-degree murder.

Dr Bernard Finch and Carole Tregoff The trial began in courtroom no. 12 of the Los Angeles county court in December 1960. Dr Finch, forty-two, and twenty-three-year-old Carole Tregoff were accused of murdering Dr Finch's wife, Barbara, and of conspiracy to murder.

The deputy district attorney opened the case for the prosecution, showing that Mrs Finch had been found on the night of 18 July 1959 on the lawn of their expensive home in West Corvina, to the east of Los Angeles. She had been shot in the back and had two fractures of her skull.

A key witness was the blonde Swedish maid Marie Lidholm. She spoke of many angry scenes between Dr Finch and his wife and of Barbara telling her she thought her husband wanted to kill her.

The Finches had been married eight years, but Dr Finch and shapely Carole Tregoff, who was his secretary, had become lovers. Mrs Finch had heard about it and was suing for divorce. Under Californian law, the property would normally be shared equally, but where the divorce was granted for adultery, extreme cruelty, or desertion the court had the power to grant the innocent party a major proportion of the property. Barbara was claiming the whole of the property, plus legal fees and substantial alimony. This caused considerable friction between the two.

Marie Lidholm described how, at about 11.30 on the night of the murder, she heard Mrs Finch's car drive into the garage. A few minutes later she heard her scream for help. Rushing into the garage she saw Mrs Finch lying on the floor. Then Dr Finch appeared – the couple had been living apart – and slammed Marie against the garage wall. Barbara got up and ran away across the lawn, while Marie dashed inside to phone the police. While she was doing this she heard a single shot.

The prosecution produced John Cody, a disreputable young man who by his own account lived by his wits. He claimed that Carole Tregoff contacted him and she and Dr Finch paid him

$1,400 to kill Mrs Finch, but he merely pocketed the money and did nothing.

The deputy district attorney also produced what he called a 'murder kit': a bag containing a flashlight, two lengths of rope, an ampoule of Seconal and some Seconal tablets, two hypodermic syringes, surgeon's gloves, bandages and a carving knife which he said Dr Finch had left at the murder scene.

Dr Finch said in evidence that it was merely part of his doctor's bag. He and Carole went to see his wife and waited for her to come home. When she arrived and saw them she produced a gun. He struggled with her and wrenched the gun away. The maid then arrived and he put down the gun to try and stop her screaming. Barbara snatched up the gun and ran off with it; thinking that she was going to shoot Carole, he chased her and took the gun off her again. As he was throwing it away it went off and his wife sustained her injury.

The gun was never found.

The jury of five men and seven women considered this some-what incredible story for eight days before announcing they were unable to agree on a verdict.

A new trial was ordered which, with a new judge, opened in July 1961, and was virtually a rerun of the first. Again the jury, this time of eleven women and one man, could not agree, much to the annoyance of Superior Judge LeRoy Dawson. He had them back in court and told them that in his opinion they ought not to believe the evidence of Dr Finch and Carole Tregoff. The doctor's attorney protested vigorously and was fined $500 for contempt of court – this conviction was later set aside and the judge reprimanded. But the jury still could not agree, even after deliberating for twenty days, and there was a third trial.

It began in January of the following year. This time Dr Finch had a different attorney, there was a new judge, and a new deputy district attorney prosecuted. The jury, this time of ten men and two women, took only four days to reach verdicts. Dr Finch was convicted of first-degree murder and Carole Tregoff of second-degree murder. The jury also had to determine the sentences, but they did not feel able to give Dr Finch the death sentence and awarded him life imprisonment instead. Both defendants thus had the same sentence.

Dr Finch was paroled in 1971 and Carole Tregoff two years earlier.

Dr Benjamin Knowles was also accused of shooting his wife. He was a medical officer in the African territory of Ashanti. In 1928, after a quarrel, his wife was found injured with a gunshot wound in the abdomen. He said, and she agreed with him, that she had sat on the gun and it had accidentally discharged. But when she died he was tried without a jury, convicted of murder and sentenced to death. On appeal in England the sentence was quashed on the grounds that the trial judge had not considered the possibility of manslaughter.

John Floyd   Thomas Bloodworth rushed out of the apartment, his face white and his hands shaking. 'Blood,' he gasped. 'Everywhere!'

It was the morning of Wednesday 26 November, 1980, and Bloodworth, who worked on the local newspaper *Times-Picayune*, had called to find out why his friend and colleague William Hines, who lived alone in the French quarter of New Orleans, had not turned up for work. Another tenant had let Bloodworth through the gates and, since Hines's apartment door was ajar, he went in. But when he saw the bloodsplashed walls he looked no further, but called the police.

Detectives found no sign of a break-in. Hines's viciously slashed body was discovered in the bedroom. It was apparent that he had been pursued through the apartment by the murderer, who had slashed him as he ran, finally seizing him from behind to cut his throat. The police had no clues; an absence of fingerprints and no forensic evidence of any kind. And they were shortly to have further problems.

On the following Friday in the early hours of the morning a young black man, Rodney Robinson, rushed out of his room in the expensive Fairmont Hotel and died on the carpet in the corridor. His throat had been cut and he had been slashed and stabbed many times, just like William Hines. He died without uttering a word. There was again very little for the police to work on – no fingerprints or other forensic evidence. No one had seen anything, except a security guard who had noticed a black man rushing out of the rear door of the hotel soon after the murder, which turned out to be a false alarm.

It took nearly a year of patient police work before the break came. Following an underworld tip-off, on 19 January 1981, John Floyd – sometimes known as 'Crazy Johnny' – a white, unemployed drifter was arrested.

His trial opened on 5 January 1982 before Judge Jerome M. Winsberg. There was no jury. Defence counsel Walter Sentenn had deliberately asked for there to be none. Perhaps he feared that the details of the bestial killings would so horrify a jury that they might be unduly influenced against his client.

John Floyd was a young man who lived mostly off the charity of his friends. A drug addict, he frequently mixed an explosive combination of drugs and booze and was extremely violent. Several witnesses testified to his outbreaks of unprovoked aggression in bars he frequented.

But the main plank in Assistant District Attorney David Plavnicky's prosecution case was the confessions Floyd had made to both murders while in police custody. He claimed to have met the two men in the same way, casually in the French quarter, and after asking for money had been befriended by them. After drinking with Hines he was invited back to the newspaperman's flat. An argument had broken out and Floyd had killed him. Similarly with Robinson. He had given Floyd a lift to a bar before taking him back to his hotel room, where another argument led to the lethal assault.

Walter Sentenn, who believed passionately that the police

had arrested the wrong man, suggested that the confessions had been obtained by beatings. John Floyd went into the witness box to claim that he had been knocked to the floor and kicked in the head by police officers during interrogation.

But he couldn't explain why he had not asked for hospital treatment after the assaults, nor could he explain how he had been able to describe the interior of Hines's flat or the colour of the carpet in Robinson's bedroom. And a videotape, made by a local New Orleans television station, of Floyd being escorted by police officers soon after his confessions, showed the prisoner with no signs of injury.

To sustain a first-degree murder charge, which carried the death penalty in the state of Louisiana, the prosecution had to prove the accused had either murdered during a felony, committed multiple simultaneous homicides or killed a law officer. Plavnicky could prove none of these and had to go for second-degree murder, which carried a sentence of life imprisonment with no chance of parole for forty years.

At the end of the trial Judge Winsberg retired for ninety minutes before pronouncing; for the murder of Rodney Robinson – not guilty! But in the case of William Hines he found the defendant guilty.

David Curtis Stephenson, Grand Dragon of the Ku Klux Klan, went on trial in Hamilton, Ohio, for murder in October 1925. In March 1924 he kidnapped young Madge Oberholtzer and so savagely assaulted her on a train that she took poison and died. The prosecutor argued that Stephenson was a murderer 'just as if he'd plunged a dagger into her heart'. The jury agreed and sentenced him to life imprisonment.

Leo Frank   The unfortunate Leo Frank was not the victim of circumstances of his own making, but of the political situation which existed in the poor South of the USA just before the First World War. The American Civil War had been over for nearly fifty years, but on Confederate Memorial Day, Saturday 26 April, 1913, in Atlanta, Georgia, factories were closed, there were parades and the people remembered the war which they had lost to the hated Yankees.

It was on this day that Mary Phagan, within a week of her fourteenth birthday, failed to come home. Her body was found the next day in the basement of the National Pencil Factory where she had worked, and where she had called in the previous day at just before noon to collect her pay packet.

She had suffered a severe blow to the back of the head, but had died from strangulation by a length of cord which had been tied tightly round her neck. Nearby were two pencil-scribbled notes purporting to have been written by Mary and pointing the finger of suspicion at the black nightwatchman. But since she would hardly have had time to write notes before being strangled they were regarded as obvious forgeries.

Twenty-nine-year-old Leo Frank was under suspicion from the beginning. The manager of the factory, he had been one of the last people to see Mary when he gave her her money in the almost deserted building. Furthermore he was cordially disliked by the Southerners because he was a rich Northerner, his uncle owning the factory. He was also a Jew, and Jews were hated in the South almost as much as they were in Germany before the Second World War.

His trial, however, which began on 28 July 1913 in Atlanta, was not quite as one-sided as it might have been. His family and many members of the Northern Jewish community put large sums of money into the defence. The best lawyer in Georgia, Luther S. Rosser, was hired and both the Pinkertons and William J. Burns, the most famous private detective agencies of the times, worked on the case.

But prosecutor Hugh Dorsey had a star witness. Jim Conley was a twenty-seven-year-old black who had been a sweeper and general handyman at the factory. He claimed to have seen Frank at 'unnatural practices', at that time a serious crime in Georgia, with girls from the factory in the manager's office. He testified that Frank had told him he'd killed Mary and that he helped the manager carry the body into the basement. He also said Frank had forced him to write the notes.

Dorsey also produced an affidavit from Frank's maid and cook, in which she said that she heard Leo confess the murder to his wife. The servant afterwards repudiated the affidavit, saying that she could neither read nor write.

It seemed that most of the witnesses against Frank had been either beaten or bribed to give evidence. But the main obstacle to the defence obtaining a verdict in their favour was undoubtedly public opinion. Many newspapers published articles attacking Frank and a mob collected outside the courtroom whenever he appeared, calling continually for his blood.

After the longest trial in Georgia's history, the jury of twelve men took less than four hours to bring in a unanimous verdict of guilty and Frank was sentenced to death. Conley was convicted of being an accessory after the fact but served less than a year in jail. After many appeals had been turned down, the state governor, John Slaton, in a courageous act – which was nevertheless political suicide – granted Frank a last-minute reprieve, and wrote a 10,000-word commentary pointing out the inconsistencies of the prosecution case.

Frank was smuggled out of prison in Atlanta to the state penitentiary at Milledgeville, but four weeks later he was attacked by a fellow convict and his throat slashed. His life was saved by the prison doctor, but his luck was not to last. On the night of 16 August 1915, seven cars full of heavily armed men arrived outside the jail. The telephone wires were cut, the barbed wire breached and the staff held at gunpoint.

Leo Frank was taken away and lynched. Newspapers praised the action and the Mayor of Atlanta said it was a just penalty. Not one of the party was ever charged although many gave newspaper interviews.

On 4 March 1982, when all the major figures in the case were dead, Alonzo Mann, who had been a fourteen-year-old office boy at the factory at the time of the murder, made a statement. He said that he had been standing in a stairwell soon after the crime and had seen Conley carrying the body, on his own, down to the basement. Conley had threatened to kill him if he reported what he'd seen. But it was not until March 1986 that the state of Georgia finally pardoned Leo Frank.

Arthur Beard was drunk when he raped and suffocated a thirteen-year-old girl. At Chester Assizes in 1919 he was convicted and sentenced to death. The court of appeal considered that as Beard was drunk he was not capable of acting with 'malice aforethought', the formula of words used to describe the state of mind necessary for murder, and reduced the finding to manslaughter. But the House of Lords again reversed the verdict. They considered that he might not have had the intention to kill, but he clearly had the intention to commit rape, a felony. And up until 1957 in English law, causing death in committing a felony was murder. He was reprieved just the same.

John Wayne Gacy 'I shan't be long, Mum. Just going to talk to this contractor guy about a summer job.'

Mrs Elizabeth Piest had come to pick up her fifteen-year-old son from his evening job at a pharmacy in Des Plaines, an outer suburb of Chicago. She waited in the warmth of the shop while her son was outside talking to the small, plump man in the big car. It was 11 December 1978, and a bitterly cold night.

She waited a long time, but young Robert did not reappear. Later that night Mr and Mrs Piest went to the Des Plaines police. Enquiries at the pharmacy revealed that the contractor, who had recently worked there, was John Gacy, who owned his own company, PDM Contractors. The next day the police called at his house in West Summerdale Avenue. He admitted seeing the boy, but claimed they spoke only for a few minutes.

Further investigations, however, revealed that ten years before Gacy had been convicted on a charge of sodomy after a series of attacks on teenaged boys in Waterloo, Iowa. He had been sentenced to ten years in jail, but his conduct was so good, he had such a buoyant, outgoing personality and anxious-to-please manner, that he was paroled after only eighteen months.

His parole officer allowed him to move to Chicago and he lived for a time with his widowed mother before occupying the bungalow in West Summerdale Avenue.

The Chicago police subsequently had a number of complaints from male prostitutes who claimed Gacy had picked them up and assaulted them. But by this time Gacy was becoming a local celebrity. He became a worker for the local Democratic

Party and was photographed with Rosalynn Carter, the wife of the President, and with the Mayor of Chicago. He became a hospital volunteer and entertained children dressed as Pogo the clown. Needless to say the complaints from homosexuals were not taken very seriously by the police, even when one, Jeff Rignall, protested that Gacy had alternately chloroformed and raped him over a period of several hours and the chloroform poisoning had left him with permanent liver damage.

The Des Plaines police went back to Gacy's bungalow with a search warrant and discovered several bodies of teenagers and young men packed into the crawl space beneath the house. The total number eventually came to twenty-nine, and Gacy then admitted that he had dumped four more bodies, including Robert Piest's, in the Illinois River.

In fact he readily confessed to all the homicides, committed in a little under seven years, but claimed that some were accidental, and others were self-defence. He showed no remorse at all.

At his trial in February 1980, the prosecution argued that Gacy was simply an evil man. The defence lawyer, Robert Motta, claimed that his client was insane. He had already told psychiatrists that he was the victim of 'multiple personalities' and had an alter ego called 'Bad Jack' who would take him over late at night, and especially when he had been drinking, and who was really responsible for the crimes. The defence actually produced Jeff Rignall as a witness and got him to agree that a man who would do such things to him was not sane. A succession of psychiatrists testified that Gacy was psychotic and suffering from personality disorders.

But the prosecution countered with the question, could a man commit thirty-three murders and still not be aware that he was doing wrong? And evidence was brought to show that Gacy had induced two of his former lovers to help dig trenches in the crawl space, which he said were for pipes, but which were really for graves.

The jury took only two hours to agree that Gacy was not insane. He was convicted of first-degree murder, sentenced to death and executed by an injection of lethal poisons at Statesville penitentiary near Chicago on 10 May 1994.

Gacy's house on West Summerdale Avenue had been gutted by the police in their search for bodies and it was finally demolished.

Carl Panzram admitted killing twenty-one people and sodomizing over a thousand in a lifetime of burglary, robbery, rape and murder in the USA, Europe and Africa. In 1928, while awaiting trial in Washington, USA, he wrote his autobiography. Serving a sentence of twenty-five years in Fort Leavenworth he killed the laundry foreman and was sentenced to death. When prison reformers sought to prevent this he wrote to President Hoover demanding his constitutional right to be hanged. 'I believe the only way to reform people is to kill them,' he wrote. He was taken at his word and hanged in September 1930.

William Gardiner   William Gardiner was tried for the murder of twenty-three-year-old Rose Harsent in November 1902 at the Suffolk Assizes in Ipswich Shire Hall. Prosecuting counsel was Henry Fielding Dickens KC, one of the sons of the famous Charles Dickens, and the defence was in the hands of Ernest Wild, as yet not a KC, but destined for a brilliant career.

Mr Dickens opened his case. Rose Harsent had been the servant of a retired couple who lived in a large house in the Suffolk village of Peasenhall. Her body had been found on Sunday morning, 1 June 1902, in the kitchen. She was lying on her back and had been stabbed in the upper part of her chest and her throat had been cut. An attempt had also been made to burn the body and nearby were broken pieces of a medicine bottle which smelled strongly of paraffin. An autopsy revealed that Rose was six months pregnant.

A subsequent search of Rose's attic bedroom, which was

reached by stairs leading from the kitchen, revealed a number of letters. One was an unsigned letter of assignation, obviously written by the killer, telling Rose to put a light in her window and he would come to her at midnight.

There were also two letters written by William Gardiner, a thirty-five-year-old married man with six children, who was a foreman carpenter at the local seed drill manufacturing works. He was an important figure in the local Primitive Methodist Chapel, a class leader, superintendent of the Sunday School and the organist. The letters were friendly but not romantic, and referred to a scandal which had rocked the village more than a year before.

Mr Dickens called two young men of the village, William Wright and Alfonso Skinner, who said they had seen Rose and William go into a small chapel and stay there for nearly an hour. The two listened outside and heard sounds indicating that the activity inside had little to do with Sunday School. Although William denied any impropriety and claimed the young men were lying, the scandal damaged him, and he resigned from his religious posts, but after an enquiry he was reinstated.

Mr Wild launched an attack on Wright in cross-examination, insinuating that he was well known in the village for spreading malicious gossip, but Skinner, who told the same story, came out of his examination relatively unscathed.

The broken bottle found near Rose's body was identified as one which had contained medicine prescribed for Mrs Gardiner's sister, and when Gardiner was arrested a clasp knife found in his pocket had traces of mammalian blood on it.

Mr Dickens produced a handwriting expert who said that the writing on the assignation note, although disguised, was remarkably similar to Gardiner's own handwriting.

William Gardiner went into the witness box and denied everything. He wasn't, and never had been, Rose's lover. He claimed that on the night of the murder he and his wife had gone to sit with their next-door neighbour, because there was a storm at the time and she was frightened of thunder. He was there from 11.30 till 1.30 in the morning. This was supported by the neighbour.

Mrs Gardiner said in her evidence that after they came home and retired for the night her husband never left her bed that night, and she would have known if he had, because she had slept very little because of having to get up and see to the children.

The jury were undecided. Apparently eleven were for a guilty verdict, but one stood out for an acquittal. Since in those days the verdict had to be unanimous, a new trial was ordered. This was very similar to the first, with no new evidence being put forward by either side. Again the jury were deadlocked.

But the Director of Public Prosecutions, instead of ordering a third trial, obviously felt that there was insufficient evidence to obtain a conviction and Gardiner was released.

He and his family soon left the village, where most people were convinced he was guilty, and for many years he and his wife kept a confectioner's and tobacconist's shop in Norwood, South London. He died in 1941.

Was he guilty and got away with it because he had a loyal wife? In those days a woman who lost her husband could well find herself destitute. Or was he an innocent man trapped by circumstances and prejudice? Rose almost certainly had several lovers, any one of whom might have killed her. The only certain thing is that the argument will go on.

James Roland Robertson was a serving Glasgow policeman when he was tried, in November 1950, for killing a woman, probably by first knocking her unconscious and then running over her with a car. He claimed that it was an accident, but he had panicked because he'd had a child by her. He was found guilty by a majority verdict, permissible at that time in Scotland, and was hanged on 16 December.

Sheila Garvie and Brian Tevendale The trial was one of the most sensational ever held in Scotland. Three people were accused of the murder of thirty-five-year-old Max Garvie: Sheila, his thirty-two-year-old wife, her lover Brian Tevendale, twenty-two, and his friend Alan Peters, who was twenty. And, as is often the case where a number of people are involved in a murder, they accused each other of being responsible.

Mr Ewan Stewart QC, the Solicitor General, opened the proceedings for the prosecution at Aberdeen Sheriff Court in November 1968.

Wealthy Maxwell Garvie farmed at West Cairnbeg, some twenty-five miles south-west of Aberdeen in the foothills of the Grampian Mountains. He was an accomplished pilot, a leading light in the local Scottish National Party and had a voracious sexual appetite, which apparently included both men and women. Early in the 1960s he founded a nudist club near Aberdeen, the place becoming known to the locals as the 'kinky cottage', and he became interested in wife-swapping. A foursome which developed in 1967 included Brian Tevendale, who was to become attached to Sheila Garvie, and his sister Trudy Birse, who was married to a policeman, but began a relationship with Max Garvie.

Max's sister gave evidence at the trial that Sheila and Brian Tevendale finally went off together to Bradford in Yorkshire. Max had pleaded with his wife to come back, agreeing to give up Trudy Birse, and Sheila returned to West Cairnbeg. A few weeks later she bumped into Brian while shopping in the nearby town of Stonehaven. A month after that, Max was dead.

The Rev Kenneth Thompson, the Garvies' local priest, said that he had attempted to counsel the pair over their failing marriage. He also reported that Sheila had visited him on the day she was arrested and told him that her husband had perverted sexual tendencies.

Brian Tevendale did not give evidence, but a statement he

had made to the police was read out. In it he claimed that after a drinking session with Sheila and Max they had returned to the farmhouse at West Cairnbeg. He said that Sheila told him Max had taken her upstairs, produced a gun and demanded anal sex with her. After a struggle Max had been shot. All Brian did was to get rid of the body, which he dumped in a culvert in the grounds of Lauriston Castle – a nearby ruin – and covered it with stones. It was not found for six months.

Alan Peters's version was that he had driven his friend Tevendale to West Cairnbeg on the night of the murder. Sheila let them in and did not appear surprised to see them. Brian had loaded a gun and he and Alan went upstairs to where Max was lying asleep in bed. Tevendale struck the sleeping man several times on the head, then put a pillow over his head and shot him through the pillow.

Sheila Garvie, giving her evidence, protested that she had not known that Tevendale was going to kill her husband. Indeed she said she had been woken up by him, and made to stand outside the bedroom while Tevendale murdered Max inside the room. But she could not explain away satisfactorily her helping to get rid of clues after the murder and her continuing affair with him. Her mother, who knew part of what had happened, became so disgusted with the association that she went to the police.

The jury took less than an hour to find that the case against Alan Peters was not proven – a Scottish verdict which has no parallel in English courts, and which means roughly what it says, that there is some suspicion attaching to the accused, but the case has not been proved and the prisoner must be released. Brian Tevendale was found guilty of murder, and so, on a majority decision, was Sheila Garvie. Both were sentenced to life imprisonment.

Forty-three-year-old Freda Rumbold was tried for murder at Bristol Assizes in November 1956. Her husband had been found shot to death in bed. Freda claimed it was an accident, but a pathologist told the court that he thought Albert Rumbold had been asleep when the 12 bore shotgun was discharged. Freda was convicted of murder and sentenced to death. She was later reprieved.

Gary Gilmore 'Down on the floor,' said the gunman.

The terrified gas station attendant, Max Jensen, who had just been ordered into the toilet, obeyed.

The gunman stood astride the young man, who was lying face down on the floor, and, bracing himself with one hand on the wall, leaned over and put a 0.22 Browning Automatic pistol to the back of Jensen's head. Quite calmly he pulled the trigger twice. Then he walked out of the gas station with $125 he had taken from Jensen.

It was a Monday night, 19 July 1976, in Orem, a small town some thirty miles south of Salt Lake City, Utah, and the gunman was thirty-six-year-old Gary Gilmore.

Gilmore had spent half his life in prison, but in 1974, when he was serving a nine-year sentence for armed robbery, he began corresponding with his cousin Brenda Nichol. His letters were well written and persuasive – he had a high IQ – and illustrated with his own drawings, for he was a brilliant draftsman.

Brenda agreed to sponsor him and he was paroled nearly five years early, in April 1976. He went to live with Brenda's parents, Vern and Ida Damico, in Provo, a larger town than Orem and a little further south.

But Gilmore found it very difficult to settle down on the outside. He quarrelled with his employers and fell out with Vern. Then he met nineteen-year-old Nicole Baker and moved in with her and her two young children. But he began shoplifting, drinking heavily and drug taking. Rows between them became frequent and he began to assault her. She in turn started going out with other men. On 13 July he threw her out of the house and she went to stay with her mother. Gilmore began searching for her and it was during this period that he committed his two random murders.

He had already stolen a number of guns from shops and on the evening of the day after he shot Max Jensen, he went into the City Center Motel, in Provo, and confronted the manager, Benny Bushnell. He shot him in the back of the head and walked out with the cash box under his arm. But this time he was seen leaving. The police were notified and Gilmore was soon picked up.

He admitted both killings, but refused to sign a confession. Nevertheless, at his trial in October 1976 in Provo, the prosecution case was strong. A shell found by the side of Benny Bushnell's body was proved to have come from Gilmore's Browning pistol.

Gilmore's attorney had previously sought a plea bargain. His client would admit first-degree murder in exchange for a life sentence. But District Attorney Noall Wootton had looked at Gilmore's record. 'This man', he said, 'is too dangerous to live.' And he decided to seek the death penalty.

The defence called no witnesses and Gary Gilmore was dissuaded from giving evidence himself. The jury took only eighty minutes to bring in a verdict of guilty.

By the time the trial came on Nicole had been to see Gilmore in prison and they had resumed their relationship. When the prison authorities attempted to stop her coming because she wasn't a relative Gilmore went on hunger strike until she was readmitted. However, he would not allow her to give evidence for him at the hearing to determine the sentence.

Gilmore himself was the only witness. But his evidence was given in an offhand manner showing no remorse, and under cross-examination he was very hostile, refusing to answer some questions, and answering many others with single words. The jury pronounced the sentence of death.

Asked to choose his manner of dying – hanging or shooting

– he said he preferred shooting. He then declared that he did not wish to go through the usual process of appealing. His lawyers went ahead anyway with a motion for a new trial, but at the hearing Gilmore withdrew the motion and fired them.

The US Supreme Court had stopped executions in the USA in 1967 and only again allowed them in July 1976, in exceptional circumstances. Gilmore's decision to insist on the death sentence caused considerable controversy and a number of pressure groups began to fight the execution.

On 15 November Nicole smuggled sleeping pills in to Gilmore, concealed in a balloon in her vagina, and both took them later that night. But the amount wasn't sufficient to kill either of them and they recovered.

An independent film producer, Larry Schiller, became interested, visited Gilmore in prison and taped many hours of interviews with him and others associated with the case.

Gilmore finally had his way and at 8.07 a.m. on Monday 17 January, 1977, he was executed by firing squad in Utah state prison.

Schiller invited American novelist Norman Mailer to write Gilmore's story from the tapes he had made and Mailer's book *The Executioner's Song* was published in 1978. It won the Pulitzer prize.

Harvey Glatman   The motorcycle cop braked to a halt as his headlight picked out two figures struggling at the side of the road. It was just outside the small town of Tustin, California, some thirty-five miles from Los Angeles, and in those days – October 1958 – the suburban sprawl had not yet reached it.

The cop pulled out his gun and told the couple, a man and a woman, to stand still. She quickly told the policeman that the man had attacked her in his car. He took them both to the police station in Santa Ana and in doing so solved a series of murders which had been puzzling police in the area for some time.

On 30 July 1957, nineteen-year-old Judy Dull had disappeared from the Hollywood apartment she shared with two other girls. She was very pretty and much in demand as a photographic model, and she had gone out that afternoon with a young man her friends described as thin, with glasses and large sticking-out ears. He said his name was Johnny Glynn and he wanted her to pose for him. She never returned and Johnny Glynn could not be traced.

Five months after her disappearance a ranch hand found a partially buried skeleton in the desert some 130 miles east of Los Angeles. This was eventually identified as Judy Dull.

In March the following year a young divorced woman, Shirley Bridgeford, who had two children and lived with her mother in Sun Valley, went out on a date with a man she met through an introduction agency. She didn't come back. The man had given his name as George Williams, but his description sounded very similar to Johnny Glynn's.

July brought another disappearance. Twenty-four-year-old Ruth Mercado, who worked as a photographic model and a stripper, went missing from an apartment block on West Pico Boulevard, Los Angeles.

Three months later Lorraine Vigil, who had a Wilshire flat, accepted a modelling job with a thin young man with glasses and sticking-out ears who said his name was Frank Johnson. He drove her out to Anaheim, where he said his studio was, but he didn't stop there and when they finally came to a halt it was near Tustin and it was dark. He produced a gun and tried to tie her up, but she struggled. The gun went off, grazing her thigh, but bravely she managed to fight her way out of the car and when he dropped the gun she grabbed it. That was when the policeman arrived.

The young man, when taken to the police station, readily admitted that his name was Harvey Glatman and he was a TV repairman who lived on the fringe of Hollywood. He had a history of burglary and robbing women at gunpoint. After taking a lie-detector test, he confessed to killing the three girls.

Judy Dull he had taken back to his apartment, telling her he had been commissioned to produce a picture of an innocent girl, bound and gagged, for a detective magazine; she allowed him to tie her up. He took pictures of her in revealing poses, then raped her. He then took her out into the desert, made her lie face down on a blanket and tied her ankles together, looping the end of the rope round her neck. He pulled on it until she strangled.

He was tried in September 1959, pleading guilty to the murders of Shirley Bridgeford and Ruth Mercado. He had taken Shirley to the desert, made her sit on the blanket while he photographed her bound and gagged, and then strangled her as he had Judy Dull.

Glatman had gone to Ruth Mercado's apartment with an offer of a photographic assignment, but she had baulked on seeing him at the door and he had produced a gun and forced his way in. He had raped her in her flat, then taken her into the desert about thirty miles from where he had killed Shirley Bridgeford. He spent the day with her, photographing and raping her, and expressed concern, because he said he actually liked Ruth a lot, that he had to kill her. Glatman led the police to where he had buried the bodies of Shirley and Ruth.

His attorney tried to persuade him to enter a plea of guilty but insane. He refused, preferring to die rather than spend a life behind bars.

Harvey Glatman went to his death in the gas chamber at San Quentin prison. 'I knew it would end like this,' he said.

In 1935, Robert James's wife Mary was found face down in a fishpond in their garden in Los Angeles. Apparently she had drowned in six inches of water. The police were not suspicious until an anonymous letter caused an investigation and the truth came out. James had tried to kill her first by tying her up and putting her foot into a box containing rattlesnakes, but she had survived being bitten several times, so he drowned her in the bath tub. He was convicted and sentenced to death.

Barbara Graham　It had all the ingredients of a Hollywood film: a pretty girl, gangsters and murder, and indeed Barbara Graham's story was made into a major epic, starring Susan Hayward.

Actually three people went on trial in Los Angeles in August 1953. Big Jack Santo, the so-called brains of the outfit, but really no more than a ruthless gangster; his equally moronic assistant Emmett Perkins, and Barbara Graham, thirty-two years old, who had convictions for prostitution and drug use and who had lived for some years on the fringes of crime in Chicago and San Francisco.

Together with two others, Baxter Shorter, a safe blower, and John True, who said he was a deep-sea diver, they had planned to rob the house of sixty-three-year-old Mabel Monahan in Burbank. Mrs Monahan was crippled, lived alone and was reputed to have a great deal of money and jewels in the house. But she was reluctant to let anybody in, so Graham was to go to the front door to allay the woman's suspicions and gain entrance by asking to use the phone.

According to True, Graham duly went to the front door first, but when he arrived she had the woman by the hair on the doorstep and was hitting her in the face with a gun. The gang found no money or jewels in the house and ran, leaving a badly beaten-up old lady, tied up and with a pillowcase over her head. Her body was found next day by the gardener. She had choked to death.

Baxter, who was questioned first by the police, told them all about the raid, but for some reason he was not taken into custody and was subsequently abducted at gunpoint by Santo and Perkins from the hotel where he was staying and never seen again.

True was also picked up by the police and he went on the witness stand to give his version of the murder. His story was confirmed by an underworld character who had been asked by Santo to take part, but had refused.

The next witness, Sam Sirianni, was to prove devastating to Barbara Graham. In prison she had met another girl and the two exchanged love letters. The girl said she had a friend who might be able to provide Barbara with an alibi – for a price. When this man came to see Graham she admitted having been with Santo and Perkins on the raid and said she also needed an alibi for the day Baxter had disappeared.

In court, Sirianni said he was an undercover Los Angeles detective and the conversations with Barbara had been taped. In vain her attorney complained that it was entrapment of the worst kind. The prosecution claimed that they had to fight 'fire with fire' and even admitted to having done a deal with John True.

The jury of nine men and three women took five hours to find the three defendants guilty of murder in the first degree, which automatically meant the death penalty. They were all executed in the gas chamber at San Quentin prison, Barbara Graham on 3 June 1955, only the third woman to suffer the death penalty in California.

Madame Hera Bessarabo was also a drug user. In July 1920 she shot her husband in their Paris apartment and with the help of her grown-up daughter Paule stuffed his body in a trunk, which the police finally traced to Nancy. Both women were arrested, but at the trial in February 1921, Paule implicated her mother and was herself acquitted. Mme Bessarabo was sentenced to twenty years imprisonment.

Ronald Geeves Griggs   'You have for a long time', began Mr Gurner KC, prosecuting counsel, 'been on very intimate terms, committing adultery, with Miss Condon?'

'Yes,' came the quiet voice of Ronald Griggs.

'You were infatuated with her?'

'Yes, yes.'

Thus did Mr Gurner establish the motive for the murder. And a compelling motive it was.

Ronald Griggs, twenty-six, and his wife of only a few weeks, twenty-year-old Ethel, arrived in the small Australian town of Omeo, 190 miles from Melbourne, in May 1926; he was the new Methodist parson.

He travelled around to visit his far-flung country parishioners on a motorcycle and sidecar, and one he began to see quite frequently was nineteen-year-old Lottie Condon. She was the daughter of a rich farmer who lived about ten miles away and she was often to be seen riding in his sidecar.

She even stayed with Griggs and his wife at the parsonage sometime during December, but it appears that Ethel, who was already pregnant, had some idea that an affair was in progress for she objected strongly to Lottie being there and complained when she caught her husband stroking the girl's forehead.

This didn't prevent Griggs going off soon after to conduct a service at Ensay, a town some thirty miles away, and taking Lottie with him. They stayed at the house of a local farmer and had separate rooms, but on Sunday night Lottie went into Ronald's room, in her own words: 'by arrangement. We had discussed the matter. Misconduct took place that night.'

Relations between Griggs and his wife continued to deteriorate and in July she asked for a divorce. But he persuaded her to wait six months, to go back to her home in Tasmania and think things over. Ronald and Lottie, after a period when they stayed apart, resumed their affair in September and intercourse took place once a week either at her home or in the parsonage.

Ethel returned on the last day of the year, and soon after was taken ill. She died a couple of days later. The local doctor thought that she had been upset by the voyage from Tasmania and that this had started a nervous vomiting which produced exhaustion and heart failure. He gave a certificate stating that death was due to hyperemesis, exhaustion and secondary cardiac failure. But rumours soon began to circulate in the little town. The police were informed and Ethel Griggs's body was exhumed.

It was found to contain fifteen-and-a-half grains of arsenic, the lethal dose being about three grains. Dr C. H. Mollison, coroner's surgeon of Melbourne, gave it as his opinion that the poison had been administered in two doses, an important finding as it would seem to eliminate suicide.

Lottie Condon admitted her affair with Ronald Griggs when questioned by the police. Griggs at first denied it, but when shown Lottie's statement, he too said that it was true.

The trial of Ronald Griggs for the murder of his wife began in March 1927, at the Supreme Court in Sale. The prosecution brought evidence to show that although no arsenic was found in the parsonage, there was a tin labelled 'white arsenic' in the blacksmith's shop on the Condon farm, to which Griggs would have had access.

The prosecution did not call Lottie Condon although her statement was read out in court. Ronald Griggs went into the witness box and calmly denied having anything to do with his wife's death. He gave evidence with candour and apparent honesty and was not shaken by cross-examination.

The defence was in the hands of Mr G. Maxwell KC, a tall, upright man, then nearly seventy years old and almost totally blind. His final speech to the jury, which has sometimes been said to be the most important part of a trial, was a masterpiece. It has been claimed that it was worthy of the great Sir Edward Marshall Hall himself.

Maxwell told the jury that the newspapers and small town public opinion had already condemned Ronald Griggs to be hanged, before he even went into the witness box. And he pointed out that under the law a man had a right to be considered innocent until proved guilty beyond a reasonable doubt. He said that although there was a motive and the means could have been at his disposal there was nothing connecting him directly with Ethel Griggs's death. No poison had been found in the house and no one had seen him with any.

It obviously made some impression on the jury, for after deliberating for six hours on one day they returned on the next to say that they could not agree. A new trial was ordered for 16 April, this time at the Supreme Court in Melbourne.

The new trial was much the same as the first, with no new evidence on either side. The jury took six hours to come to a unanimous decision. The verdict was not guilty.

Ronald Griggs was discharged, and as he was led away a girl's voice came from the back of the court: 'I want to see him.' But whether it was Lottie's voice and whether she actually did see him is open to doubt. Certainly Griggs was disgraced. He tried to obtain another ministry under an assumed name, but was found out and dismissed. He slipped into obscurity.

Dr Charles Friedgood killed his wife by injecting her with the drug demerol, which made it look as if she had died of a stroke, and he signed the death certificate to that effect. But his grown-up family were not convinced and the police arrested him as he was boarding a plane for Europe. He was tried by a New York court in January 1977 and convicted of murder. He made history: the following year New York State made it illegal for a doctor to sign a death certificate for a relative.

Joseph Albert Guay On Friday 9 September, 1949, flight number 108 of Quebec Airways was en route from Montreal to Comeau Bay on the north shore of the St Lawrence River in Canada. Some twenty minutes after it had left Quebec City an explosion ripped it apart and it nosedived into the ground in wooded country near Cap Tormente. All twenty-three people on board were killed.

This had a sequel in February 1950, when Joseph Albert Guay, a thirty-two-year-old Quebec jeweller, was tried at the Criminal Assizes in Quebec City on a single count: that of the murder of his wife Rita who had been on board the aircraft.

Senior Crown prosecutor Noel Dorian called a succession of engineers and scientists whose meticulous work on the fragments of the crashed aircraft showed conclusively that the explosion was not accidental, but had been caused by a bomb containing dynamite. They were even able to pin-point the actual dry battery used to detonate the device and to confirm that the plane did not carry batteries of that type.

Baggage handlers were called to prove that the device must have been placed aboard during its stop in Quebec City. Records of the parcel destinations showed that one was addressed to a non-existent person in Comeau Bay and the baggage clerk remembered that it had been handed in by a dark, middle-aged woman. A taxi-driver gave evidence that he had driven a woman of this description to the airport with just such a parcel, and he was able to identify her. She turned out to be a Mrs Marguerite Pitrie.

Mrs Pitrie gave evidence at Guay's trial. She said she had known him for some years and had helped him when he was starting up in his jewellery business by finding him female customers. According to her, Guay had asked her to buy him some dynamite as he wanted to blast tree-trunks on a friend's country property. Then he had come with a parcel, saying it was a religious statuette, and asked her to take it to the airport. After she had done this and the explosion had been reported in all the papers, he produced a newspaper article which reported that the police were looking for a dark, middle-aged woman. He told her that if she took sleeping pills and left a confession he would look after her children. She had taken some pills, but not enough apparently, and when she came out of hospital she was arrested.

On cross-examination Mrs Pitrie proved a very difficult witness. She frequently clashed with Defence Attorney Gerard Levesque, mimicked him from the witness box and when she apparently got tired of his questions sat down and began to fire them back at him.

Her brother Genereux Ruest, a crippled watchmaker, described how he had made a clockwork detonator from plans supplied by the jeweller and claimed that Guay told him it was to kill fish. But afterwards Guay threatened him and warned him not to talk to the police.

The last witness was nineteen-year-old Marie-Ange (in English, Angel Mary) Robitaille, a beautiful dark-haired girl who had met Guay when she was only sixteen. They had started going out together, but Guay's wife found out and told her parents. Marie gave up Guay for a time, then resumed her relationship, left home and lodged with Mrs Pitrie so that Guay could visit her. Later they set up house together in a town called Seven Islands, but the girl eventually went back to her parents. A distraught Guay had threatened to kill himself, at one 'stage waving a revolver about, and she had called the police. The record of this minor offence was one of the things which led the authorities to Guay, as an alert detective linked his name with that of a passenger on the crashed aircraft.

The prosecutor claimed that Guay had decided a solution to his problem was to kill his wife; he had insured her life for $10,000 just before she took off.

The jury agreed and after a trial lasting three weeks took just seventeen minutes to bring in a verdict of guilty. Guay was sentenced to death.

Such was the horror and revulsion generated in the public mind by the outrage, in which children as well as adults were killed, that the authorities brought both Genereux Ruest and Marguerite Pitrie to trial. Ruest was duly convicted of murder in December 1950, and in March 1951 the verdict against Pitrie was guilty of murder. All three went to the scaffold.

An interesting sidelight on the case was that, had the plane not been a few minutes late leaving Quebec City, it would have been well out over the St Lawrence River when it exploded and the wreckage would have landed in deep water. It would have been just about impossible then for experts to prove that the explosion was not accidental and the deadly three would have got away with murder.

H

Archibald Hall (Roy Fontaine) Before his trial in May 1978, Archibald Hall, who liked to be called Roy Fontaine, was examined by a psychiatrist who, although allowing for the fact that Hall when he was younger had twice been sent to mental institutions, declared him sane – perhaps because most of his murders were committed to keep him out of jail.

Hall had spent much of his adult life in prison for burglary, embezzlement and theft. When he was free he liked the high life and often worked as a butler, for which his perfect manners and cultured speech made him much in demand.

During the summer of 1977, when he was fifty-three and working for Lady Peggy Hudson, an elderly widow, at her eighteenth-century manor house in Kirkleton, Dumfriesshire, he was joined by David Wright. Wright was a twenty-six-year-old burglar from Birmingham with whom Hall, who was bisexual, had had a homosexual affair in prison.

He persuaded Lady Hudson to take Wright on as an odd-job man, but the burglar soon began stealing her jewels; in particular, when she was away he stole an antique ring which he gave to a girl in the village. Hall managed to get it back, but the two had a furious row and Wright got drunk and threatened Hall with a rifle. The next day Hall took Wright rabbit shooting, waited until his companion's gun was empty then shot him in the head. He buried the body under some stones near a stream.

Soon after this the police informed Lady Hudson of Hall's criminal background and he was sacked. But he soon got another job, using forged references, as a butler to a retired MP, Walter

Scott-Elliot, who lived with his much younger wife in Knightsbridge in London.

The Scott-Elliots were very wealthy and Hall planned to rob them with a couple of confederates: Mary Coggle, forty, an ex-girlfriend of his, now working as a part-time prostitute, and a friend of hers, thirty-nine-year-old Michael Kitto, who was a petty thief and easily dominated by Hall. He showed Kitto round the house one night and, thinking Mrs Scott-Elliot was away, went into her bedroom. But she had returned and was in bed and started screaming. In a moment of panic Hall smothered her with a pillow, assisted by Kitto.

Persuading Mary Coggle to impersonate Mrs Scott-Elliot by wearing one of her fur coats, they drove north with the old man in a drugged state, and the body in the boot, and buried it near Perth. Then Hall and Kitto killed Walter and buried his body in a wood at Glen Affric, south of Inverness.

They then holed up in a cottage rented by Hall at Newton Arlosh, not far from Carlisle. But Mary Coggle began making drunken phone calls to friends in London and Hall was afraid she would give them away. He killed her with a poker, and he and Kitto dumped her in a stream near Lockerbie.

The pair were now joined at the cottage by Hall's younger brother Donald, who was also a petty criminal. Hall had always hated Donald and, seizing the opportunity when the young man offered to show them how he could be tied up with only six inches of string, promptly chloroformed him. Hall and Kitto drowned him in the bath, put the body in the boot of a car they'd hired and drove north.

But Hall had made the mistake of changing the car's number plates because he thought that YGE 999R was too conspicuous. They stopped at the Blenheim Arms Hotel at North Berwick. The proprietor thought they were a couple of conmen who might leave without paying the bill and informed the police, who checked and found the car had false number plates. They then found the body in the boot.

Kitto soon told the police the whole story and the bodies of Mr and Mrs Scott-Elliot and Mary Coggle were recovered. Eventually Hall, after making a number of suicide bids, led the police to where he had buried David Wright.

Tried in Edinburgh in May 1978 for the murders of Walter Scott-Elliot and David Wright, Hall pleaded guilty. The judge, Lord Wylie, gave him life, while Kitto, who also pleaded guilty to assisting in the murder of Scott-Elliot, was jailed for fifteen years

Both men were then tried at the Old Bailey in London for the murders of Mrs Scott-Elliot, Mary Coggle and Donald Hall, whose killings had taken place in England. Hall admitted killing Coggle and his brother, but denied killing Mrs Scott-Elliot, while Kitto admitted the murder of Mary Coggle but pleaded manslaughter to the killings of Donald Hall and Mrs Scott-Elliot.

Kitto was sentenced to fifteen years, but Judge James Miskin recommended that Archibald Hall should never be released.

The gang who robbed the Colombo Racecourse in Sri Lanka, in January 1949, substituted one of their own men for the driver who regularly took the takings to the bank. The regular driver was later discovered in the jungle tied to a tree, a gas mask placed over his head with the air tube blocked. He had died of suffocation. The gang was soon rounded up and four men, Wijedasa, Seneviratne, Premalal and Munasinghe, were tried in January 1950 at Colombo Assizes. All four were convicted of robbery and murder, and executed.

The Hall-Mills Case   The trial and indeed the whole case was bedevilled by two factors, the influence of newspapers and the effects of local American politics.

In 1922 New Brunswick was a small town some thirty-five miles from New York, but in the neighbouring state of New Jersey. One of the wealthiest, most influential families in town was the Stevens family. Frances Stevens had married the Reverend Dr Hall, a minister of the episcopal church. At the time of the murders he was forty and she was forty-seven and they lived in a palatial residence with Mrs Hall's bachelor brother, fifty-year-old William, who was somewhat slow mentally.

On the morning of Saturday 16 September two bodies were discovered just outside the town in a disused crab apple orchard much frequented by lovers. Dr Hall was lying on his back beside the body of thirty-four-year-old Mrs Eleanor Mills, who had been a member of the minister's church choir. Dr Hall had been shot once in the head and Mrs Mills three times in the head. Her throat had also been cut and the upper part of the windpipe, the larynx and tongue – the organs used in singing – had been removed. Scattered over and around the bodies were some torn-up love letters written by Mrs Mills to Dr Hall.

The trouble was that the murders had been committed just inside the Somerset County border where it joins Middlesex County, in which New Brunswick is situated. Neither police force really wanted to be involved in a potentially explosive case involving influential local people and each tried to get the other to accept responsibility. As a consequence, the investigation was confused and slipshod to say the least.

But the New York papers made the case a nationwide sensation, involving as it did religion, sex and murder. Mrs Mills's husband sold some of Dr Hall's letters to his wife to the newspapers and all kinds of witnesses came forward to sell their stories to the papers for substantial sums.

One of the most significant was a lady, known as the 'Pig Woman', who lived on a smallholding nearly a mile and a half from the site of the murders. She had gone out on the Thursday night the two disappeared, searching for thieves who had been stealing her crops. Near the orchard she saw two people in a car, an elderly woman with grey hair and a man she took to be a black man. William Stevens had tight curly hair and a swarthy complexion. Later she said she heard men and women arguing, then a flashlight went on and she saw two men fighting. The light went off and she heard a shot and a woman began screaming. She started to run off and heard three more shots. She claimed to have recognized Mrs Hall and her brother Henry Stevens.

The police case was presented to a grand jury – somewhat similar to committal proceedings in Britain before magistrates – in November. After a seven-day hearing the jury of local people decided to take no action.

There the matter rested for three and a half years. Then the editor of a New York paper claimed to have evidence that a maid, previously in Mrs Hall's service, had said she had been bribed to give false evidence to the grand jury. The newspaper also stated that some police officials had taken bribes and destroyed evidence against Mrs Hall.

The governor of New Jersey ordered the case to be reopened and appointed Senator Alexander Simpson, a well-known lawyer, to investigate and take appropriate action. Eventually Mrs Hall, Henry Stevens, William Stevens and a cousin, Henry Carpender, were arrested.

Senator Simpson desperately tried to have the jury drawn from a county other than the ones around New Brunswick, but he was resisted by a formidable battery of lawyers provided by the Stevens family and others and led by Senator McCarter, probably the most widely known trial lawyer in the state, and Simpson lost the motion. The trial eventually began in November 1926 in Somerville, the county town of Somerset County, and the jury was drawn from local people.

Mrs Hall, Henry Stevens and William Stevens were only indicted for the murder of Eleanor Mills. But right from the start Simpson, who did not have a particularly strong case, was in trouble. Many of his witnesses now changed their testimony, saying they could no longer remember, and the planks of his carefully constructed case began to disappear. The Pig Woman, who by this time was dying of cancer, was brought in her hospital bed into the courtroom, gave her evidence in a faltering voice and was in no condition to resist the severe cross-examination she was subjected to.

In the final speech of the defence Senator McCarter attacked Simpson as an officious meddler who had led an army of snoopers into Somerset County, which four years earlier had held his clients blameless. This was greeted with a cheer from the public benches and even the jury smiled in encouragement. Simpson must have known he was beaten before he even began his final speech for the prosecution. He persevered with great determination, but it was no use, the jury acquitted all three defendants.

A rumour went round afterwards that Mrs Hall, the Stevenses and the Carpenders had spent over $400,000 on the defence, a huge amount of money in those days. None of them bothered to deny it.

Yvonne Chevallier's husband had just been promoted to Minister of State in France for Technical Education, Youth and Sport in August 1951, when one Sunday morning in their bedroom she shot him four times in the chest. When their young son rushed into the room she calmly took him downstairs and handed him over to a servant before going back upstairs to shoot her husband again. Rather surprisingly the court regarded this as a 'crime of passion', due to her husband's infidelities, and acquitted her.

James Hanratty   'Take this.' She held out a pound note to the gunman, then shouted, 'Take the car and go!' Turning she knelt by the body of her boyfriend, thirty-one-year-old Michael Gregsten, whom the gunman had shot.

It was the early hours of Wednesday 23 August, 1961. The night before, Valerie Storie and Michael Gregsten had been sitting in the latter's Morris Minor in a cornfield at Dorney Reach, near Maidenhead, when a man with a gun tapped on the window and forced his way in. He made them drive about for several hours until they reached a layby on the A6 road between Luton and Bedford, near Clophill, called Deadmans Hill. There he shot Gregsten twice in the head, raped Storie and forced her to drag her boyfriend's body out of the car.

As she knelt on the ground the gunman emptied his gun at her and drove away in the car. But Valerie Storie survived, paralysed from the waist down.

The police, possibly due to an underworld tip-off, soon had two suspects, both having stayed at the Vienna Hotel, Maida Vale, though at different times. They were Peter Alphon and a small-time car thief called James Hanratty. The murder revolver had been found under the back seat of a London bus, and cartridges from bullets fired from it were found in the room Hanratty had occupied in the hotel the night before the abduction.

To begin with Alphon seems to have been the chief suspect, but after Valerie Storie failed to recognize him at an identification parade – she picked out a Spanish sailor instead – the police turned to Hanratty.

He was arrested on 11 October and Valerie Storie, at an identification parade at Stoke Mandeville Hospital three days later, said that he was the man who had shot Michael Gregsten.

His trial began in January 1962 at Bedford Assizes. The prosecution, led by Graham Swanwick QC, did not have a very strong case. Their main witness was Valerie Storie, though she had to admit she had only seen her attacker's face once, and that only fleetingly, when he was raping her. Other identifications, of Hanratty driving the stolen car in an erratic manner, were equally suspect. Another witness, a friend of Hanratty's, said the prisoner had once told him the back of a London bus was a good place to hide things. A well-known 'grass' claimed that Hanratty had confessed to him while they were together in prison, but this was denied by two other prisoners.

Hanratty's best defence should have been his alibi. He said he had been in Liverpool on the night of the murder, but could not identify where he had stayed and mentioned only a sweetshop he had been in where he had asked directions. A lady from a sweetshop in Liverpool remembered a man like Hanratty asking for directions but she couldn't remember which day it had been.

One week into the trial, however, Hanratty told his defence counsel, Michael Sherrard QC, that he was changing his alibi. Now, he claimed to have spent the night in the North Wales seaside town of Rhyl. At such short notice it was almost impossible for the defence team to obtain corroborating evidence, since Hanratty couldn't remember exactly where he had stayed in the town. But somehow they did.

They found a boarding house which had a room exactly fitting Hanratty's description of it – an attic room with a green bath – and the landlady, Mrs Jones, remembered a young Londoner resembling Hanratty's photograph occupying it, on the night of the murder. But she collapsed under the searing cross-examination of Graham Swanwick, one of Britain's most experienced barristers. Her books were in a terrible state and nothing could be proved from them. Other residents of the hotel at the time of the murder said they couldn't remember Hanratty being there at all.

The jury were unimpressed by the alibi and brought in a verdict of guilty. Hanratty was sentenced to death. The Court of Appeal upheld the verdict and sentence, the Home Secretary refused to grant a reprieve and Hanratty was hanged in Bedford prison in April 1962.

Five books have so far been published on the case. All except the first concluded that Hanratty was innocent and the author of that book, Louis Blom-Cooper, has since accepted publicly that the conviction was unsatisfactory.

Controversy has raged round the case for years. Peter Alphon publicly confessed to the murder in Paris in 1967, but an inquiry under barrister Lewis Hawser in 1974, which was held in secret, concluded there was no doubt of the guilt of James Hanratty.

The Home Office has promised to release all the papers on the case in 2061, a hundred years after the event, so we might have to wait until then to find out what really happened.

Jean Harris Dr Herman Tarnower was a very successful doctor who had raised himself from humble beginnings in Brooklyn to a lucrative practice in the expensive suburb of Purchase, Westchester County, New York. Having invented the Scarsdale Diet, the book of which was a bestseller, he was a wealthy man. He was also the eternal bachelor, who at sixty-nine had had many girlfriends. One of these was fifty-seven-year-old Mrs Jean Harris, the headmistress of the exclusive Madeira School for girls in McLean, Virginia.

They had been lovers for fourteen years, but now Tarnower seemed to be tiring of her and, in the opinion of Mrs Harris, wanted to supplant her with a younger woman, Mrs Lynne Tryforos, a thirty-seven-year-old divorcee.

On the night of 10 March 1980, Jean Harris made the five-hour drive from her home in Virginia to Tarnower's house in Purchase. When she arrived at about eleven o'clock she was not surprised to find the house in darkness. Dr Tarnower retired to bed early. She entered by the garage, which was open, and went up the spiral staircase to the doctor's bedroom. In her hand she carried a 0.32 Harrington and Richardson revolver.

A little later shots were fired, the intercom button was pressed, and when Mrs van der Vrekens picked up the phone in the servants' quarters she heard screams, firing and Mrs Harris's voice. She quickly got in touch with the police. When they arrived Jean Harris was just leaving.

Dr Tarnower was lying in the space between twin beds. He had been shot in the hand, the chest and the back. He died later in hospital.

Mrs Harris obtained the services of Joel Aurnou, a former Westchester judge, and was released on bail. The story put out by Aurnou and his associates before the trial, and which seemed to be accepted by the media, was that Dr Tarnower was excessively promiscuous, an unfeeling brute who had toyed with the sensitive Mrs Harris then discarded her for a younger model.

The trial became the sensation of the decade and opened in White Plains, New York, in November 1980. Jean Harris's version was that she had gone to the doctor's room to commit suicide. Tarnower was asleep, but she woke him up. When she raised the gun to her head he lunged across the bed to stop her and was accidentally shot in the hand. They wrestled with the gun while he tried to phone for help, but again it went off and he collapsed on the floor between the beds. She attempted to shoot herself, failed again, and went downstairs.

Aurnou presented her as 'a very fine lady', and brought witnesses from her school to prove the point. He wanted to show her as the vulnerable woman, depressed and exhausted by troubles at her school, and in despair after rejection by her lover. But in the witness box she came across as self-confident, aggressive, even overbearing. Far from being overawed she ticked off the judge, admonished prosecuting counsel and complained about her own attorney.

Prosecution attorney George Bolen had an ace up his sleeve. He read out what came to be known as the 'Scarsdale Letter', written by Jean Harris to Dr Tarnower on the day of the murder. It was penned ostensibly to tell the doctor that she would be going to his testimonial dinner, even though he apparently preferred the company of, as she put it, 'a vicious, adulterous psychotic', and, she went on, she didn't care, 'even if the slut comes – indeed, I don't care if she pops naked out of a cake with her tits frosted with chocolate!'

She rambled on, obsessed with money and how upset she

was because he had cut her out of his will. She claimed she took money from his wallet to pay for new clothes to replace ones she says her rival, whom she refers to as 'your psychotic whore', fouled with excreta.

Quite a lot of the letter was a diatribe of hate showing a woman at her worst, and it effectively destroyed the picture of her Aurnou was trying to present of a strong, upright citizen who would never stoop to deliberately shooting her lover.

It was a long trial, lasting over three months, and the jury, containing eight women, took eight days to come to a conclusion. They found her guilty of second-degree murder, which implies no premeditation, but does not rule out the intent to kill.

Before she was sentenced she said to the judge: 'For you and Mr Bolen to arrange my life so that I will be in a cage for the rest of it, and that every time I walk outside I will have iron around my wrists, is not justice; it is a travesty of justice.'

The judge gave her the mandatory fifteen years to life.

Patrick Hassett Thirteen-year-old Candice Williams was a pretty girl of West Indian parentage. Her body was found on the stairway leading to the roof of a twelve-storey block of council flats in the Erdington area of Birmingham, on Tuesday 25 July, 1978. She had been raped and strangled with one of her own shoelaces.

Post-mortem examination of the girl's stomach showed that she had eaten a yellow fruit, probably a peach, just before she died and a shopkeeper nearby remembered a young man, accompanied by a girl, buying two peaches. Apart from this there was little to link anyone with the crime.

One of the thousands of men interviewed by the police was nineteen-year-old Patrick Hassett who lived nearby, but at the time there was nothing to connect him to the murder.

Two years later, in the same area, there were two more rapes of young girls. Another man was eventually convicted of the crimes, but the exposure of the cases in the newspapers before the man was charged made an ex-girlfriend of Hassett's go to the police. She said that just after the Candice Williams murder he had had scratches on his neck and had asked her to give him an alibi, which she had refused to do.

Hassett was promptly arrested. His blood group proved to be the same as the murderer's, who had left his semen in Candice Williams, but it was a very common blood group. Pubic hairs taken from him were also very similar to those found on the body, but there was nothing else to connect him to the crime and he was eventually released.

The following year he was convicted of dragging a woman into his car and assaulting her and served eighteen months. Soon after his release he viciously beat up a young girl in his van in Tamworth and received a ten-year prison sentence.

In 1988 he was visited in prison by police officers anxious to see if the newly developed so-called genetic fingerprinting technique could help to prove that Hassett was the killer of Candice Williams. Understandably, he refused to give intimate samples such as blood, saliva or hair, as was his right, and since he was not in police custody the officers could not insist on it. They could do nothing except wait.

Hassett was released in February 1991, and immediately rearrested. He was taken to the Erdington police station and again asked for intimate samples. He again refused, except for hair from his head, which could have been taken by force if necessary. A police surgeon took some head hair samples which were analysed at the Birmingham forensic science laboratory.

Meanwhile, Hassett, under the rules of the Police and Criminal Evidence Act (PACE), had to be bailed. When he surrendered to his bail he was charged with the murder of Candice Williams.

His trial began in March 1992. The prosecution had to prove that the DNA profile from Hassett's body cells, obtained from his hair, matched that of the semen samples collected twelve years before, which were still preserved in the laboratory.

Mark Webster from the forensic science laboratory showed the jury a video to illustrate the way that dark bands – looking something like a bar-code placed on its side – from each sample can be compared by placing them side by side.

It can safely be said that no two people ever have the same ordinary fingerprints, even identical twins. But the same is not true of genetic fingerprinting. The scientist has to show in every case presented in court that the DNA profile match is statistically significant. That is, you would have to take a very large number of people to have the chance of finding among them two with the same DNA profile.

The first experiments Webster conducted showed only that there was a probability of one in 3,200 that someone other than Hassett was the murderer. This was not acceptable, but the scientist was able to use a different technique which showed that the odds really were one in 12,000 that a match could be obtained with someone other than Hassett.

It was enough to convince most of the jury and he was convicted of the murder of Candice Williams by a majority of ten to two. He was sentenced to life imprisonment.

Bruno Hauptman   On 21 May 1927, the young American, Charles Lindbergh, landed a small aircraft at Le Bourget airport in Paris and became the first man to fly the Atlantic alone. Overnight he became a national hero, receiving in quick succession the Distinguished Flying Cross and the Congressional Medal of Honour.

Five years later he was Colonel Charles Lindbergh, the owner of a large mansion standing in 500 acres near Hopewell, New Jersey, roughly halfway between New York and Philadelphia. He was married with a twenty-month-old son, Charles Lindbergh Junior.

The baby disappeared from his cot on the night of 1 March 1932, and the kidnapping created immense publicity and considerable outrage. A ransom note was left and eventually $50,000 paid, through the agency of a Dr John Condon, a retired teacher in the Bronx, New York, who had inserted an advertisement in his local paper offering to act as an intermediary. He received a note from the kidnappers and on the evening of 2 April, at St Raymond's Cemetery in the Bronx, he and Lindbergh paid over the money to a shadowy figure.

Four weeks later two truck drivers discovered the body of a baby in some woods, five miles by road, but only a mile in a straight line, from the Lindbergh house. The body was identified as Charles Lindbergh Junior. It was estimated that the child had died from a fractured skull soon after being kidnapped.

Two and a half years later, Bruno Richard Hauptman was arrested in the Bronx and found to be in possession of some of the ransom money. His trial began in January 1935, in the county courthouse at Flemington, New Jersey.

The prosecutor was thirty-seven-year-old David Wilentz, the Attorney General of New Jersey, who had never before appeared in a criminal trial, let alone one for murder. His opening statement was vicious and vehement and plainly intended to appeal to the crowd outside the courthouse – which continually shouted: 'Put the Dutchman in the hot seat' – as much as to the jury. Hauptman, however, was not Dutch but German.

Wilentz was opposed by Edward Reilly, a seasoned trial lawyer from New York. He had a drink problem and his monumental hangovers usually prevented him performing at his best until later in the day.

The prosecution described how part of the ransom money had been paid in gold certificates, which were subsequently in the process of being withdrawn by the government and thus were fairly rare. In September 1934, the manager of a filling station in New York took one and, because he was not sure he could cash it, noted down the number of the customer's car. The ransom certificate numbers had all been recorded and the police were soon alerted. They traced the car and found hidden in Hauptman's garage a total of $14,600 in gold certificates, which were all part of the ransom.

A wood expert testified that he had examined a crude ladder found near the Lindbergh home which was said by the prosecution to have been used by the kidnapper to climb up to the nursery window. He laboriously traced the wood back to a timber yard near Hauptman's home. A rail of the ladder was also shown to have been cut from a floorboard in Hauptman's house.

Both Dr Condon and Lindbergh said that they recognized the voice of the man in the graveyard as being Hauptman's. Eight experts gave evidence that the handwriting on the ransom notes was undoubtedly that of Hauptman. And a telephone number written on a door in his home turned out to be that of Dr Condon.

The prosecution case looked strong. The defence, conversely, sounded weak. Hauptman's explanation was that a friend of his, Isidor Fisch, had left a box with him and gone off to Germany where he had since died. Hauptman later found money in the box and, as Fisch was dead, decided to spend some of it. The story sounded contrived, but his claim that as a professional carpenter he would never have made such a crude ladder sounded more reasonable. The defence also disputed the handwriting evidence, which is often unreliable, and claimed that the identification evidence was flimsy.

Hauptman said that he had been working at the Majestic Apartments in New York on the day of the kidnapping, but timesheets and payroll records for the period did not support his alibi. And he admitted that he was an illegal emigrant to the USA, who had served a term of imprisonment for robbery in Germany as a young man.

Wilentz's closing speech reached heights of vituperation rare even for an American courtroom. 'What type of man', he ranted, 'would murder the child of Charles and Anne Lindbergh? He wouldn't be an American ... The authorities have found an animal lower than the lowest form in the animal kingdom, Public Enemy Number One of this world, Bruno Richard Hauptman.'

Not surprisingly Hauptman was found guilty and sentenced to death. And after a number of appeals had failed he was electrocuted in Trenton state prison, New Jersey, on 3 April 1936.

Even before his execution there was considerable disquiet about the trial and the Governor of New Jersey, Harold Hoffman, himself campaigned on Hauptman's behalf, believing that the carpenter was innocent, but his efforts were unpopular and he lost office in 1938. Many books have been written on the subject, one of the most recent being Ludovic Kennedy's *The Airman and the Carpenter*. In it he suggests there was fabrication of evidence, such as the ladder rail alleged to come from Hauptman's floorboard and the documents from the Majestic Apartments which he claims were doctored by the police. The telephone number on a door in Hauptman's apartment was afterwards discovered to have been put there by a newspaperman.

The modern theory seems to be that Isidor Fisch, a well-known crook in the New York underworld, used the gullible Hauptman to help him launder 'hot money', since the carpenter used to buy and sell on the New York stock exchange, and may have done so with money he obtained from the real kidnappers. Certainly Fisch paid for his passage to Germany in 1933 with part of the ransom. The kidnap was probably the work of more than one man. Some of the Lindbergh servants may well have been implicated, since a dog in the house never barked when the intruder climbed in the window, and one of the maids committed suicide when she was questioned by the police.

We shall probably never know what really happened except

that almost certainly an innocent man was executed.

Guillaume Seznec was a Normandy businessman who, in October 1924, was tried for the murder of a fellow businessman. Largely due to the evidence of Inspector Pierre Bony he was convicted and sentenced to life in French Guiana. He returned to France after twenty years and died in 1954. Meanwhile, Bony collaborated with the occupying Germans during the war and, after being shown to have protected gangsters, was later shot by firing squad. Before he died he confessed to having framed Seznec.

Gordon Hay　Fifteen-year-old Linda Peacock was found strangled in a cemetery just outside the large village of Biggar some thirty-five miles south-east of Glasgow. She lived a mile and a half from the village and had disappeared the previous day, Sunday 6 August, 1967, after having been given a lift into Biggar at about eight o'clock in the evening.

Police enquiries established that she had talked to an old gentleman at the door of his house in the village soon after 9.30 that night and he had the impression that she was killing time. She then walked off in the direction of her home, which would have taken her past the cemetery. Witnesses saw a man and a girl outside the cemetery at just after ten o'clock, and one saw what she thought was a couple actually inside, near a gravestone. Other witnesses heard screams coming from the cemetery at about 10.20.

Linda had received two heavy blows to the head causing wounds which had bled heavily. She had been strangled by a ligature which had afterwards been removed. She had not been raped but her clothes had been pulled up exposing her breasts and there was a bite mark on the right one.

Close to the cemetery there was a residential school for problem boys. They were not locked in, but they were closely supervised. Intensive police interrogation eventually broke one of the boys, who told them that seventeen-year-old Gordon Hay had been missing from 9.55 till 10.45, and a boathook, which one of the boys had brought back from camp the previous day, could not be found. When it was discovered examination established that it could have caused the wounds to Linda's head, but no traces of blood could be found on it.

Hay was brought to trial in February 1968. A friend of Linda's gave evidence that the day before the murder she had been with her at a fair and Linda had stopped to talk to some boys from the school. The friend walked on, but she identified the boy Linda talked to – it was Gordon Hay.

The main evidence for the prosecution was that given by Dr Warren Harvey, a consultant to the Glasgow Dental Hospital. The bruise marks on Linda's right breast had been photographed; twenty-eight boys from the school had had their teeth impressions taken at the dental hospital and Dr Harvey was asked to say if any corresponded to the bite marks on the murdered girl's body. He had immediately eliminated all but five and asked for additional impressions to be taken from these five.

At this stage Professor Keith Simpson of Guy's Hospital, London, had been consulted. He had been one of the first to investigate the use of bite marks for evidence. He suggested that more evidence would be needed to convince a jury, so Dr Harvey made casts of the teeth in acrylic resin and, when a suitable female body became available in the mortuary, made trial bites on the breast. Of the five bite marks he picked out the one made by number 11: Gordon Hay.

Since this was the first time this type of evidence had been presented in a Scottish court it was strenuously opposed by the defence. On the second day of the trial the judge dismissed the jury and asked two other judges to sit with him to determine whether the evidence should be allowed. In the end they decided that it should and the jury heard how Dr Harvey had found in the tips of Hay's canine teeth minute pits which gave character-istic bite marks. He had examined the mouths of 342 youths between sixteen and seventeen, looking at over 1000 canines, and had come across only two with this condition.

The defence really had no counter to the forensic odontology evidence. Hays went into the witness box to deny even having known Linda, and his story of never having left the school was supported by some of his friends. But they admitted having discussed the evidence amongst themselves before coming into court.

The jury took two and a half hours to reach a verdict of guilty and since the accused was under eighteen at the time of the offence he was ordered to be detained during Her Majesty's pleasure.

When the police enquired about Elsie Cameron in December 1924, Norman Thorne, a young chicken farmer in Crowborough, Sussex, who was her boyfriend, admitted that she was dead, but claimed that he had not killed her. He said she had been depressed because he would not marry her, and that he found her hanging from the beam of the hut where he lived. He cut her down, dismembered the body and buried it under the chicken run. But Sir Bernard Spilsbury said he could find no evidence of hanging and the police found no rope marks on the beam. Thorne was found guilty and hanged in 1925.

Robert Healey The Fall and Rise of Reginald Perrin was a television series which began each episode with the same incident: Reggie Perrin leaving his clothes on a beach to make people think he had committed suicide. When on 31 July 1986 the clothes of Robert Healey were found on the beach at Prestatyn, together with a suicide note, and it was learned that his wife and thirteen-year-old step-daughter were also missing, the press inevitably called it the Reggie Perrin case.

Robert Healey was a thirty-seven-year-old self-employed

driving instructor. He had been married to his present wife, forty-year-old Greeba, for only eight months. Letters he left in his home at Stockport, Cheshire, suggested that theirs was not a happy marriage.

The police found bloodstains in his house which matched the blood groups of his wife and step-daughter, and his car turned up in a car park in Birmingham the day after his disappearance. It was also discovered that he had recently obtained a copy of his brother-in-law's birth certificate. It looked very much as if he was trying to obtain another identity. Ten days after his supposed death a bloodstained quilt was found in a ditch near Chester. The blood on it was of the same type as that of his wife and step-daughter.

On 15 August, the bodies of Greeba Healey and her daughter Marie were found in a shallow grave near Caerwys, North Wales, only about five or six miles from Prestatyn. Healey's wife had suffered severe head injuries and his step-daughter had been suffocated. Both had had sexual intercourse before death.

The day after the two bodies were discovered Healey gave himself up in London. His trial for murder began the following March in Liverpool Crown Court.

Healey's defence was largely contained in an exercise book he had been using as a diary. In it he claimed that although he killed Greeba and Marie he didn't know it was going to happen. He continually felt that he was like a piece of furniture, to be moved around by his wife, who constantly criticized and ridiculed his love-making. And one night after a particularly humiliating episode he had gone downstairs feeling ill. He picked up a rolling pin and found himself attacking his wife. Marie came into the bedroom and he said that he tried to push her out, so that she would not see her mother lying on the floor.

But Dr Donald Wayte, a pathologist, described Marie's injuries as more like those he had seen on crush victims in road accidents, and prosecuting counsel accused Healey of simply inventing his story to obtain sympathy.

A witness described how she had gone on holiday with the Healeys to Majorca only a month before the killings. She said she thought Healey exhibited an unhealthy interest in young Marie, although she had to admit that she said nothing to Greeba at the time.

The jury returned after three hours with a unanimous verdict of guilty, and Healey was sentenced to life.

It was then revealed – circumstances which the jury could not know about during the trial – that he already had a conviction for indecent exposure and inciting a thirteen-year-old girl to commit an act of gross indecency. In his diary he chronicled the deteriorating relationship between him and the young girl. He may well have been sexually abusing Marie and his wife may have found out about it. Had she reported him to the police, in view of his other conviction, he could have gone to prison, which might have been the real motive for the Reggie Perrin murder.

William Sanchez de Pina Hepper was a BBC translator, had been an American spy in Spain and was a noted painter. In February 1954, at his studio in Brighton, he raped and strangled an eleven-year-old girl. He was arrested in Spain, extradited and tried at Lewes Assizes in July. His defence was insanity, but he was convicted of murder and hanged at Wandsworth prison in August 1954.

Sarah Ann Hearn　This was another case where the accused tried to fake a suicide, but it developed into one of the most famous English courtroom battles of the century.

It began peacefully enough with a middle-aged couple, Mr and Mrs William Thomas of Lewannick, near Launceston, North Cornwall, taking a friend on a motor-car outing to the nearby seaside resort of Bude in October 1930. The friend, Mrs Sarah

Ann Hearn, had been living with her elder sister, Miss Lydia Everard, nearby, but her sister had died some months ago. Mrs Hearn brought along tinned salmon sandwiches and chocolate cake. They duly ate these at a café in Bude, and on the way back Mrs Thomas was violently ill. When they reached home a doctor was called and Mrs Thomas was transferred to hospital in Plymouth where she died on 4 November.

At the funeral, remarks seem to have been passed about Mrs Hearn's involvement in her friend's death and she subsequently disappeared, after writing a letter to Mr Thomas which hinted at suicide. Her hat and coat were found on the cliffs at Looe, on the south coast, and one of her shoes was washed up on a nearby beach. But a picture of her in a newspaper alerted a gentleman in Torquay, who had just engaged a new cook, and Mrs Hearn was arrested.

She was tried in June 1931, at Bodmin Assize Court, for the murders of Mrs Thomas and Miss Everard. And there was displayed an array of legal talent rarely seen in that part of the world. For the prosecution Herbert du Parcq KC led Patrick Devlin, who subsequently became a famous judge, and the defence was in the hands of Norman Birkett KC, assisted by Dingle Foot, whose father was MP for Bodmin.

The eminent pathologist Dr Roche Lynch, senior analyst to the Home Office, stated that Mrs Thomas had died from arsenic poisoning. By the examination of organs from her exhumed body he was able to calculate that she had received a dose of ten grains, the lethal dose being two to four grains. Miss Everard also had large quantities of arsenic in almost every part of her body, including the hair and nails.

These findings were immediately attacked in cross-examination by Norman Birkett, who pointed out that the amounts Dr Lynch had mentioned were still very small concentrations of arsenic. In fact the soil of Lewannick itself contained greater concentrations of the poison than had been found in the bodies.

And he got the witness to agree that during the exhumation, which took place in a snowstorm, had only a very small portion of soil accidentally found its way into one of the sample jars, it would go a long way to account for the amounts found.

The prosecution were able to show that Mrs Hearn had bought an arsenic-containing weedkiller from a chemist's shop in Launceston. But Birkett pointed out that this was blue, and any placed in the salmon sandwiches would have noticeably stained the white bread.

Birkett called only Mrs Hearn as a witness. Her calm demeanour and forthright manner impressed the jury. She denied poisoning the two women, but admitted that the talk at the funeral had frightened her and led her to attempt suicide, which she afterwards could not go through with. Having badly damaged the prosecution case through his cross-examinations, Birkett went on to attack it in his final speech for the lack of motive shown and its many inconsistencies.

Du Parcq's final speech was marred by a period when he was plainly unwell and eventually he fainted in court. He was able to continue after a rest, but it clearly affected the summing up of his case.

The judge told the jury that there was insufficient evidence to prove murder in the case of Miss Everard and a verdict of not guilty was duly recorded. It took only sixty minutes' deliberation for the jury to reach a similar verdict on the charge of murdering Mrs Thomas.

During the trial, when Birkett had finished his final speech, he sat down exhausted and turned to his junior counsel, Dingle Foot.

'Cases like this take years off a man's life,' he said.

'Perhaps,' replied Foot, 'but they add years to the client's.'

Norman Birkett had a reputation for successful defences in poisoning cases and another lady he appeared for was Beatrice Annie Pace. She was tried at Gloucester Assizes in 1928 for the murder of her husband, a sheep-breeder at Coleford, by poisoning him with arsenic. Birkett pointed out that the sheep dip Pace used contained arsenic and that it was by no means unknown for sheep dippers, especially ones with heavy moustaches like Pace, accidentally to poison themselves. The case was stopped by the judge and Beatrice Pace was set free.

Garry Heidnik When forty-three-year-old Garry Heidnik was tried in the city hall in Philadelphia, in June 1988, he was charged with eighteen separate offences. These included two counts of first-degree murder, kidnapping and rape, various assaults, involuntary deviate sexual intercourse, making terroristic threats, criminal solicitation and possession and abuse of a corpse.

If that were not enough, the man himself was one of the strangest figures ever to step into the dock at a murder trial. Tall and thin, he had an IQ of 'near genius level' as one psychologist reported. Heidnik had amassed a considerable fortune on the stock exchange and owned a new Cadillac and a Rolls-Royce, three other cars and a van. Yet he did no regular work, communicating with his stockbroker by telephone, and chose to live in a small house in one of the seediest, most rundown parts of Philadelphia.

But perhaps the most incredible thing about the whole case was the story told by witness Josefina Rivera in court.

She was a twenty-five-year-old black prostitute who, on the night of 26 November 1986, had a row with her boyfriend and left the apartment they shared. She didn't come back for four months. Then she appeared on his doorstep in an hysterical state, emaciated and dressed in filthy rags. She said that on the night she left she had been picked up by a man driving a new Cadillac and they went back to his house for sex. Afterwards he overpowered and handcuffed her, and dragged her down to the basement. He explained that he wanted a large family and intended to capture about a dozen women and make them all pregnant.

Over the succeeding weeks he added another five girls to

his harem. Some were prostitutes and some were of very low intelligence. It appeared that Heidnik, although white himself, preferred black girls. Far from treating them as part of a family he kept the girls chained up in his cellar, supplying very little food and subjecting them all to a regime of beatings and sexual abuse. He dug a pit in the cellar and shackled a girl inside it if he considered that she had misbehaved, ramming a lid down on it so she had very little air.

One victim, Sandra Lindsay, a retarded woman, particularly annoyed him and he kept her suspended from an overhead beam by her wrists for a week, forcing food into her mouth at intervals. She eventually choked to death. He then took the body upstairs where he dismembered it. The girls soon smelt the odour of roasting flesh, and when one of the others, Deborah Dudley, displeased him he took her upstairs to show her Sandra's head cooking in a pot.

Deborah remained defiant and he put her, together with two others, into the pit and poured water over them. Then he replaced the lid, through which holes had been bored, and forced Josefina to push a live electric wire down the hole to touch the girls or their chains. The wire made contact with Deborah's chains and she was electrocuted.

Heidnik decided not to dismember the body this time. He made Josefina help to carry it to a car and together they drove to a remote part of New Jersey where they buried it on waste land.

By now Josefina was desperately trying to win Heidnik's confidence, pretending to enjoy sex with him and sympathizing with his desire to produce a family. Eventually she was able to persuade him to let her go to visit her children, and she rushed round to her boyfriend's apartment. He called the police, Heidnik's house of horror was raided, and the two remaining girls were released.

Heidnik's defence attorney, A. Charles Peruto Jr, naturally hoped to show that his client was insane. Heidnik had a history of mental illness, having been invalided out of the army with schizophrenia when he was young and having spent many periods in asylums. But Judge Lynne M. Abraham told the jury that having a mental illness is not necessarily the same as saying that a person is legally insane, which implies that they did not know at the time that what they were doing was wrong.

The prosecution were able to show that during the time he was holding his victims captive, torturing and killing them, he was at the same time manipulating stocks and shares by phone through his broker.

The all-white jury of six women and six men took two-and-a-half days to find Heidnik guilty on both counts of first-degree murder and guilty on nearly all the other charges. In Pennsylvania the jury also decides the sentence in the case of first-degree murder. Heidnik was sentenced to death twice and on the other charges to 120 years in jail.

Dr John Hill   Dr John Hill apparently had everything. From humble beginnings on a farm in southern Texas he was, by March 1969, one of the top plastic surgeons in Houston. He had been married to Joan, the adopted daughter of one of the richest men in town, oil tycoon Ash Robinson, for twelve years and had a nine-year-old son. They lived in a large mansion in the exclusive River Oaks suburb.

But Dr Hill also had a mistress, Ann Kurth, for whom he rented an apartment. Joan Hill had learned of her husband's extra-marital activities and was being difficult . . .

On Friday 14 March the Hills went to a benefit dinner and the next day had two friends to stay the weekend. On Sunday morning Joan was sick after breakfast, had diarrhoea, and went back to bed. The next morning she was no better and her father, who lived nearby and had come round to see her, thought she had influenza.

By Tuesday morning her maid was becoming worried about

her; she called Joan's parents and also rang Dr Hill at his office at the hospital. He came home and took his wife to a small hospital in which he had a financial interest. There she was found to be in an advanced state of shock with a barely recordable blood pressure. She died early on Wednesday morning.

A cursory autopsy was performed by the hospital pathologist, who gave the cause of death as 'acute pancreatitis' and the body was embalmed ready for burial.

But Ash Robinson was far from happy and reported the matter to the district attorney of Harris County, who ordered another autopsy to be done by the coroner. But the embalming had made it very difficult to determine the exact cause of death and this official reported it as due to 'virus hepatitis'.

The oil tycoon was still not satisfied and believed that his son-in-law had in some way killed his daughter. He employed private detectives and lawyers to investigate the circumstances of the death and got in touch with Dr Milton Helpern, the famous New York pathologist. Luckily the Harris County coroner had been one of Helpern's students and Helpern was invited to perform yet another autopsy.

This one was attended by no less than twelve doctors, representing Dr Hill and Harris County, but the outcome was no more conclusive than before. The New York pathologist concluded that death had resulted from some acute inflammatory and probably infectious disease and the entry portal was probably the alimentary tract. He did make a comment, however, that the failure to provide adequate medical attention at home and the delay in hospitalization aggravated a situation which proved fatal. The local coroner agreed and recommended a grand jury investigation.

By this time Dr Hill had married Ann Kurth, and this was seen as a possible motive for the doctor conniving at the death of his wife. It took three separate grand juries – the first two recommended no action should be taken – before he was finally sent for trial. The indictment was based on an old Texas statute by which he was charged with 'murder by omission', in that he had killed her by failing to provide and withholding proper medical attention. The trial date was set for February 1971, and at that time he could have faced the death penalty if convicted.

When the trial began Dr Hill had divorced Ann and found himself another woman Connie Loesby. This proved to be a disastrous move on his part, for whereas in Texas law a wife couldn't testify against her husband, Ann could and did.

First the prosecution put on the friends who had stayed with the Hills over that fatal weekend. They testified that the doctor had brought home some éclairs, cream puffs and tarts and selected which pastry should be given to each person, even to his wife.

Ann went into the witness box to say that a week before the death she had noticed some pastries in the refrigerator, which Hill had told her not to touch. She had also seen some petri dishes – used in laboratories to culture microbes – in the bathroom, which the doctor had said were for an experiment he was conducting. In addition, Ann claimed that he had tried to kill her by crashing their car and soon afterwards by injecting her with a syringe.

It was then that the prosecution made their mistake. 'What made you think that the injection would be harmful?' enquired the prosecutor.

Ann replied promptly, 'Because he told me how he had killed Joan with a needle.'

Richard Haynes, the defence attorney, was instantly on his feet. He objected that this direct accusation of murder was not what Dr Hill was being charged with, and since the defence had had no chance to prepare themselves against it, a mistrial should be declared. The judge agreed and the trial was abandoned.

Legal manoeuvring on the part of the defence ensured another delay and the new trial was not scheduled until November 1972. By this time the Supreme Court of the United States had ruled against the death penalty. Since Dr Hill had high hopes that at the new trial he might be found not guilty, he was almost home and dry.

Then fate, or someone else, took a hand. By September 1972 Hill had acquired a new wife, Connie. Returning home one day from a convention they entered the house in River Oaks, where a gunman lying in wait shot Dr Hill.

Through the gun, which he threw away, the police were able to trace and arrest the killer. He jumped bail and, being followed into a café by a police sergeant, after an exchange of shots, was himself killed. Two women, a brothel madame and a prostitute, were charged with complicity in the murder of Dr Hill and they named Ash Robinson as having paid for the contract. But although both were convicted and received terms of imprisonment the oil tycoon was never indicted.

Dr Hill's wife Connie, his mother and his son, brought a civil action against Robinson, but it failed. The brothel madame refused to testify.

The prostitute took a lie detector test which indicated that she was telling the truth; Ash Robinson, however, also took a lie detector test which seemed to show that when he said he had nothing to do with it, he also was telling the truth.

Dr Arthur Waite, a New York dentist, also married the daughter of a millionaire. First, in January 1916, he killed his mother-in-law by putting diphtheria and influenza germs in her food. Then in March he tried the same thing with his father-in-law, but eventually had to resort to arsenic. A relative became suspicious and an autopsy was done before Dr Waite had time to have the body cremated. He was convicted and electrocuted in May 1917.

Audrey Marie Homan 'Mike,' came the thin voice over the phone, 'I've been poisoned with arsenic.'

It was the voice of his sister Carol Hilley speaking from hospital in Anniston, Alabama, and to Mike Hilley it sounded like the end of a story which had begun four years ago, in 1975. As it turned out, he was wrong.

In May 1975 his father had died, in Anniston, of what was diagnosed as infectious hepatitis. Soon after, his mother, Audrey Marie, embarked on a spending spree which was to land her in debt. She continued to write cheques on empty bank accounts and was soon in deep financial trouble. She then took out a $25,000 insurance policy on her nineteen-year-old daughter Carol. Soon after this Carol began suffering stomach trouble with frequent vomiting. Marie Hilley took her daughter round a series of hospitals, without waiting very long in any one, and no one could find out what was wrong.

Some of Carol's relatives in Anniston began to get suspicious. Freeda Adcock, Frank Hilley's sister, had always been uneasy about her brother's death, particularly since she had learned from him just before he died that Marie had been giving him secret injections.

When Marie was finally arrested and charged with passing dud cheques, Freeda persuaded a young hospital doctor to consider the possibility that Carol might be suffering from some sort of poisoning. He soon found out that it was arsenic.

In October 1979, Frank Hilley's body was exhumed and found to contain a substantial amount of the same poison. Mike Hilley and his wife Teri had also lived with his mother for a while after his father's death and Teri had suffered two miscarriages. They now considered that they might have received small doses of arsenic.

Marie Hilley was arrested, charged with poisoning her husband and daughter, and allowed out on bail. She promptly disappeared.

A few months later a lady calling herself Lindsay Robbi Hannon met middle-aged John Homan in Fort Lauderdale, Florida. They moved north to New Hampshire, near the Canadian border, and eventually got married, obtaining jobs in the nearby town of Keene. Robbi soon began to complain of crippling headaches, which she said were due to a rare and possibly fatal blood disorder. Telling John she would go and stay with her twin sister Teri for treatment she went to Texas. In November 1982, shortly after Robbi arrived, Teri reported her death in the newspaper. She then got in touch with John and was soon flying up to New Hampshire to console him.

It is difficult to say if Homan believed this incredible deception – Teri when she arrived had blonde hair and was thinner than Robbi who had been a brunette – but many people in Keene did not, easily recognizing Teri as Robbi. Some got in touch with a local reporter who, suspecting some sort of insurance fraud, contacted the police. Teri was interviewed and suddenly, as if becoming tired of the charade, admitted who she was.

Her trial began in May 1983, in Anniston. The young prosecutor, Assistant District Attorney Joe Hubbard, who hadn't left school when the case began in 1975, had a difficult task. He had to prove that the gentle-looking, demure middle-aged lady was 'a cold calculating diabolical killer', as he put it.

Carol, the first witness, wouldn't look at her mother as she gave details of what she remembered of her father's death and the progress of her own illness. Freeda Adcock revealed how in Marie's belongings she had found a bottle of rat poison containing arsenic and a medicine bottle containing a solution of arsenic in water, while Lieutenant Carroll of the Anniston police reported finding an empty pill bottle in Marie's handbag when she was arrested which still contained traces of the poison.

Defence attorney Wilford Lane countered by putting Mike Hilley on the stand, who said that he did not believe his father would have allowed his mother to give him an injection. But Hubbard destroyed this evidence when he made Mike admit that he had written to the coroner some time after his father's death saying that he believed his mother was responsible.

Audrey Marie Hilley was convicted on 9 June 1983 of poisoning her husband and attempting to poison her daughter. She was sentenced to life imprisonment.

But that was not the end of this incredible story.

Four years later she convinced a gullible prison governor to allow her a three-day parole. Meeting the ever faithful John Homan in February 1987, she went with him to a hotel in Anniston. Marie then disappeared leaving John a letter saying a man named Walter was taking her to Canada. But she didn't go that far. She only wandered up the railway line towards her childhood home. Five days later she appeared, wet through and dishevelled, collapsed on the porch of a house near the tracks. She was quickly taken to hospital suffering from exposure, but died of a heart attack before she reached it. Audrey Marie Homan never admitted to any of her misdeeds and died keeping her own counsel.

Robert Hoolhouse   At first sight it looked like a pretty open and shut case. Sixty-seven-year-old Mrs Margaret Dobson of High Grange Farm, Wolviston, County Durham, had been found raped and murdered on a farm track near her home. Death was due to stab wounds to the chest and neck.

The most obvious suspect was twenty-year-old Robert Hoolhouse, a farm labourer whose family had quarrelled with the Dobsons and been ordered off High Grange, where they had been living in one of the cottages. He said he had an alibi for the time of the murder, which the police believed had occurred between 4.30 and 5.30 on the afternoon of Wednesday 19 January, 1938, but this was soon shown to be false and he rapidly changed it.

He had bloodstains on the sleeves of his shirt and jacket and also on the jacket lapel, the peak of his cap, his overalls and raincoat. One bloodstain on his cuff was shown to be group O, the same as Mrs Dobson, and Hoolhouse refused to take a blood test. Pubic hairs found on his shirt front could well have come from Mrs Dobson. And there were scratches on his face. He also rode a bicycle of the same kind as the murderer's.

Hoolhouse was brought to trial at Leeds Assizes in March 1938. As the judge was to point out, the evidence against him was purely circumstantial. Half the young men in the area rode similar cycles to Hoolhouse; nearly half the population had blood group O; and his explanation that he had cut himself shaving could have accounted for some of the stains. Since he often worked as an assistant on a threshing machine he could well have had other people's blood splashed on his clothes.

The false times he claimed in his alibi were also easily explained, as the young man had been practically accused of the murder by another farmhand, who subsequently went to the police, and it is by no means unknown for quite innocent suspects to tell lies if they are afraid they will be accused.

Hoolhouse claimed he received the scratches on his face in a fall from his cycle. Mrs Dobson had been wearing woollen gloves at the time she was murdered, making it unlikely that she was able to scratch her assailant.

The pubic hairs on the young man's shirt were one of the weakest links in the prosecution's chain of circumstantial evidence. He was known to have had at least one girlfriend, so their presence could not be said to be conclusive proof that he had just raped an old lady. Nor was semen discovered on his clothes, whereas Mrs Dobson's pubic area had been matted with it.

There were footprints round the body, most of which were Mr Dobson's, since it was he who had found his wife. But one of his overlaid an earlier footprint which might well have belonged to the murderer; this, however, was much too large to have been made by Hoolhouse.

The young man's counsel, Arthur Morley KC, called no witnesses for the defence. In retrospect this seems a curious decision, since Hoolhouse claimed he was home by 5.00 p.m., some miles away from the murder scene, and was apparently seen there by his father and a neighbour. Perhaps Mr Morley felt he had already effectively demolished the prosecution case.

Certainly the judge, Mr Justice Wrottisley, in his summing up seemed to agree. He pointed out to the jury that though the evidence was consistent with Hoolhouse being the murderer, it was also consistent with his not having committed the crime. He went on to say: 'If . . . you think that it all amounts to this, that very likely that young fellow did it, but we cannot be certain – if that is the frame of mind you are left in, then your duty is to say "Not guilty." '

Most people in court seemed to be of the opinion that this would be the verdict, but the all-male jury, possibly influenced by the violence and horror of the crime, brought in a verdict of guilty. Hoolhouse was sentenced to death and, after an appeal was rejected and the Home Secretary refused to order a reprieve, was hanged in Durham jail on 26 May 1939.

Rupert Furneaux in his book *Robert Hoolhouse* claims that the evidence on which the young man was convicted was slim and that he did not receive the benefit of a reasonable doubt. And it is hard not to agree with him.

Rupert Stuart, a twenty-seven-year-old Australian aborigine, was rather luckier. In 1959 he was tried at Adelaide for the murder of a nine-year-old girl, and after confessing that he had raped and murdered her while drunk was convicted and sentenced to death. An appeal that the verdict was against the weight of evidence was rejected. Another appeal that Stuart did not know enough English to make a proper statement was also rejected. His lawyers then appealed to the Judiciary Committee of the Privy Council in London. This final appeal was also rejected, but by this time the sentence had been commuted to life imprisonment.

Arthur and Nizamodeen Hosein   The trouble with circumstantial evidence is that it leaves so many questions unanswered. The Hosein brothers were convicted on purely circumstantial evidence, but it has never been satisfactorily explained how two such bungling kidnappers managed so successfully to conceal the death of Mrs Muriel McKay.

She was the wife of Alick McKay, the deputy chairman of the *News of the World*, and when she disappeared from her home in Wimbledon on Monday 29 December, 1969, it was soon realized that she had been kidnapped in mistake for Rupert Murdoch's wife, since Alick McKay had been using his chairman's Rolls-Royce.

Telephone messages demanded a million pounds ransom and these were followed by letters from Muriel McKay, written in captivity, confirming her terrible position and asking for co-operation from her husband. Two attempts were made by disguised policemen to deliver the ransom. The first, after placing the suitcase containing the money near some paper flowers, was called off when a Volvo containing two black men circled the area but drove off without stopping. The second was aborted when the same Volvo passed the drop-off spot four times but did not stop. By this time the police had noted the number of the car and it was traced to thirty-three-year-old Arthur Hosein, who lived at Rooks Farm in the village of Stocking Pelham, near Bishop's Stortford.

Arthur and his twenty-one-year-old brother Nizamodeen, who also lived at the farm, had originally come from Trinidad. They were arrested and, in September 1970, tried at the Old Bailey on charges of murder, kidnapping and making demands with menaces.

The prosecution was in the hands of the Attorney General, Sir Peter Rawlinson, who had been junior counsel in the prosecution of Ruth Ellis in 1955 (*see* p. 326).

When the Attorney General had finished his opening statement, Nizam's counsel, Douglas Draycott QC, said that his client wanted to make certain admissions, without actually making a confession. In his statement, read by Mr Draycott, he admitted making enquiries about Rupert Murdoch's Rolls-Royce, placing the paper flowers by the first drop-off point, driving the Volvo when they went to collect the suitcases and writing a note of the number of a car, which was to be the second ransom hand-over point.

Arthur tried to put all the blame on his younger brother, claiming that he had seen him at the farm meeting several suspicious-looking people. One, he thought, was the Labour MP Robert Maxwell, who later bought the *Daily Mirror*. But Arthur Hosein's fingerprints had been found on a newspaper which had been left at Mrs McKay's home when she was kidnapped and on several of the letters she had written to her husband.

He showed a good deal of arrogance in the witness box, arguing with and jeering at the Attorney-General when counsel lost his place in his notes and becoming almost hysterical with rage at times under cross-examination.

The jury took just over four hours to find the brothers guilty of every charge made against them, though they added a plea for leniency for Nizam. The younger brother said nothing on hearing the verdict, but Arthur launched into a tirade accusing the judge of racial discrimination and claiming justice had not been done. Mr Justice Sebag Shaw sentenced both of them to life imprisonment for the murder and gave Arthur an additional twenty-five years and Nizam fifteen years for kidnapping. Each also received a fourteen-year sentence for blackmail and ten years for sending threatening letters.

What happened to Mrs McKay remains a mystery. One theory is that she was cut up by the brothers and fed to their pigs, but though the police searched every inch of Rooks Farm and its surroundings no trace of her was ever found. And to this day the Hoseins have never broken their silence.

Donald Hume   One of the most remarkable trials of the twentieth century, this one showed very clearly how the behaviour in
court of the defendant could affect the outcome.

Stanley Setty was a forty-six-year-old Iraqi-born Jew who
traded in second-hand cars, and anything else he could turn his
hand to, from the kerb and the cafés around Warren Street,
London, in 1949. He disappeared on 4 October and on 21
October a package containing his body, minus the head and legs,
was washed up on the Essex marshes. Having identified him by
his fingerprints, the police were soon visiting an associate of
Setty's, twenty-nine-year-old Donald Hume. He was arrested and
his trial began at the Old Bailey in January 1950.

The prosecution, led by Christmas Humphreys KC, had a
wealth of evidence to present. Hume, who was well known to
the staffs of small airports around London, was seen taking off
in a single-engine Auster from Elstree aerodrome on the day
after Setty disappeared with a couple of heavy parcels. He was
noticed landing at Southend two hours later with an empty plane.
The next day he took off from Southend with a very heavy parcel
– he refused an offer of assistance with it – and subsequently
landed at Gravesend airport with no package aboard.

There was also ample evidence of bloodstains in Hume's flat.
A large bloodstain was found on the back of the sitting-room
carpet and traces of blood were discovered between the cracks
of the floorboards in the dining-room. Where there was enough
to test, it was typed as the same blood group as Setty's.

In addition to this Setty was known to have withdrawn £1,000
in fivers from his account just before his disappearance and the
bank had kept a record of the consecutive serial numbers. One
was used by Hume to pay for a hired car and some of the others
were paid into his bank account.

But Hume had a story to explain all this. Admitting in the
witness box that not all the deals he did were honest, he said
that he had previously met three suspicious characters, called

Max, Greeny and Boy. Hume described them in detail and reported that they had asked him to get rid of some parcels by dropping them into the sea from a plane. They said that they were plates used to make forged petrol coupons, but when the three turned up at his flat with the packages Hume rapidly realized that they contained something more sinister than forgery equipment.

One of the parcels leaked blood on his floor, but he was too scared of the men to argue and duly dropped the parcels as they asked. They paid him with five-pound notes.

It was a preposterous story, but given the world Hume obviously moved in it could just have been true and he appeared in the witness box to be a man who, if not absolutely honest, was also not obviously a murderer. It was enough to confuse the jury. After retiring for two-and-a-half hours they came back to say that they were hopelessly divided, and the judge dismissed them.

Then for some curious reason Mr Humphreys decided not to ask for a new trial, but to proceed on the second indictment, that of being an accessory after the fact. A new jury was then sworn in. The prosecution offered no evidence on the murder charge and Hume was acquitted. Since he had already admitted disposing of Setty's body he pleaded guilty to being an accessory. Mr Justice Sellers sentenced him to twelve years.

Hume served eight, and when he was released confessed to the *Sunday Pictorial* that he had in fact murdered Setty, knowing that he could not be charged again with the same crime.

But the money that he received for his story was soon gone and he embarked on a series of bank robberies both in this country and in Switzerland. He shot and seriously injured a bank manager at Brentford, near London, and also severely wounded a cashier at a bank in Zurich. The Swiss official managed to set off the alarm and Hume was pursued out of the bank. When a taxi-driver tried to stop him Hume shot and killed the man.

One year and eight months after being released Hume was

again brought to trial for murder, in Switzerland, but this time he was convicted and sentenced to life imprisonment.

In 1976, after sixteen years in a Swiss prison, he was released and flown to Britain. When he landed he was examined by two psychiatrists and taken to Broadmoor, the prison for the criminally insane.

Joe Hunt   A business and social club was formed in Los Angeles in March 1983 by twenty-four-year-old whizzkid Joe Hunt, in order, among other things, to trade in the stock market. He persuaded young wealthy businessmen to put up money for commodity trading. When he decided that they needed more capital someone suggested they try Ron Levin.

Levin was a forty-year-old homosexual businessman who was attracted to the handsome young men of the Boys Club and agreed to put up $5 million. But he was a conman and persuaded a brokerage house to set up a dummy account for Hunt to trade. At first the whizzkid made a loss, but soon he turned this into a substantial profit. Then Levin told him to stop trading and used the impressive account figures himself to set up a real account with another broker without having to put up any cash.

When Hunt discovered that he had been tricked and had not made any money at all he went to Levin's luxury apartment in Beverly Hills with Jim Graham, a small-time black crook who posed as an ex-Mr Universe, football player and karate expert. At gunpoint Levin was forced to sign a cheque for $1.5 million, then he was shot and his body buried in remote Soledad Canyon. Hunt left a sheaf of documents forged to show that the $1.5 million was to obtain an interest in one of Hunt's companies. But Levin had the last laugh, from beyond the grave, when the cheque bounced.

The whizzkid later confessed this murder to a meeting of his club, but such was his power over them that none of them went to the police. They were still short of money and another member

Above: Leopold and Loeb, sentenced to life imprisonment for the murder of Bobby Frank, with their lawyer Clarence Darrow (centre). (*Popperfoto*)

Below: Solicitor Mr Leigh Taylor and Mr Geoffrey Lawrence QC (left) at the trial of Dr John Bodkin Adams. (*Topham*)

Above left: Dr John Bodkin Adams, acquitted of the murder of Edith Alice Morrell. (*Popperfoto*)

Above right: Widow Marie Besnard was found not guilty of the murders of twelve people after three trials. (*Popperfoto*)

The trials and acquittal of George Ince show how the massive juggernaut of the legal system could be stopped in its tracks by a single man. (*PA News*)

The hook-ended knife with which August Sangret stabbed and killed his pregnant girlfriend Joan Pearl Wolfe. (*Topham*)

Officials dredging the canal during the Ronald Light case.
(*Hulton Deutsch*)

Graham Backhouse's
self-inflicted wounds.
(*Topham*)

Dean Corll, mass
homosexual murderer.
(*Topham*)

Claus von Bulow was found guilty on two counts of attempted murder, and then acquitted after a second trial. (*Rex Features*)

Defence lawyer Alan Dershowitz at the second trial of Baron Claus von Bulow. (*Rex Features*)

Peter Sutcliffe. (*Express Newspapers*)

Alice Crimmins at Queens Criminal Court, where she was tried for the murder and manslaughter of her son and daughter. (*Range*)

Pamela Smart was sentenced to life imprisonment for helping to murder her husband Gregg. (*Rex Features*)

Above: O. J. Simpson was aquitted of murdering his wife Nicole and her friend Ronald Goldman. (*AP*)

Right: Blood-stained sheets are strewn along the entryway of the Los Angeles condominium where Nicole Brown Simpson and Ronald Goldman were murdered on 12 June 1994. (*AP*)

of the group, Reza Eslaminia, whose father Hedayat was an Iranian exile of reputed wealth, suggested that they kidnap his father, force him to transfer money to Reza then kill him. Graham, Reza, a friend of Reza's, Ben Dosti, and some others broke into the Iranian's San Francisco apartment, chloroformed him and packed him into a trunk. By the time they reached Los Angeles with the trunk the old man had suffocated.

Some club members were becoming appalled at the violence and went to the police. Dean Karny, who had been a close friend of the whizzkid, reported that Hunt had given him details of the Levin murder, and he confessed his own part in the Eslaminia killing. The district attorney gave Karny full legal immunity and the young man led the police to Soledad Canyon where the Iranian's body had been dumped. After much searching a jawbone was found, which was identified as having belonged to Hedayat Eslaminia, but no trace of Levin's body was ever found.

In May 1985 Jim Graham was tried for the murder of Ron Levin, but apart from the evidence of Dean Karny there was little against him and the trial ended with a hung jury.

November the following year saw the opening of Joe Hunt's trial for Levin's murder. Again Karny went into the witness box, but the prosecution had no body and no weapon and for a while it looked as if the outcome would be the same as in Graham's trial. But prosecutor Fred Wapner then produced seven pages of yellow legal paper which Hunt had inadvertently left inside the sheaf of documents he had carefully placed in Levin's apartment. The top sheet was headed: 'At Levins – To Do' and was a memo of procedure to complete the extortion of money from Levin and to accomplish the murder. Mr Wapner called it 'a recipe for murder'. It was enough to convince the jury and Hunt was found guilty of first-degree murder.

At the subsequent hearing to determine the penalty, the jury gave the convicted man life imprisonment without the possibility of parole.

Meanwhile Jim Graham was tried again for the murder of Ron Levin and again the jury were undecided. This time the district attorney agreed to drop the murder charge if Graham would plead guilty to being an accessory after the fact and possession of an illegal weapon.

Reza Eslaminia and Ben Dosti were tried in October 1987 for the murder of Hedayat Eslaminia. Dean Karny again told his story; this time he had actually been there while the murder was done. Both defendants were convicted of second-degree murder and sentenced to life imprisonment.

In November 1988 Joe Hunt sacked his attorney and conducted his second defence – against the charge of murdering Hedayat Eslaminia – himself. After many delaying tactics he was finally brought to trial in April 1992, but in December, after a record twenty-six days' deliberation, the jury failed to reach a verdict and a mistrial was declared. The following January the charges against Hunt of murdering Eslaminia were dropped.

Dean Karny has been given a new identity by the Federal Witness Protection Programme. This means that he must remain undercover for the rest of his life, and among other things he can never again see his family.

Dr Bennett Clarke Hyde Dr Clarke Hyde had an ambitious plan: murder nine people and his wife would inherit close to $3 million, which in 1909 was an enormous fortune.

His wife's uncle was Colonel Thomas B. Swope, the founder of Kansas City, who had become a multi-millionaire in real estate. The old man – he was eighty-two – had made a will by which his fortune was to be shared out among his descendants, his two sons and his sister-in-law's four daughters, of whom Dr Hyde's wife was one. If any died, their share was to be distributed among the others. They all lived together, including Dr Hyde and his wife, in a large mansion at Independence, close to that part of Kansas City which is in Missouri.

First there was the problem of Swope's old friend and adviser, James Hunton, who was the estate's administrator. In September, Hunton developed a fever and Hyde diagnosed typhoid. In a few days Hunton was dead. Not long after, Thomas Swope himself was stricken, and though an anti-toxin was administered and nurses were in round-the-clock attendance, the old man died in convulsions on 3 October.

The doctor now decided to complete the job with one last stroke and after a dinner party at the mansion near the end of November, nearly everyone – except Dr Hyde and his wife – was taken ill. Once again Hyde postulated typhoid and in December Chris Swope, one of the colonel's sons, died in convulsions in the same way as his father had done.

By now the nurses were becoming suspicious. They reported to Mrs Swope, 'People are being murdered in this house', and she asked a former prosecuting attorney to investigate the matter. By February the following year he had enough evidence to indict Dr Hyde for three murders.

The trial took place in April 1910. Three doctors reported on autopsies they had done on the exhumed bodies of Thomas Swope and James Hunton. Strychnine, a poison causing convulsions, had been found in both. A number of nurses went into the witness box to claim that they had seen Dr Hyde substitute pills of his own for those supplied by the chemist, and give the patients unauthorized injections when he thought he was not being observed.

A local doctor, Dr Stewart, a colleague of Dr Hyde, claimed that the defendant had borrowed typhoid bacilli from him, and a local chemist said Hyde had purchased cyanide on three occasions, saying he wanted to kill rats. Unfortunately the poison book containing the doctor's signature was destroyed in a fire before the trial began.

The prosecution theory was that Hyde had first introduced typhoid germs into his victims and then, when they were ill, finished them off with strychnine or cyanide to confuse the symptoms. The trial lasted a month and the jury took three days to bring in a verdict of guilty of first-degree murder. Dr Hyde was sentenced to life imprisonment. But Dr Hyde's wife was a wealthy woman in her own right and she financed lawyers to fight her husband's case. A year later they won an appeal and a new trial was ordered. Dr Hyde was allowed bail, the bail money being provided by his wife.

The second trial was abandoned due to the illness of one of the jurymen, and a third was ordered. The jury still could not agree and a fourth was begun in January 1917, nearly seven years after the first. But when the defence asked for dismissal of the charges on the grounds that Hyde had been tried three times without a definite result, the prosecution did not object. They had run out of money to carry on the case. The costs of the three previous trials had nearly bankrupted Jackson County.

Dr Hyde owed his freedom to his wife's money. But she was no fool. When a decent interval had elapsed she divorced him. Dr Hyde died in 1934 without, as far as we know, attempting any more murder schemes.

George Ince The trials of George Ince for murder were among the most spectacular to have occurred in British courts this century. And they showed how the massive juggernaut of the legal system could be stopped in its tracks by a single man, and not a lawyer at that.

The first trial began in Chelmsford Crown Court in May 1973. Ince was charged with murdering fifty-one-year-old Muriel Patience, attempting to murder her husband, fifty-four-year-old Robert, and her daughter Beverley, twenty; wounding Robert and Beverley, and stealing £900 in cash and cheques.

Robert and Muriel ran the Barn Restaurant and Nightclub at Braintree, Essex, and at 2.00 a.m. on 5 November 1972, Muriel and her daughter returned to the house next door, where they lived. They were confronted by two men and held at gunpoint until Bob came home. The intruders demanded the keys to the safe. Bob Patience at first said they were in the restaurant. The gunman then shot Muriel in the head. Her husband gave up the keys and the gunman rifled the safe. He forced Bob and Beverley to lie face down on the floor then shot them both through cushions. Beverley received a back wound, which she survived, and Bob only a slight head wound, since he moved his head at the instant the gun was fired. Muriel died.

The Essex police appealed to the East End criminal fraternity for help and someone mentioned the name of George Ince, who had convictions for violent brawling and shop-breaking, though none since 1961.

At both the East Ender's trials the main prosecution evidence was that of identification. Bob Patience had not picked out Ince at the identification parade, but he claimed that after seeing the back view of him at the magistrates court he was convinced Ince was the man. And he lost no opportunity during his evidence to point to the man in the dock and state categorically that this was the man who had shot his wife.

This clearly upset Ince who interrupted quite often and eventually leaped to his feet shouting: 'Why don't you tell the truth?'

The star prosecution witness was undoubtedly Beverley Patience. Unlike her father, she had seen the gunman at close quarters for some considerable time. Also unlike him she had originally picked out Ince's photograph from a series shown her before the identification parade, and she had immediately identified Ince at the parade. Although in the box she was nervous and tentative, somehow her words carried conviction. She was subjected to several outbursts by Ince and eventually the judge, Mr Justice Melford Stevenson, ordered Ince to be removed from the court until Beverley had completed her evidence.

In some ways Melford Stevenson was not the best choice for judge. Having been a brilliant counsel, as a judge he had a reputation for harsh sentencing and being prickly in court. He and Ince clashed several times and on the fifth day of the trial the East Ender, after conferring with his two counsel, Victor Durand and Robert Flasch, in a sensational move sacked them both.

This gave him the opportunity to speak on his own behalf and say things that his counsel wouldn't. Ince accused the judge of being rude and biased and said that he didn't want Durand to represent him unless another judge heard the case. He wasn't, however, entitled to a new judge, and Melford Stevenson told him so. The judge also decided that the trial should proceed without Ince's defence and the bizarre affair continued with no defence reply being made to the prosecution's final speech.

All this clearly affected the all-male jury, some of whom may have felt some sympathy for the lone man battling against what he regarded as the superior forces of the law. After six-and-a-half hours' deliberation they came back to say they were hopelessly deadlocked on all six charges.

The new trial began five days later, with a new judge, Mr Justice Eveleigh, and Ince having reinstated his counsel. The prosecution evidence was the same, but this time the East Ender produced an alibi witness. A mysterious woman, known as Mrs Doris Grey, claimed that she was Ince's mistress and had spent the night of the murder with him. What the jury did not know was that Mrs Grey was better known as Mrs Charles Kray. She had changed her name by deed poll in 1969, after her husband had been sent to prison for ten years, at the same time as his more famous brothers Ronnie and Reggie had received life sentences (see p. 190).

It took the new jury three hours to find Ince not guilty and he was hustled away shouting abuse at the police officers in court.

Three weeks after the trial a petty criminal told the Kendal police that a man he'd recently lodged with in Ambleside possessed a gun and had confessed to murdering Muriel Patience. The gunman, John Brooks, was arrested and ballistics proved that his gun was indeed the murder weapon. A friend of his, Nicholas Johnson, was tracked down by the Essex police and confessed he'd been there when Brooks shot Mrs Patience. He even showed the police where they had buried bank bags taken from the safe and a cigarette lighter stolen from the house.

In February 1974 Brooks was convicted of murdering Mrs Patience and Johnson convicted of the lesser charge of manslaughter.

By this time, however, George Ince was in prison, sentenced in November 1973 for hijacking, with four other men, a consignment of silver bullion at Mountnessing, Essex. He did receive a letter from the Chief Constable of Essex, Sir John Nightingale, apologizing for his being accused of the murder. And he did get to marry his Dolly Grey – although he had to be let out of prison for an hour in 1977 to do it.

Philip Yale Drew, an American actor with a touring company performing at Reading's County Theatre in June 1929 was identified by several witnesses as being seen coming out of a tobacconist's shop just before the shopkeeper was discovered brutally murdered. He suffered a 'trial by inquest' without being charged with committing any crime. Luckily the jury returned a verdict of murder against some person or persons unknown, but the case led to a revision of the Coroners Act and inquests today cannot be used as mini-trials.

J

William Jennings The remarkable thing about the trial of William Jennings in May 1989 was that it happened at all, for the murder of which he stood accused had occurred twenty-seven years before.

Stephen Jennings was three years old when he disappeared in December 1962. His family occupied a small terraced council house in the little village of Lower Gomersal, near Batley, West Yorkshire. His parents had three other children, Paul, Susan and baby Barry, all under five. According to his father, William Jennings, who had been looking after the children while his wife took the baby to a clinic, Stephen, Paul and Susan had gone out to play at a neighbour's in the morning, but only Paul and Susan returned for their midday meal.

After a few hours' frantic searching by the police and many local men, including Stephen's father, no one believed that the child would be found alive, because of the bitter weather. Searching was also a very difficult task, for the whole area was pitted with abandoned mineshafts, old and disused railway lines and depressions in the ground now filled with water. There were numberless places where the child could have slipped and fallen into a deep pit or drowned in a water-filled hole.

It was one of the coldest winters within living memory. It snowed in the area just after Christmas, making the search impossible, so it was called off.

From the start the police and many local people had been suspicious of William Jennings's story and of his assertion that the child must have been abducted by gypsies. The family had a bad reputation in the village for neglect and abuse of their children. It was believed that Jennings had taken a dislike to young Stephen because he was conceived while Jennings was in prison serving a sentence for larceny. In July of the year he disappeared, Stephen had been taken to hospital with badly scalded feet, which had occurred when he was alone with his father, but Jennings was not charged.

Later, in 1965, young Barry was discovered emaciated and in a distressing condition in his cot and Jennings and his wife were each jailed for eighteen months for neglect of the child.

There was still no sign of young Stephen. Then, twenty-five years after he disappeared, his body was found. In April 1988 a local man, who had taken part in the search, was walking his dog when he found a small human skull and some other small bones beneath some stones. The spot was only three-quarters of a mile from the old Jennings home.

The bones were carefully excavated by an archaeological team from Bradford University, and scientific examination revealed that they were the skeleton of a three-and-a-half-year-old child. A greenstick fracture of the wrist corresponded to one Stephen was known to have suffered a few weeks before he disappeared, and a pair of child's sandals found with the bones were identical to a pair Jennings had reported the boy wearing on the day he went missing. By this time the child's old home had been pulled down, Jennings and his wife had divorced in 1972, and he was living in Albrighton, Wolverhampton.

The police kept the finding of the bones secret for the time being, even persuading a local journalist who had heard about the excavation not to publish his story. They hoped that the surprise might force a confession from Jennings, because there was nothing to connect him directly with the disappearance, and if he didn't confess they could never get a conviction.

Officers from the Batley police and the Kirklees force went to Jennings's home by car. He was told the news then immediately arrested 'on suspicion', which meant that he would have to be released unless he confessed. But he continued to deny any involvement all the way back to Batley, except for the last twenty minutes when he went quiet. Then suddenly he broke down.

He said that in a fit of temper, because the child had soiled his bed, he'd knocked him through the banisters and Stephen had fallen downstairs. He'd picked him up and put him to bed, but the child had stopped breathing. Afraid that his wife would come back and find the boy dead he put him in a sack and dumped the body near a stone wall, piling stones on top of it.

During his trial at Leeds Crown Court, Jennings's counsel appealed for a manslaughter verdict on the grounds that the death was accidental. But according to expert witnesses, the bones revealed that the boy had suffered a severe beating which would have killed him anyway. William Jennings was convicted of murder and sentenced to life imprisonment.

Had he been convicted in 1962 he might well have received the death sentence.

K

Edmund Kemper   Ed Kemper was just fifteen when he shot his grandmother and grandfather on their seven-acre farm in the foothills of the Sierra Nevada, near Tollhouse, California. It was August 1964.

He spent the next five years at the Atascadero Hospital for the criminally insane, classified as a paranoid schizophrenic. But he is an intelligent man and there soon learned enough about psychology to be able to conceal the raging demons within him and he was released in 1969.

A giant of a man, at six feet nine inches, he was refused a job with the police force because he was too tall and obtained a position with the California Division of Highways. But he soon began cruising the highways on his own account picking up girl hitch-hikers.

In 1972, when he was living in Alameda, a suburb of San Francisco, he began killing an occasional one, usually driving her to a quiet destination and despatching her by stabbing or shooting. Then he would take the body back to his apartment and dismember it, sometimes having sexual intercourse with the corpse in the process. He would dispose of the pieces by dumping them in remote canyons or by throwing the parts over a convenient cliff. Very occasionally body fragments would be found and sometimes even identified, but Kemper was never even suspected.

He murdered six young girls in this way between May 1972 and February 1973. But he realized he was coming to the end of his tether and fantasized about killing a large number of people in a final gesture to the world in general.

What he actually did was to kill his mother, with whom he had had a love-hate relationship all his life. He battered her to death with a hammer while she lay asleep in her apartment near Santa Cruz during the Easter weekend of 1973. He then phoned her best friend, saying he was going to arrange a dinner for the two women that night, and she agreed to come over. When she arrived he strangled her and cut off her head. He then drove 1,500 miles to Pueblo in Colorado and from there phoned the Santa Cruz police to tell them what he'd done.

Kemper's trial opened in Santa Cruz in October 1973. James Jackson, his defence counsel, had a difficult job. His client had already made detailed confessions about all his murders, which he remembered in great detail. These had been taped by the police and were played back in court. And although much of the trial was taken up by the evidence of medical witnesses, they were all for the prosecution. Jackson could get no psychiatrist or psychologist to give evidence that his client was insane.

The parade of prosecution medical experts called Kemper everything from a sex maniac to a sadistic psychopath, but all claimed that he was sane. The murder of the girls, they suggested, was merely working up to the killing of his mother.

The jury took five hours – relatively rapid by American standards – to find Kemper guilty on all eight counts of first-degree murder. The death penalty having been suspended until the beginning of 1974, Kemper received eight life sentences with the recommendation that he never be released.

In 1935 Dr Buck Ruxton, who lived in Lancaster, also cut up the bodies of two women; his wife, whom he killed after a quarrel, and the maid, who unfortunately saw him. He dumped them in a ravine near Moffat in Scotland. But Scotland is not California and the pieces were soon discovered. Parts had been wrapped in an edition of the *Sunday Graphic* which was sold only in Morecambe and Lancaster and a photographic superimposition of a portrait of Mrs Ruxton fitted perfectly on to an X-ray of the head of one of the victims. Ruxton was tried at Manchester Assizes in March 1936, found guilty and hanged.

Randy Kraft When the two policemen stopped the Toyota Celica on the San Diego Freeway in Orange County, near Los Angeles, in the early morning of 14 May 1983, they expected to have caught yet another drunk driver. They did not guess that they would solve a mystery which had been puzzling California police for the past ten years.

For, beside the driver, thirty-eight-year-old computer analyst Randy Kraft, was the dead body of a young Marine from the nearby El Tor air base. He was sitting in the passenger seat with his hands tied with his shoelaces and his genitals exposed; he had been strangled with his own belt.

Kraft was taken into custody and a thorough search made of his car. Bottles of beer were found, together with containers of pills, which turned out to be tranquillizers, anti-depressants and painkillers. And under the floor mat on the driver's side the investigators discovered a large envelope containing photographs. They were all of young men, some clothed and some naked, most of whom looked to be asleep – or dead.

In the car boot, inside a ring binder, the police came across a list. Although it was obviously in code it made chilling reading, for Detective Jim Sidebotham of the Sheriff's Department guessed what it was.

Over the past ten years or so bodies had been turning up at regular intervals along the freeways in California. They were all young men. Some had been identified as prostitutes, some as Marines. A few had clothes on and others were naked, but they had all been strangled, and in many cases the bodies had been mutilated, often before death.

The police assumed that the victims were hitch-hikers, who were rendered unconscious by the use of alcohol and drugs, then tied up, raped and tortured before being strangled and dumped by the roadside. They couldn't be sure that they were all the work of one person, but similarities with many of the corpses led to the murderer being called the 'Freeway Killer'.

The list Detective Sidebotham had found seemed to contain references to sixty-seven murders, a record at that time for serial killers.

The trial obviously created severe problems for the district attorney's office at Orange County. The large number of murders would raise difficulties for the prosecution, defence and the jury, and it was eventually decided to limit the charges of murder to sixteen. Even so it was not until September 1988, after Randy Kraft had been in prison for five years, that the prosecution were ready to proceed.

A succession of pathologists described to the jury – selected on the basis of a fifteen-page questionnaire as well as the interview – their examination of bodies picked up from the freeways since December 1972. Horrifying details of emasculation and objects being forced into the rectum, as well as nipples been burnt with a car cigarette lighter, revolted the jury. But a thumbprint found on a broken bottle used to mutilate one of the victims was clearly that of Randy Kraft.

A search of the bungalow in Long Beach which he had shared with a male lover for the previous ten years turned up a camera and an electric shaver which could be proved to be the property of two of the murdered men. The lover plainly had no idea that Kraft was engaged in such fiendish pursuits.

The defence relied on a series of alibis and the assertion that the murders had been done by other people – not such a wild suggestion, as it turned out.

But the character of the calm, pleasant-looking computer consultant was damaged irretrievably when the shambling figure of Joseph Francher gave evidence. He described how thirteen years before, as a young boy, he had been drugged and raped by Kraft, and he claimed this had ruined him, as his subsequent life of crime indicated. Whether this was strictly relevant to the murders remains a moot point. But it certainly affected the jury of ten women and two men. Although it took them eleven days to come to their verdicts they found Randy Kraft guilty of all sixteen murders.

In the subsequent hearing to decide if he should receive the death penalty, Kraft gave evidence himself, which he had refused to do during the trial. But it made no difference. The jury recommended the death sentence.

William G. Bonin was arrested in June 1980 and accused of being another freeway killer, in California. He had already served two terms of imprisonment for kidnapping, rape and child molesting. A youth called Gregory Miley gave evidence at the trial, which began in November 1981, that he had helped lure youths and young boys into Bonin's van, where Bonin raped and killed them, then dumped their bodies on the freeways. Bonin was finally convicted of ten murders and sentenced to death. Miley received twenty-five years.

Ronald and Reginald Kray   When the East End twins Ronnie and Reggie Kray went on trial for murder and being an accessory to murder, it turned into the longest criminal trial in English history. It was also one of the most publicized and there was a brisk trade on the black market for tickets to the public gallery. Many show-business and entertainment figures were in attendance and Judy Garland sent the twins a good luck telegram.

Yet these were two of the most vicious and brutal criminals ever to operate in London. They can be said to have begun their careers of crime in 1952 when they were called up for national service. They had been noted amateur boxers in their youths, and Ronnie was soon in trouble for striking an NCO. Both served sentences for assault and going absent without leave and were eventually discharged.

They then rented a billiard hall in Mile End and soon

acquired a reputation for violence. Their readiness to fight rival gangs and to beat up anybody who crossed them or gave what they fancied was an insult, served a dual purpose. It established them in the lucrative business of protection rackets and made the victims too frightened to go to the police or give evidence against them. They introduced the trick of pretending to shake hands and using the free hand to smash the other person's jaw. They also used guns and knives with equal facility.

In the early days they did not always escape the law. Ronnie nearly beat an Irishman to death and received a three-year prison sentence for GBH, and Reggie was sentenced to eighteen months for threatening violence to a protection racket victim.

In 1960 they acquired a controlling share in Esmeralda's Barn, a successful casino in fashionable Belgravia, and began to rub shoulders with the rich and with well-known personalities.

By 1965 the Krays were in competition with the Richardson gang from South London, who included torture as part of their repertoire of violence. In March 1966 the Richardson outfit raided a pub in south-east London and a member of the Kray gang, usually known as 'The Firm', was shot and killed. The next night Ronnie heard that George Cornell, an associate of the Richardsons, was drinking in the Blind Beggar pub in the White-chapel Road, the Krays' territory. He immediately went there armed with a 9mm Mauser automatic and his 'minder', Ian Barrie, and shot Cornell through the head. The police could find no witnesses, or anyone who would say anything about the shooting.

For eighteen months Ronnie, who had already once been certified insane, during a prison sentence, and was an active homosexual, goaded his twin to perform a cold-blooded killing also, until Reggie decided to despatch Jack McVitie. The victim was a gang member who had taken money to kill a former associate of the Krays, Leslie Payne, but had failed to do so. On 27 October 1967, McVitie was invited to a party, and when he

arrived Reggie placed a gun to his head and pulled the trigger.
The gun failed to fire. Ronnie grabbed the man from behind and
Reggie stabbed him with a knife until he was dead. Once again
the police could find no witnesses willing to testify.

In 1966 the twins were involved in a bizarre murder. Frank
Mitchell, known as 'The Mad Axeman', an old friend of Ronnie's,
was in Dartmoor prison. He was a trusty and allowed out quite
often, and in December he was simply picked up by the Firm
outside the prison and hidden in a flat in East London. From
there he wrote letters to the newspapers complaining that he had
not been given a release date. The Krays didn't want to conceal
him indefinitely, however, and expected him to give himself up
eventually. He refused, and though the brothers claimed that he
was smuggled out of the country, an eye witness subsequently
revealed that he was taken away in a van, shot and his body
disposed of.

The activities of the Krays were becoming an embarrassment
to the police, and in September 1967 a special squad of fifteen
detectives was formed, headed by Detective Superintendent
Leonard Read, known as 'Nipper'. The detectives began collecting evidence against the Krays. They met Leslie Payne, who had
once been the Krays' financial expert but was now afraid the
twins were trying to kill him; he gave the police a 200-page
statement. Read also guaranteed immunity to anybody who
would testify against the twins and gave a promise that no statement made would be used until the brothers were safely under
arrest.

When the trial finally went ahead in January 1969, twenty-
eight criminals gave evidence against the Krays. Their strangle-
hold had finally been broken. Only three men remained loyal:
their elder brother Charles and a friend of his, Freddie Foreman,
who refused to give evidence against them, subsequently received
ten years each for their part in disposing of Frank Mitchell's body.
Ian Barrie also refused to give evidence and he was sentenced

to twenty years for his involvement in the murder of George Cornell.

After sixty-one days the jury pronounced the twins guilty of murder and being accessory to murder. Each received life with a recommendation that they should serve not less than thirty years.

They were tried separately for the murder of Frank Mitchell, but there was not enough evidence to convict them.

Ronnie's history of insanity kept him confined in Broadmoor until his death in 1995. Reggie has been in a number of prisons and hopes soon to be paroled.

Denise Labbé and Jacques Algarron The famous French writer Jean Cocteau called it 'the trial of the century', but all it really accomplished was to illustrate the danger of trying to apply literary theories to real life.

In May 1954, when Jacques Algarron met Denise Labbé, the 'Superman' philosophy of the German philosopher Nietzsche was still a potent force, as it had been to Leopold and Loeb (*see* p. 202).

Algarron was a cadet at the military college of Saint-Cyr and Labbé was a secretary. They met at a dance in Rennes in north-west France. He was an arrogant and dominating man and she was docile and submissive – as it turned out, a fatal combination. There is evidence that he scratched and bit her in their love-making, and from her letters to him, she seems to have enjoyed it. He explained to her his concept of the 'extraordinary couple', which they could become if they were willing to make sacrifices for each other, but it appeared that she was the one who was to do the sacrificing.

Both had been promiscuous before they met. He had several illegitimate children and she had a two-year-old daughter, Cathy, whose father was a doctor. Algarron suggested that, to prove her love for him, she sacrifice her child's life. She agreed.

Labbé found it difficult, however, and made several unsuccessful endeavours, including two attempts to drown her daughter in a river, before she finally pushed little Cathy's head into a bucket of water and held it until she drowned.

Her mother and the child-minder Labbé used when she was

out at work, Mme Laurent, were suspicious of her behaviour and when the child died Mme Laurent went to the police. They discovered that, at the spot where Denise had said the baby fell into the river (after one of her attempts to kill the child), there was a five-foot-high fence, making it impossible for it to have been an accident.

Labbé was arrested and held in prison for a month. When she learned that Algarron had been seen flirting with another woman, she confessed everything.

They were tried together for murder in May 1956, and three of the most famous counsel in France at the time appeared in court. Francisque Gay prosecuted, and Denise Labbé was defended by Maurice Garçon, while René Floriot defended Jacques Algarron.

When Labbé was questioned by the judge and asked to give her story – the normal procedure in French trials – she was timid, spoke in a halting voice and frequently broke down in tears.

Algarron on the other hand was confident and assured and claimed that he had not intended that Labbé should take him seriously. When asked why he had done nothing after she had made her first attempt to murder her child he said he had thought she was play-acting.

His lawyer, René Floriot, brought five of Algarron's mistresses to the witness box; they all said he was a normal lover and very kind and gentle with children. But it was noticeable that all the women were smart and sophisticated and presumably much less susceptible to his wild ideas and not so easily dominated as Labbé.

Her counsel, Maurice Garçon, replied by bringing Mme Laurent to the stand. She said that Labbé had been a kind and devoted mother until she met Algarron. Garçon also read out some of the young man's letters. They were full of intellectual argument and obscure literary references and must have utterly baffled the jury of seven simple farmers from the local region.

They took only three hours to bring in verdicts of guilty against both the accused, but with extenuating circumstances in the case of Denise Labbé. She was sentenced to life imprisonment and Jacques Algarron received twenty years with hard labour.

From May 1967 to December 1985, Marybeth Tinning, who lived in Schenectady, New York State, had nine children, one of whom was adopted. All of them died: one aged five, two when they were two, and the rest before they were one year old. There were six autopsies, and the causes of death were variously given as natural causes, unknown, or Sudden Infant Death Syndrome, or, in Britain, 'cot death'. Eventually neighbours grew suspicious and the police investigated. Marybeth was interviewed by detectives and confessed to killing three of her children by putting a pillow or a cushion over their faces. She was tried for the murder of only one, in June 1987. By this time she was denying everything, but her confession was put before the jury and she was convicted. She was sentenced to twenty years to life.

David Lashley Twenty-four-year-old Janie Shepherd disappeared on the night of Friday 4 February, 1977. The daughter of a wealthy Australian couple who lived in Sydney, Janie was staying in London and disappeared on the way to see her boyfriend who lived in Knightsbridge.

Her car was found the following Tuesday near Notting Hill Gate. The Mini was covered in mud, and the police estimated from the petrol left in the tank that it had been driven some seventy-five miles. Inside, the roof lining had been slashed and there was evidence of a struggle. Detectives also found some of Janie's clothes in the car.

The police believed that she had been abducted and perhaps killed. Her parents came over from Australia and began helping the police search the countryside around London. But ten weeks after her disappearance there was still no sign of Janie and her heartbroken parents went back home.

Six days later the body of Janie Shepherd was found in woods on Nomansland Common, near Wheathampstead, Hertfordshire. It was considerably decomposed, but she was identified from her jewellery, and after a post mortem pathologist Professor James Cameron was able to conclude that she had died from compression of the neck.

An examination of police files of men convicted of abduction and rape turned up Barbados-born David Lashley, who had been sentenced in 1970, when he was thirty-one, to twelve years imprisonment for rape, robbery and indecent assault. A tall and powerful man, many of his attacks had been on women in cars. He had been paroled in 1976 after coming to the aid of a prison warder during a riot. But he had an alibi for the night Janie Shepherd disappeared.

In June 1976, however, just weeks after Lashley had been released and nearly eight months before the Shepherd abduction, another woman reported she had been attacked, raped and her wrist badly slashed in her car less than half a mile from where Janie's car had been found. On a hunch the police put Lashley on an identification parade and the woman immediately identified him. He was sentenced to eighteen years.

He was now safely in prison, but the police were still convinced that Lashley was the murderer of Janie Shepherd. His friends and relatives confirmed his alibi, however, and there was nothing to connect him with the crime.

In 1988 Janie's mother wrote from Australia asking for any fresh information on her daughter's murderer and the Home Office decided to reopen the case. Lashley was due for parole in February 1989. Then a prisoner came forward to say that Lashley had confessed the Janie Shepherd murder to him. When Lashley walked out of the prison gates, he was immediately rearrested and his trial for murder opened at St Albans Crown Court in February 1990.

The main prosecution witness was Daniel Reece who had

been friendly with Lashley in Frankland prison in County Durham. He said that Lashley had become angry after reading in a newspaper how a black man had been jailed for raping a white woman. 'He should have killed her,' he snarled. 'If I had killed the one in 1976, like I killed Janie Shepherd, I would not be here now!'

Lashley then told him how he grabbed the Australian girl when she came out of a supermarket in Queensway and forced her at knifepoint to drive to an underground car park in Notting Hill where he tied her up and raped her. He killed her by holding her neck with one hand and pressing his closed fist against her windpipe. This method of killing agreed with the findings of the autopsy, which had never been made public.

Reece also said that Lashley told him he had tied the body into the front seat of the Mini, driven to Hertfordshire and dumped the body. When he returned to London, he had thrown some of Janie's shopping into gardens near where he left the car. Items of food which the check-out girl at the supermarket remembered her buying were indeed found in gardens in the area.

The police were also able to show that Lashley was quite familiar with the locality where the body was found, having been a van driver for a Hertford firm in the 1960s.

Lashley's aunt went into the witness box to repeat the alibi she had given him in 1977. But the jury took only two-and-a-quarter hours to bring in a unanimous verdict of guilty.

Janie Shepherd's mother was in court to hear the judge, Mr Justice Alliot, sentence David Lashley to life, with the words: 'In my view you are such an appallingly dangerous man that the real issue is whether the authorities can ever allow you your liberty in your natural lifetime.'

John M'Guigan, a twenty-four-year-old Irish vagrant, was sent for trial in November 1935 in Edinburgh, accused of shooting to death a young man near Perth and raping his fiancée. A handkerchief used to tie the girl's hands was proved to be his and she identified him as the man who raped her. He was convicted of the rape, but since the shot had been fired from some bushes the jury brought in a verdict of not proven on the murder charge. M'Guigan was sentenced to ten years.

Marlene Lehnberg and Marthinus Choegoe Marlene Lehnberg was only nineteen when, in November 1974, she turned to murder. A beautiful girl, she had already taken a few tentative steps towards a modelling career, but had not left her rather humdrum job as a receptionist at an orthopaedic workshop attached to a hospital in Cape Town, South Africa. This was partly because she was in love with the chief technician, forty-seven-year-old Christiaan van der Linde. They met during their lunch hours, and had twenty minutes or so together after he had taken her to her boarding house after work at nights.

But this arrangement did not satisfy the girl. Christiaan did not seem inclined to leave his family and became upset when Marlene telephoned his wife, Susanna, to tell her of the affair and ask her to divorce him. Susanna refused. Marlene then thought she would leave Cape Town altogether, but Chris persuaded her to stay.

Marlene decided to have Susanna murdered, and searched for an assassin. Marthinus Choegoe, thirty-three, was a ludicrous choice. Known as a 'coloured' – that is not white or black, but of mixed parentage, or possibly even of Asian descent – he had lost a leg in a car accident and could not get around very easily except on crutches. Marlene met him when he came to the orthopaedic workshop to obtain a new artificial leg. He was extremely poor and lived in a shanty town just outside the city. He was easily dominated by the young white girl, who had a much higher social position and who promised him a car, money and even sex as rewards for killing Susanna.

Choegoe twice managed to hobble as far as the house where

Susanna lived, but did nothing when he got there and was picked up by police the second time for loitering suspiciously. After being routinely beaten-up, however, he was allowed to go free.

Marlene saw that he could not do it unaided and on 4 November took him in her car to the house in the suburbs. She was armed with a gun she had stolen from a fellow boarder and Marthinus had a hammer. According to his subsequent confession Marlene went to the front door first and was allowed in. He followed painfully and was let in by the white girl.

He saw her fell the older woman by striking her on the jaw with the gun. She then told him to strangle Susanna. He tried, but as the woman lay half-conscious on the floor Marlene shouted at him to stab her with some scissors.

After it was all over they rushed back to her car. The young girl then drove all the way to Johannesburg to try and establish an alibi, while Choegoe went back to the shanty town.

By a process of elimination the police finally reached Marlene. They had already heard from another receptionist that she seemed to have a contact with a coloured cripple called Marthinus, and when they taxed her with it she confessed. She claimed, though, that she had only driven Choegoe to the house and he had gone in alone. He was soon picked up and he too made a confession.

They were tried together for the murder of Susanna van der Linde and sat as far away as possible from each other in the dock. The court proceedings began in March 1975 at the Cape Town Criminal Sessions. Huge crowds queued up each day for the few seats in the public gallery and the press dubbed it the Scissors Trial.

There was no jury, the case being heard before a judge, Mr Justice Marius Diemont, and two assessors. The Attorney General prosecuted, and Marlene Lehnberg was defended by Mr Dennis Delahunt, while Marthinus Choegoe was represented by Mr Roelof van Riet.

Both defence lawyers had hopeless positions. Letters the girl had written to her lover showed ample motive for murder, and their confessions established their guilt. Marlene's counsel tried hard to show that she had been led by her lover, and Marthinus's representative attempted to lay all the blame on Marlene. It was really a question of whose confession the judge would believe.

Eight days after the start of the trial the judge read out his 5,000-word judgement, which lasted nearly an hour. It ended with the verdict: 'guilty as charged', for both of them.

Tension began to mount. Would it be life or death for them?

Now their counsel spoke again, this time pleading mitigating circumstances. Each went into the witness box to be examined again. The Attorney General replied to the arguments, pleading that there were no mitigating circumstances.

Again Justice Diemont conferred with his assessors, this time for an hour. Then he came back to deliver his second assessment, going through all the points raised by counsel. The judgement for each again was: 'I find no mitigating circumstances.'

And the sentences? 'To be hanged by the neck until you are dead.'

But this was not the end. Next came the applications, made to the same judge, for leave to appeal to the Appellate Division. This time a parade of psychiatric witnesses appeared, for Marlene to try and prove that she was psychotic, and for Marthinus to prove that the trauma of losing his leg and his subsequent life had affected his behaviour.

This time Judge Diemont gave a different judgement. Marlene was refused leave to appeal. Her sentence must stand. But the judge considered that Marthinus was at such a great disadvantage that his moral guilt was diminished. He was given leave to appeal.

But a later petition on Marlene's behalf for leave to appeal was granted and the appeal court set aside the death sentence on account of her age. She was sentenced to twenty years, Marthinus to fifteen years.

In November 1926, Arthur Stout's stepmother was found dead on her farmhouse kitchen floor near Axtel Ridge, Ohio, apparently strangled, and with curious half-moon indentations on her neck. Stout, who lived on a neighbouring farm, was charged with her murder. His young housekeeper, Inez Palmer, visited him regularly in jail and showed the sheriff a note she said came from Stout's father. In it the old man confessed to the murder. The father's body was subsequently recovered from a well. But the sheriff thought the note was a forgery and when the half-moon impressions on the murdered woman's neck were found to correspond to the heels of Inez Palmer's high-heeled shoes, she confessed. But Arthur Stout, who was known to be on bad terms with his stepmother, was shown to be an accessory, and he also was sentenced to life imprisonment.

Nathan Leopold and Richard Loeb   Both defendants pleaded guilty, yet the trial still took nearly two months to complete. It occurred in 1924 in Chicago, a city which had a gangland killing nearly every day, yet the single murder of a young boy so incensed the public that the death penalty was demanded. And the trial, which was really to determine the sentence, became one of the most famous in American history.

The case began with the discovery of the naked body of a fourteen-year-old boy, Bobby Franks, stuffed into a concrete drainpipe at the edge of Wolf Lake in the city, in May. Bobby's father, a wealthy Jewish businessman, had already received a ransom note saying that his son had been kidnapped.

It took only a week for the police to track down the murderers. A pair of spectacles found near the body had a special hinge, and only three such pairs had been sold: one to a lawyer who was in Europe; another to a lady who still had hers; the third to a wealthy young man of nineteen called Nathan Leopold.

He quickly confessed. He and his eighteen-year-old friend Richard Loeb had decided to perpetrate a murder in furtherance of Leopold's Nietzschean 'Superman' philosophy and Loeb's desire to commit the perfect crime. The victim, they decided, would be selected at random, except that he would be an easy target, a young boy, and they would demand a ransom after they had killed him to raise some money, which they hardly needed.

They picked up Bobby Franks, whom Loeb knew slightly, outside a school for boys with wealthy parents. In a car they had hired, they stabbed him to death with a chisel, then dumped the body. The ransom note, previously typed on a stolen machine, was then posted. But their carefully laid plans went badly wrong; they left the murdered boy's foot sticking out of the pipe and the body was quickly discovered.

The confessions made by the boys were substantially the same, except that each accused the other of actually stabbing Bobby Franks to death. It was shown later, and afterwards admitted by him, that Loeb had done the killing.

Both came from very rich Jewish Chicago families. Leopold was considered a brilliant student, the youngest ever to receive a degree from the University of Chicago; he had already distinguished himself at the law school. Loeb was apparently not quite so clever, though he too had graduated early from the University of Michigan. But he was the dominant figure of the pair and in their homosexual relationship Leopold adored him.

Their families obtained the services of Clarence Darrow, easily the most famous lawyer of his time in Chicago and possibly in America. Darrow was well known as a defender of the underdog, and many people thought he compromised his principles by working for rich clients, but Darrow was a passionate opponent of the death penalty and in this case his strategy was aimed at that alone.

If Darrow had used a defence of insanity he would have had to enter a plea of not guilty. The case would then have been tried by a jury. With the confessions before them the verdict would almost certainly have been guilty. In the state of Illinois the jury also determined the sentence and such was the public feeling against the two boys, because of the sheer appalling callousness of the crime, Darrow had no doubt that the sentence would be death.

So he took a gamble. By having his clients plead guilty he ensured that they could not escape conviction. But the case would be heard by a judge, without a jury, who would determine the sentence. Darrow could then offer evidence in mitigation and hope that he could save the boys' lives.

Darrow began his defence by calling psychiatrists (they called them 'alienists' in those days). The prosecuting counsel, state's attorney Robert Crowe, objected strongly, saying that insanity pleas had not been invoked and therefore the defence could not call medical experts. But Judge John R. Caverly said that it was his duty to hear any evidence the defence presented. Darrow had won the first round.

His experts testified to the abnormality of the two boys, suggesting that their cloistered childhoods, influenced in one case by an hysterical governess and in the other by a very dominating nurse, had led to a retreat from reality, and to an intense and dangerous attachment between them.

The prosecution's psychiatrists, on the other hand, gave their opinions that though Leopold and Loeb might show some abnormalities they were both entirely sane.

The climax of the proceedings came with the summing-up speeches. Robert Crow's lasted for two days and Darrow's eleven-hour epic went into three. Always one of the most eloquent pleaders, Darrow kept it simple, but the power of his oratory had everyone, including the judge, in tears as he pleaded for mercy.

The judge gave his decision on 10 September 1924. Chiefly because of the defendants' ages, he said, he would not sentence them to death. Instead he gave them life imprisonment and would recommend that they never be paroled. He then gave them an additional ninety-nine years on the kidnapping charge. It meant that they would never normally be released.

Richard Loeb never was. In January 1936, when he was thirty, he was injured in a razor attack in prison and died of his wounds. Nathan Leopold, together with Loeb while he was still alive, developed correspondence courses with other prisons and together they wrote a mathematics textbook which was used successfully in many American prisons. After Loeb's death Leopold continued his educational work, became a hospital nurse and wrote a book on birdwatching, and an autobiography. He was paroled in 1958, having served thirty-three years, and went to Puerto Rico to work as a hospital laboratory technician. He got married, and died of a heart attack in 1971.

Many people assumed Darrow had been attracted to the case by the offer of an enormous fee, but in fact he asked the Chicago Bar Association to propose a suitable fee, and he had to wait seven months after the trial to get that!

Christopher Craig and Derek Bentley were not so intellectually advanced as Leopold and Loeb. In fact Bentley was illiterate and considered by some to be educationally subnormal. They decided to break into a London sweet warehouse in November 1952, but were seen and caught on the roof by the police. Craig had a gun and shot a policeman, but at sixteen he was too young to hang. Bentley was nineteen and had not been armed or anywhere near Craig when the shot was fired, but because the police swore he shouted: 'Let him have it, Chris', he too was convicted of murder – and hanged.

Thomas Ley and Lawrence Smith   The trial of Thomas Ley and Lawrence Smith began at the Old Bailey in March 1947, and was presided over by the newly appointed Lord Chief Justice of England, Lord Goddard. He was a down-to-earth judge who nevertheless could be a stickler for etiquette. Senior Treasury counsel Anthony Hawke, who was prosecuting, had the temerity to refer to one of the accused as 'Mr Ley' during his opening speech. 'You will not use any prefixes, Mr Hawke,' snapped Lord Goddard and henceforth it became plain 'Ley'.

Thomas Ley had been taken to Australia as a child when his father died and his mother emigrated from Bath. He started at the bottom as a solicitor's clerk and worked his way up to a partnership. Then he went into politics and rose to become minister of justice for the state of New South Wales. He also won a seat in the federal parliament. But unsavoury rumours began to circulate about him. He was involved in dodgy business deals, and an accusation that he had bribed a candidate in an election collapsed only when the accuser suddenly disappeared. In 1929 he left Australia and came to England.

He brought with him his mistress, Mrs Margaret Brook, leaving his wife behind. By 1946 he was sixty-seven and immensely fat, and sexual relations with Mrs Brook had ceased some ten years before. But he had become insanely jealous of her. He was convinced that she was having sexual relations with thirty-five-year-old Jack Mudie, a barman, who had a flat in the same house as her daughter and whom she had met only once.

On 30 November 1946, Mudie's body was found with a rope round its neck in a shallow trench at the bottom of a chalkpit near Woldingham in Surrey. He had died of asphyxiation. A letter found in his room, sent by solicitors acting for one of Ley's companies, led the police eventually to the ex-minister.

At the trial, John Buckingham, the owner of a car-hire service, said that he had been approached by Ley and an associate of Ley's, Lawrence Smith. They told him they wanted to hire a car to kidnap a blackmailer. A man had seduced a woman friend of Ley's and her daughter and was now blackmailing them. Ley wanted to kidnap the man, force him to sign a confession, then give him money and send him abroad.

Buckingham persuaded a friend of his, Mrs Bruce, to pose as a wealthy lady requiring a barman to serve drinks at a party. Mudie agreed to act as barman and Mrs Bruce and Buckingham's son drove him to the rear entrance of Ley's house in Beaufort Gardens, in London, where Smith and Buckingham senior were waiting. According to the car owner they simply pushed Mudie into a front room and left him, Buckingham collecting £200 from Ley on the way out.

But Lawrence Smith, who turned out to be a foreman joiner working on some alterations to Ley's house, had a slightly different story. He said that he gripped Mudie when he came through the rear door and Buckingham threw a carpet over the man's head. Smith then secured it with rope and Buckingham 'jumped' the prisoner along the passage into another room where they sat him in a chair. Buckingham then departed, and Smith left about ten minutes later, when he heard some other men arrive. ,

Sir Walter Monckton, the high-priced counsel retained by Ley, put the ex-minister in the witness box, where he simply denied mentioning Mudie to Smith, Buckingham or Mrs Bruce and produced a somewhat nebulous alibi of having been at the Liberal Club that evening.

Then Sir Walter produced an incredible witness – one Robert Cruikshank, who claimed he had gone to Ley's house on the night of the murder to try and get a job, found the back door open, and wandering about inside had seen a man tied up in a chair. For no good reason he began pulling on the ropes. The inference seemed to be that he might have killed Mudie accidentally. But Lord Goddard was frankly incredulous and Cruikshank's story sounded even more preposterous under cross-examination by Hawke.

It was plain that Ley was heavily involved in Mudie's murder; but had Smith left, as he said, not knowing what was to happen to the barman? The lie was given to this when the prosecution produced two gardeners who had seen a man at the chalkpit three days before the murder. When he saw them he jumped quickly into his car and drove away. They recognized the car as a Ford 8 or 10, with registration figures 101. The man who had such a car and was picked out by one of the gardeners at a police line-up was Smith.

The jury took only fifty-five minutes to find both men guilty of murder and they were sentenced to death. But Thomas Ley was examined in the death cell by a number of doctors and declared to be insane. His sentence was respited and he was transferred to Broadmoor Asylum. Smith had his sentence commuted to life imprisonment. Ley died two months later of a stroke.

Buckingham was not charged with any offence with regard to the kidnapping, but was recognized by the army as a deserter and sent to prison.

In 1927, Captain William Lancaster teamed up with Mrs 'Chubbie' Miller, an Australian woman aviator, to make a flight from London to Australia. They were both married, but fell in love and set up house in Florida. While Lancaster was in Mexico, Chubbie met an American writer, Haden Clarke, and wrote to Lancaster that they were going to be married. The flyer rushed back with a gun and a furious row erupted one night. In the morning Clarke was found shot in the head, beside two suicide notes – typed on Lancaster's machine. Lancaster was tried for murder in Miami in August 1932, but acquitted. He set off in 1933 for a record-breaking flight to South Africa, and disappeared. Twenty-nine years later a French army patrol found the crashed plane in the Sahara with the remains of the flyer beside it. His diary showed how he died in the desert, the last entry being exactly twelve months after Clarke died.

Ronald Light This was one of the trials of Sir Edward Marshall Hall. And to begin with, in the best Hollywood tradition, the case against his client looked hopeless.

Twenty-one-year-old Bella Wright had been found, at ten

minutes to ten on Saturday night, 5 July 1919, beside her bike in a country road near Little Stretton in Leicestershire. She had been shot through the head, and a spent bullet was discovered nearby.

Several people had seen Bella earlier that evening in the company of a young man with a green bicycle, but appeals from the chief constable of Leicester for him to come forward were unsuccessful. Then, seven months later, a bargeman snagged an obstruction on a canal near Leicester and brought to the surface parts of a green bicycle. Registration numbers had been filed off, but a secret one had been missed and this identified the machine as having been bought by a Ronald Light, a mathematics master at a Cheltenham school, who had previously lived in Leicester.

He claimed to have sold the cycle years ago, but was identified by nearly everybody who had seen Bella with the young man. Besides, a cycle repairer in Leicester picked him out as the man who collected the cycle on the day of the murder, after some work on it had been carried out, and remarked that it was a nice day 'for a run in the country'.

Further, a revolver holster had been recovered from the canal, containing cartridges of the type found near the girl's body. The holster was subsequently identified as having belonged to Light.

The trial was held in Leicester Castle in June 1920, and the prosecution was in the hands of the Attorney General, Sir Gordon Hewart, assisted by Henry Maddocks and a young Norman Birkett. After the first day the Attorney General was called away on urgent government business and the rest of the case was conducted by the younger counsel. Norman Birkett made an error in questioning two schoolgirls. They said they had been accosted by Light earlier in the evening, and Birkett asked one girl about the specific date in question. Marshall Hall objected that this was leading the witness. He also made short work of their evidence, showing that they had only made statements after Light had been arrested, that they'd read about the case previously, and the date had been suggested to them by the police.

But Marshall Hall reserved his big guns for the firearms expert giving evidence for the prosecution. He persuaded the gunsmith to agree that the bullet could have been fired from a rifle as well as a revolver, thereby introducing the possibility that a stray shot from someone using a rifle nearby could accidentally have killed Bella. He also suggested that a person shot at close range with a service revolver would have half their face blown off, whereas Bella had only a small entry wound under her left eye and a larger exit wound on the right side of her head. 'It depends on the velocity,' said the expert cautiously.

Marshall Hall had a policy in important cases that a client must make a written declaration that they wanted, or did not want, to go into the witness box. Light emphatically did. He then declared that he had lied to the police: he had seen Bella that evening. Had ridden with her. Then, when she visited her uncle's cottage in a nearby village, found that he had to repair a puncture and so was able to see her again when she came out. But they parted soon after.

On cross-examination he said he had panicked when he heard that she had been killed and dumped the bicycle and the revolver holster. The revolver he had left behind at a casualty clearing station in France at the end of the war. He had a good war record, and came across as an open and honest young man in a difficult situation.

The combination of his appearance, his performance in the box, and Marshall Hall's clever assertion that the girl's death might have been accidental, was enough to cause the jury to have a reasonable doubt, and they brought in a verdict of not guilty.

Marshall Hall himself regarded the case as one of his greatest triumphs, but the foremost gun expert of the day, Robert Churchill, whom the great defender consulted but did not call, believed that the bullet could not possibly have been fired from a rifle. Comparing it with the Moat Farm Murder case (below) he believed that a revolver bullet could have behaved in the same way as the bullet that killed Bella Wright. So was Ronald Light guilty after all?

In the Moat Farm Murder case Samuel Dougal, a randy ex-soldier of fifty-two, persuaded fifty-five-year-old spinster Camille Holland to buy the remote Moat Farm, near Saffron Walden, and set up house with him. But he couldn't keep his hands off the maid and Camille soon disappeared. He continued his seduction of practically every pretty girl in the neighbourhood until suspicions were aroused and the police investigated. After digging up most of the farm they discovered Camille's body buried in an old drainage ditch. She had been shot through the head. Tried in 1903 at Chelmsford Assizes Dougal said the gun went off accidentally. He was hanged the same year.

Harold Loughans   Mrs Robinson was murdered on the night of Sunday 28 November, 1943. A widow aged sixty-three, she was the licensee of the John Barleycorn Beerhouse in Commercial Road, Portsmouth, and lived alone above the pub. She had been strangled, the marks of one hand only being still on her neck when she was found, and a month's takings, which she kept in two handbags, having disappeared.

Nearly a month later two plain-clothes constables apprehended a man in Waterloo Road, London, suspecting him of handling stolen property, and he confessed to the murder. Harold Loughans, forty-two, made two written statements, one to the police in London and another to officers from Portsmouth, which gave details of the pub and the murder of Mrs Robinson and included the fact that he had strangled her with his right hand only.

But when he was in prison awaiting trial he suddenly declared that he was innocent and that the police had put words in his mouth to obtain the confessions.

J. D. Casswell, leading the prosecution at the trial at

Hampshire Assizes in Winchester in March 1944, was astonished when counsel for the defence, John Maude, said to him in the robing room, 'I'm calling an alibi for Loughans.' It was perfectly proper, for the accused did not then have to disclose his defence until the trial.

The alibi consisted of three highly respectable and reliable women and two railwaymen, who had all seen Loughans on the night of the murder on the platform at Warren Street underground station, which was used by Londoners at the time as an air-raid shelter. If he was in London he couldn't have been in Portsmouth, eighty miles away.

The jury were understandably confused, failed to agree, and a new trial was ordered at the Old Bailey for a fortnight later.

During this time Casswell, reading the alibi witnesses' statements carefully, realized that only one woman had actually seen Loughans between 12.30 p.m. and 5.15 a.m. and she could easily have been mistaken. He persuaded two policemen to drive a car from Warren Street to Portsmouth one night, stay there half an hour and return. They were back easily by 5.15 a.m.

At the second trial, however, Casswell had yet another surprise. Sir Bernard Spilsbury, the most eminent pathologist of his day, appeared for the defence and said that Loughans had a deformed right hand – he'd lost the tops of his fingers in an accident in his youth – and couldn't possibly have strangled anybody with it.

And when prosecuting counsel tried to produce his rebuttal witnesses for the alibi, the judge said: 'No, Mr Casswell. You didn't produce them at the first trial and you can't produce them now!'

Not surprisingly, the jury found Loughans not guilty. This rather rankled with Casswell and when he wrote his memoirs seventeen years later in 1961 he mentioned the case and his dissatisfaction with it. The book was serialized in *The People*. Loughans read it and sued for libel.

The case came before a high court jury in January 1963, and was virtually a rerun of the murder trial. By this time, though, Sir Bernard Spilsbury was dead and two other illustrious pathologists, Dr Francis Camps and Dr Keith Simpson, examined Loughans's right hand and claimed that it was quite capable of strangling a woman. Casswell was also able to produce his rebuttal evidence for the alibi. The two ex-policemen came out of retirement to testify about the journey they had made, and Casswell's defence, that the words used by him in the article were true, was successful. The libel action failed. In other words, the jury were saying in effect that they believed Loughans had murdered Mrs Robinson.

In May 1963, Loughans, now dying of cancer, walked into the offices of *The People* to say that he had murdered the old lady at the Portsmouth beerhouse. And he wrote the confession, which the newspaper subsequently published, with his deformed right hand.

Sir Henry John Delves Broughton was a member of the 'Happy Valley' set of British expatriates in Kenya at the beginning of the Second World War. He was tried in Nairobi in May 1941 for shooting Lord Erroll, Hereditary High Constable of Scotland, who had been his wife's lover. But the prosecution could not prove that the gun which fired the fatal bullet had been in Broughton's possession and the jury found him not guilty. In December 1942 he committed suicide in a Liverpool hotel. James Fox, in his book *White Mischief*, published in 1982, claims that Broughton told Juanita Carberry, the daughter of a friend, on the day after the murder, that he had killed Erroll.

Dr Jeffrey MacDonald In the early hours of Tuesday 17 February, 1970, the military police were called to 544 Castle Drive at Fort Bragg, North Carolina. Inside the military base bungalow they found a scene of carnage. Twenty-six-year-old Colette Mac-Donald lay on the floor of the main bedroom in disarrayed pink pyjamas, her face and head battered and with numerous stab wounds, some inflicted with a knife, some with an icepick. The top half of her body was covered with a blue pyjama top. In another bedroom lay the body of Kimberly Macdonald, aged five. She also had been clubbed about the head and stabbed. In a third, two-year-old Kristen had been stabbed thirty-three times.

Near his wife's body lay Captain Jeffrey MacDonald, a twenty-six-year-old army doctor, the only one left alive, who seemed to have only a small wound to his chest. He explained that four hippie intruders had attacked them, two white men and one black, and a white woman with long blonde hair, high boots and a floppy hat, who kept repeating: 'Acid is groovy. Kill the pigs.'

From the very beginning the army investigators were suspicious of MacDonald's story. There was very little sign of the disorder one might have expected after a frenzied attack by four intruders, and after telling his story in some detail the captain refused to take a lie detector test.

Investigators discovered that all four members of the Mac-Donald family had different blood groups. It was therefore possible to trace, from the blood spots and splashes in the bungalow, where each had been. The army opinion was that MacDonald had fallen asleep on the living-room couch watching television. When he awoke he found that one of his daughters had wet the bed. This started an argument with his wife which escalated into violence. He battered Colette with a wooden club and when young Kimberly came in to see what the commotion was about he clubbed her as well. Then, realizing what he had done, he deliberately stabbed all his family to support the story of the hippie attack, killing his youngest child in the process.

On 1 May, MacDonald was charged with three counts of murder. But the initial army investigation had been so sloppy, valuable evidence such as footprints and fingerprints having either been lost or destroyed, that Bernie Segal, MacDonald's lawyer, had no difficulty discrediting the army case. In October the charges were dropped.

During all this, MacDonald's strongest supporter had been his father-in-law, Freddie Kassab. But when he left the army and, being a media celebrity, appeared on a television chat show, Kassab realized that the story his son-in-law told of that fateful night did not square with the facts. He obtained and read the transcript of the army tribunal and went to the Castle Street bungalow to make his own investigation. Eventually he became convinced that MacDonald had killed his family.

Kassab began a crusade to get the army to reopen the investigation, which, after many months, they did, but it was not until July 1979, nine years after the murders, that Dr Jeffrey MacDonald finally went for trial in Raleigh, North Carolina.

The case turned mainly on forensic evidence. The prosecution produced the blue pyjama top found on top of Colette's body. MacDonald said he had used it to ward off blows from a man wielding an ice pick, but examination showed that the holes were round, not torn, and much more consistent with the view that MacDonald had stabbed Colette's body through the pyjama top.

The jury deliberated for six-and-a-half hours before finding him guilty on all three counts of murder. He was sentenced to three consecutive terms of life imprisonment.

Just before the trial he persuaded crime author Joe McGinniss to write his story, but when the book *Fatal Vision* finally came out it was not what MacDonald expected. McGinniss told the story of the all-American boy, handsome and popular at school, brilliant at his studies, who qualified as a doctor then joined the elite Green Beret paratroopers and finished by massacring his family.

McGinniss's theory was that MacDonald was taking the drug Eskatrol to lose weight. At the time the drug contained amphetamines, which in large doses can cause sleeplessness, hallucinations and a loss of control close to mania. Previous to the murder night MacDonald had worked a twenty-four-hour shift at a local hospital, followed by a full day's work in his army office and an hour of basketball. He was in effect a time bomb waiting to explode. And what might have been a normal domestic row rapidly escalated into lethal violence.

When the book came out MacDonald sued McGinniss for fraud and breach of contract, and after a well-publicized trial received from the writer a quarter of a million dollars in an out-of-court settlement.

Ethel Major   The trial was held in an old courtroom built inside the more ancient walls of Lincoln Castle, during October 1934. Mrs Major was defended by the redoubtable Norman Birkett, but he had a difficult task.

Ethel Brown had been born in a small village in the Lincolnshire Wolds known as Muckton Bottom. When she was twenty-four she had an illegitimate daughter, and though she never told her parents who the father was they raised the child as Ethel's sister. She married Arthur Major when she was twenty-eight and they lived all their lives together not very far from where she was born.

At first they were reasonably happy. But someone told Arthur about Ethel's daughter and the marriage began to deteriorate. Arthur took to drinking heavily and became violent. Then Ethel discovered love letters written to him by another woman.

On Tuesday 22 May, 1934, Arthur came home from his work as a gravel pit lorry driver and had some corned beef. Soon after, he collapsed with convulsions and later that night, at her father's insistence, Ethel called the doctor. The next day Arthur was rather better, but in the evening Ethel gave him some gruel and the agonizing convulsions returned. He seemed to recover again the following day, but later he was given some water. This time he did not survive the torture and died that night with Ethel looking on.

Her plans for a hurried funeral were thwarted when the police, in response to an anonymous letter sent to the coroner, stopped it. An autopsy was performed and strychnine found in Arthur's body. Ethel was arrested.

Part of the prosecution case was that it couldn't have been suicide. Medical opinion was that Major must have had at least two doses of the poison, and prosecution counsel Edward O'Sullivan argued that no man having given himself some and suffered the appalling agonies of the convulsions it causes would give himself any more.

Ethel's father, who lived only a mile or so from the Majors, testified that being a gamekeeper he possessed a bottle of strychnine, which he used to kill vermin, kept in a locked wooden box. The police found an old handbag of Mrs Major's containing a key which fitted the box.

Birkett battled long and hard for his client. He cross-examined the prosecution witnesses, bringing out the provocation she had suffered from her husband, but he was handicapped by the fact that she did not give evidence herself and he could find no witnesses to speak on her behalf.

What sealed her fate, though, was a dog. Her next-door

neighbour's dog came into her back garden the day after Arthur suffered his first attack. Another neighbour saw her come out and scrape something off a plate on to the ground for the dog to eat. Then she laughed, which was odd because she was known to detest the dog. The next day it died in convulsions. Someone put two and two together and wrote a letter to the local coroner; the police exhumed the body of the dog. It contained strychnine.

The jury of nine men and three women took only an hour to find her guilty, but with a strong recommendation for mercy.

However, the Lord Chief Justice dismissed the appeal and the Home Secretary could find no extenuating circumstances to order a reprieve. She was hanged in Hull jail on 19 December 1934.

Eva Rablen also poisoned her husband with strychnine. In April 1929 she gave him a massive dose in a cup of coffee she brought him as he waited outside in the car while she was at a Saturday night dance in Tuttletown, California. He died before a doctor could be brought. But Eva had bumped into a woman on her way out and spilled some coffee on the woman's dress. The spots tested positive for strychnine. When this leaked out, before the trial started, she changed her plea to guilty. She was sentenced to life imprisonment without the possibility of parole.

Tony Mancini   On Derby Day 1934 a female torso was discovered in a trunk in the left-luggage office at Brighton Railway Station. The following day the legs were found in a suitcase left at King's Cross Station in London. The identity of the body was never established and this, the first Brighton trunk murder, was never solved.

The second trunk murder surfaced when the police were called to a basement flat in Kemp Street, Brighton, on 14 July and found another trunk with a body in it. This one was soon identified as Violet Kaye, a well-known prostitute. She had disappeared a few weeks before from a flat in Park Crescent, Brighton, where she had been living with a young man who called himself Tony Mancini.

Mancini was also well known, at least to the London police, as a small-time crook whose real name was Cecil Louis England. He had gone from the flat where the trunk had been left, but was soon picked up in Kent. The police initially believed that they had the perpetrator of both trunk crimes, and so did the newspapers. All sorts of stories about him circulated in the press and by the time the trial began, on 10 December, at Lewes Assize Court, the general public was convinced of his guilt.

He was only charged with the murder of Violet Kaye and the uphill task of defending him was undertaken by Norman Birkett.

The prosecution produced witnesses to prove that when Mancini had been working at the Skylark Café, Violet had come in the worse for drink and they had had a row. The next day she disappeared. Mancini told a waitress from the café that she had gone to France. He gave her some of Violet's clothes and she washed some of his. On a shirt she found a small bloodstain, which Mancini said had come from a cut he received while shaving.

Violet's sister had received a telegram, apparently from Violet, saying that she was going to Paris. But telegrams were sometimes handwritten by the sender in those days and the writing was nothing like Violet's; it bore a remarkable resemblance to Mancini's.

In the opinion of Sir Bernard Spilsbury, the famous pathologist, Violet had been killed by a violent blow on the side of the head, possibly from a hammer. Just such a tool had been found, partially burnt, in the basement flat at Park Crescent. Birkett tried hard to get the eminent doctor to agree that the injury might have been caused by a fall down the stone steps to the basement, but Spilsbury would not be budged.

Birkett scored a notable success, however, by being able to

show that a blood-splashed shirt and trousers of Mancini's, which the prosecution had produced as evidence, had come into the waiter's possession only after Violet had been killed. He also forced Chief Inspector Donaldson, who had been in charge of the case, to admit that although Mancini was a known criminal he had never been convicted of violence. He also extracted an admission from the policeman that there had been many false statements about the accused in the press.

Perhaps the eminent advocate's most skilful move was to put Mancini himself in the witness box. Mancini admitted that he had come home that night and found Violet dead in bed. He packed her body in the trunk and even sent off the forged telegraph message to her sister. When asked why, he said that as a known criminal he was afraid that his story simply would not have been believed by the police.

It had a horrible ring of truth about it, and it obviously convinced the jury, who took only two-and-a-half hours to bring in a verdict of not guilty. Mancini walked out of court a free man.

Forty-two years later, on 28 November 1976, the *News of the World* published an interview with Mancini in which he confessed to the murder of Violet Kaye, knowing of course that he could not be tried again for the crime. And in May 1978 he repeated the assertion to Stephen Knight, co-author with Bernard Taylor of *Perfect Murder*. He claimed that he and Violet had a fight that night and, having floored her, he banged her head on the fender in front of the fire and killed her.

A prostitute was found strangled in an empty building in Shaftesbury Avenue, London, in October 1931. Eighteen months later Frederick Field, who was serving in the RAF, confessed to the murder after getting a newspaper to buy his story and support his defence. He was tried and acquitted. In 1936, after being arrested as a deserter, he tried it again, confessing to the murder of a widow in Clapham. As before he soon withdrew his confession, but this time he had given away too many facts which only the murderer could have known. He was convicted and hanged.

Charles Manson   10050 Cielo Drive, Beverly Hills, California, was the rented home of Roman Polanski and his actress wife Sharon Tate. In the early hours of 9 August Mrs Polanski, who was eight months pregnant, her friend and hairdresser Jay Sebring, Abigail Folger, heiress to a coffee fortune, and Wojiciech Frykowski, described as a playboy, were all murdered, and a teenager who had been visiting the caretaker and was driving away in his car was stopped and shot to death.

The following night, a couple of miles away, Leno LaBianca, president of the Gateway chain of grocery stores, and his wife Rosemary were stabbed to death with knives and a double-tined carving fork at their home.

The police did not immediately connect the two killings, nor them with another, the stabbing to death of Gary Hinman in his apartment in Los Angeles on 31 July. They had a suspect in the Hinman murder, Robert Beausoleil, who had been arrested at Spahn's Movie Ranch in the hills north of Los Angeles, the home of a group of hippies led by someone called Charles Manson.

In October the police raided the Barker ranch, an inaccessible spot in Death Valley, because a group of hippies there were suspected of stealing cars. Ten women and four men, including Manson, were arrested. One of the girls, who was the lover of Bobby Beausoleil, claimed that he had been sent to Hinman by Manson, together with Susan Atkins, who was also arrested at the ranch.

Atkins, questioned by the police, readily admitted helping Beausoleil to kill Hinman, and in jail told her cell companions about being involved in the Tate/LaBianca murders. They promptly informed on her.

A Los Angeles grand jury eventually brought indictments for

murder and conspiracy to murder against Charles Manson, thirty-two, Charles 'Tex' Watson, twenty-three, Susan Atkins, twenty-one, Patricia Krenwinkel, twenty-one, Leslie Van Houten, twenty, and Linda Kasabian, twenty-one.

The trial of Manson, Atkins, Krenwinkel and Van Houten for the Tate/LaBianca murders took place in Los Angeles in June 1970. Watson had been extradited from Texas, but was at the time incarcerated in a Californian mental hospital classed as 'presently insane'. Kasabian had turned state's evidence and was the chief prosecution witness. She had not actually killed anybody, but had certainly collaborated in and aided and abetted seven murders.

She was on the witness stand for seventeen days, telling how Manson, the leader of what he called his 'Family', governed even their sex lives. She had taken a large number of different drugs, but used mostly LSD, as did all the Family.

Kasabian reported how on the afternoon of 8 August at the Spahn ranch Manson told her and the others to arm themselves with knives and prepare for 'Helter Skelter'. These words, taken from a song by the Beatles, with whom Manson seemed obsessed, represented a war between blacks and whites, which the blacks would win; they would, however, eventually give up power to him. His Family were to murder white people so that the blacks would be blamed and the war start.

Manson saw Atkins, Krenwinkel, Van Houten and Kasabian off in a car driven by Watson and they went to the house on Cielo Drive, where Manson had apparently known the previous occupants. Tex cut the telephone wires, opened the gate, stopped a car coming down the drive and shot the driver four times. It was the teenager who had been visiting the caretaker. Soon afterwards Kasabian saw Abigail Folger being chased out of the house by Krenwinkel and Watson and stabbed to death on the lawn; she also saw Frykowski appear at the front door screaming and covered in blood. He too was chopped down with knives.

The next night they went out with Manson. Selecting a house at random, he went inside alone, tied up the occupants, then instructed the Family members to enter and kill the prisoners. Kasabian remained in the car.

During much of her testimony she was continually interrupted by objections from Manson's attorney Irving Kanarek, who became so persistent and disruptive that he was eventually convicted of contempt of court and sentenced to a night in the county jail by Judge Older. Kanarek's cross-examination of Kasabian took seven days, and would have gone on longer except that the judge ended it because the attorney kept repeating himself.

During the trial, President Nixon made a speech in Denver in which he said: 'Here is a man [referring to Manson] who was guilty, directly or indirectly, of eight murders.' In vain did his press secretary protest that Nixon meant to use the word 'alleged'. The damage had been done. Judge Older had always insisted that the jury should be kept under wraps to shield them from the incessant press coverage and the impromptu interviews that attorneys and sometimes the defendants gave the press after each day's hearing; when Nixon made his outburst he banned all newspapers from the court. But somehow one reached the defence table and during the trial Manson held it up so that the jury could see the headlines, 'Manson Guilty Nixon Declares'.

It was meant to lead to a mistrial, but it failed. The judge said that he didn't see why the bad behaviour of the defendants – Manson and the three girls often interrupted the proceedings with statements and remarks and Manson once jumped over the defence table and tried to attack the judge – should lead to their advantage.

On 16 November, twenty-two weeks after the trial began, Deputy District Attorney Vincent Bugliosi ended the prosecution case. Paul Fitzgerald, attorney for Susan Atkins and the spokesman for the defence attorneys, announced that they would call no witnesses for the defence! Immediately the girls jumped up and said they wanted to testify. It was obvious that they wanted to take all the blame for the crimes, thus allowing Manson to go free. Bugliosi refused to agree to this and after much discussion in judge's chambers only Manson gave evidence, but only before the judge, not the jury.

Things were now getting hectic. At the resumed session in open court Manson threw a paperclip at the judge and Atkins made a grab for a knife on the exhibits table. All four defendants were hustled out while Bugliosi began his final speech.

The jury of seven men and five women eventually found Manson, Atkins and Krenwinkel guilty on seven counts of first-degree murder and Van Houten guilty on two counts of first-degree murder. So ended the 'guilt trial', as it is called in California. The 'penalty trial' followed and lasted from 26 January to 17 March 1971. The same jury gave the death penalty for all four defendants, but on 18 February 1972 the California Supreme Court voted to abolish the death penalty and they were given life sentences.

Charles Watson was subsequently tried and convicted on seven counts of first-degree murder. Manson, Atkins and Beausoleil were convicted of the murder of Gary Hinman. Linda Kasabian had all charges against her dismissed.

Since 1978 Manson has regularly applied for parole, but each time it has been refused.

Bertie Manton On the morning of 19 November 1943, the naked body of a woman was found bound up with sacks and cord in just six inches of water in a muddy stream known as the River Lea in Luton. She was about thirty to thirty-five years old, but there were no identifying marks and even her dentures had been removed. Her face was severely damaged due to heavy blows, and though her picture was shown in cinemas locally even her own children did not recognize her and no one came forward to say who she was.

After three months the police were no nearer identifying her and Chief Inspector Chapman of Scotland Yard ordered a reappraisal of all the evidence collected. On a piece of cloth found on a rubbish dump the police discovered a dyer's mark, which had been missed the first time round. The dyer was located and he said the cloth was from a coat dyed for a Mrs Rene Manton of Regent Street, Luton.

Bertie Manton, a driver for the National Fire Service, said that his wife had left him on 25 November and he produced letters which he said had been written by her from London. But the letters contained the name 'Hampstead', without the 'p', and when Manton was asked to write the word he too left out the letter.

Superintendent Cherrill of Scotland Yard, the fingerprint expert, was asked to come to the house in Regent Street and after an exhaustive search finally found a thumbprint on an old pickle jar forgotten in the cellar. It matched perfectly the left thumbprint of the murdered woman.

Confronted with this, Manton confessed that he had killed his wife. They had quarrelled for years about her going around with other men, he said. She had previously gone away for six months leaving him to look after their four children and refused to tell him where she had been. On the day of her death they quarrelled after the midday meal when the children were all at school. She threw a cup of tea in his face and he hit her with a heavy wooden stool. When he realized she was dead he hid her body until the children had gone to bed then carried it to the river on his bicycle and dumped it.

Bertie Manton was tried at Bedford Assizes in May 1944. His counsel, Arthur Ward, pleaded that the attack was not premeditated and the verdict should be manslaughter. During cross-examination Chief Inspector Chapman admitted that Manton was of good character and devoted to his children, and that Rene was known to have associated with soldiers and civilians alike.

Manton himself told the story of the fateful day. But during cross-examination by prosecutor Richard O'Sullivan, he was asked: 'Did you hear Dr Keith Simpson tell the jury that there were marks upon the neck of your wife, of the application of a hand and the reapplication of a hand?'

'Yes sir. I remember taking hold of her throat and pushing her against the wall.'

O'Sullivan went on persistently. 'And the marks showed that the hand had been applied with considerable force?'

'I may have grabbed her twice, but that was in my temper.'

The prosecutor paused, then delivered the *coup de grâce*. 'You said nothing about that in your statement to the police?'

Together with the many precautions which he had taken to cover up the crime, this was enough to convince the jury that there was more to the killing of Mrs Manton than her husband said. And they brought in a verdict of guilty. Manton was sentenced to death.

A petition for mercy, initiated by his children, collected 30,000 signatures and he was subsequently reprieved, but three years later he died in prison.

Another corpse identified by its fingerprints was also found in a river, this time near Wagga Wagga, Australia, on Christmas Day 1933. The skin of both hands was missing, but a human glove – the skin from a man's hand and wrist – was found nearby. This was worn by a detective to enable fingerprints to be taken. The dead man, Percy Smith, had last been seen with a trapper, Edward Morey, who was charged with his murder. During the trial, in 1934, one of the witnesses, Moncrieff Anderson, was shot dead and his wife claimed in court that her husband, not Morey, had killed Smith. Mrs Anderson was later shown to have written love letters to Morey and she was convicted of the manslaughter of her husband. Edward Morey was convicted of the murder of Smith.

Peter Manuel The trial of Peter Manuel, thirty-one, on eight charges of murder, began at the Glasgow High Court in May 1958, and the prosecution took two days to describe the murders.

The body of seventeen-year-old Anne Knielands was found on 4 January 1956 in a copse on a golf course in East Kilbride, a satellite town outside Glasgow. Her head had been battered and semen stains were found on her disarranged clothes although she had not been raped. The police questioned some gasboard workers who had been excavating nearby and learned that one, Peter Manuel, who was a well-known local burglar, had a conviction for rape. But Manuel lived with his parents and they gave him an alibi for the night of the murder.

In the following September, Mrs Marion Watt, forty-five, her sister Margaret and Mrs Watt's sixteen-year-old daughter, were shot to death in their bungalow at High Burnside, another small community near Glasgow. The husband, William Watt, had been away on a fishing trip at the time, but he was strongly suspected by the police and on 27 September he was charged with the three murders.

By this time Manuel, who was beginning a prison sentence for attempted robbery, got in touch with Watt's solicitor saying he knew who the real murderer was, but he refused to answer questions from the police. They were having second thoughts, however, and Watt was released in December.

Manuel came out of prison on 30 November 1957, and just under a month later seventeen-year-old Isabelle Cooke, a schoolgirl, disappeared on her way home in the town of Mount Vernon, after a dance. One of her shoes and her handbag were recovered from a water-filled colliery shaft, but there was no trace of the girl.

On 6 January 1958, the police found the bodies of forty-five-year-old Peter Smart, his wife Doris and their eleven-year-old son Michael in their bungalow in Uddingston. They had all been shot through the head and a substantial amount of money had been stolen from the premises. Manuel lived only ten minutes' walk away.

After an underworld tip-off that he seemed to have acquired a lot of money recently, the police arrested him. Some stolen goods were found in his home and his father was also arrested and charged with receiving stolen goods. Manuel spent the night in the cells, then said that if the police released his father he would help to clear up some crimes of homicide.

He wrote detailed confessions to the murders of Anne Kniel-ands, the Watt family, Isabelle Cooke and the Smarts. He even led the police to where he had buried the body of the missing teenager and showed the police where he had thrown the guns, used to kill the Watt family and the Smarts, in the River Clyde. Both pistols were subsequently recovered.

At his trial, however, Manuel repudiated all his statements, saying that they had been extracted under duress. His counsel, Harold Leslie, then produced what Scottish law describes as special defences. One, known as 'Impeachment', had not been used in a murder trial in Scotland for a hundred years, and meant that Manuel would accuse William Watt of murdering his own family.

The defence also put in a plea that Manuel's confessions to the police should be ruled inadmissible as evidence. This was rejected by the judge, Lord Cameron. The next day Manuel dismissed his counsel and conducted his own defence, so that much of the prosecution evidence was heard over again and Manuel was able to cross-examine William Watt, insinuating that he really should have been tried for killing his wife, daughter and sister-in-law.

He also presented a series of complex alibis for the murders and claimed that the police were trying to frame him for the crimes. The judge praised Manuel for the skill with which he had presented his case. Nevertheless there was a great deal of evidence against him. Apart from the confessions, banknotes which he had used at pubs and which had been recovered by the police could be proved to have been part of the money stolen from Peter Smart.

The jury of nine men and six women took only two hours to find him guilty of six capital murders, the Watt and Smart families, and the non-capital murder of Isabelle Cooke. On the judge's direction he was acquitted of the murder of Anne Knielands because of the lack of evidence to corroborate his confession.

He was hanged in Barlinnie prison on 11 July 1958.

Seventeen days after his execution a Newcastle inquest jury decided that Peter Manuel had also been responsible for murdering taxi-driver Sydney Dunn.

Aircraftman Arthur Heys raped and brutally murdered a WAAF at an RAF station near Beccles, Suffolk, in November 1944. While in custody he tried to smuggle out a letter to the commanding officer, purporting to come from the real murderer. It gave details that only the murderer would know and thus was a kind of confession. He was convicted and hanged.

Master Sergeant Marcus Marymont   Sergeant Marymont, thirty-seven, was tried for murder in December 1958 by a United States General Court Martial, held at Denham in Buckinghamshire. The charges were that he had administered arsenic to his wife, forty-three-year-old Mary Hellen, and had had wrongful sexual intercourse with a woman not his wife.

Marymont had been stationed at the US Air Force nuclear bomber base at Sculthorpe, Norfolk, living in married quarters with his wife and three children. In July 1956 he met Mrs Cynthia Taylor, twenty-three, the manageress of a shop in Maidenhead.

He told her that he was divorced and his ex-wife lived in America. They began an affair, meeting once or twice a month. Mrs Taylor came under severe questioning at the trial and was made to read portions of her letters to the sergeant which had been recovered from his desk. In her evidence she said that he promised to marry her when she had obtained her divorce.

Marymont spent Christmas of 1957 with Mrs Taylor, leaving his wife and family to spend the holiday on their own. In April of the following year Mary Marymont found a letter he had forgotten to post to Cynthia in his pocket and taxed him with it. Marymont said that he would give up his lover.

On 6 June 1958, the sergeant and his wife went to a party and soon after returning Mrs Marymont became ill. She was no better the next day and was taken to the hospital on the base where she died at 9.47 that night. Dr Albert Cook, obstetrician at Sculthorpe, gave evidence that he was immediately suspicious. Although he knew Mrs Marymont had a history of gastric upsets he at once suspected poisoning.

The sergeant denied poisoning his wife. His counsel, Major William Karr, submitted that the chance of Mrs Marymont having died by her own hand or even by accident was just as likely as that her husband had killed her.

Major C. J. Lewis, prosecuting, built up an impressive case. Dr L. C. Nickolls, Director of the Metropolitan Police Laboratory, pointed out that arsenic is retained in the hair, and analysis of Mrs Marymont's hair showed that she had been given some of the poison at least six months before she died. Dr Francis Camps, the English pathologist who had carried out the autopsy and was an acknowledged expert on arsenic, gave it as his opinion that Mrs Marymont had been given a large dose of the poison just before she died. Although it could give rise to a burning sensation in the mouth, this could be disguised by a strong-tasting drink such as coffee.

Two civilian cleaners at the air force base said that one night

they had seen Marymont in the chemical laboratory and the
sergeant had called their attention to the presence of a bottle of
arsenic on the shelf, asking why it was not locked up. A pharma-
cist who kept a shop in Maidenhead reported that the sergeant
had asked if they kept arsenic, but when he was told that a permit
was required he left.

Master Sergeant Marymont was found guilty, by the panel
of fifteen American officers, of the murder of his wife and also
of misconduct with Mrs Taylor. He was sentenced to life imprisonment, which meant precisely what it said.

Appeals against the sentence were made in America and in
Britain. William Mars-Jones appeared for Marymont at an appeal
at Denham and claimed that Mrs Cynthia Taylor should never
have been compelled to give evidence against him. As a British
subject and only a witness she had the right not to give evidence
on matters which might incriminate her, as she would have had in
an English high court. Although this appeal was rejected, in 1960
the US Court of Military Appeals dismissed the charge of adultery
against Marymont and reduced his sentence to thirty-five years.

Early in 1910, Dr Hawley Harvey Crippen, an American doctor selling
patent medicines in London, poisoned his wife, whose stage name
was Belle Elmore, with hyoscine. When Ethel le Neve, Crippen's
secretary and mistress, moved into the family home at Hilldrop Crescent,
Belle's friends went to the police. Crippen and Ethel fled to Canada.
The police then found a portion of Belle's body – the head, limbs and
skeleton were never found – buried under the cellar. The runaway pair
were arrested on board ship after the suspicious captain had radioed
to London, the first time radio had been used in a murder hunt. Tried in
October 1910, Ethel was acquitted, but Crippen was convicted and
hanged.

Henry McKenny and John Childs   This story begins at the
end. In June 1979 a gang of five armed bandits robbed a security

van in the town of Hertford. In the pocket of one of a series of boilersuits the gang discarded in a public toilet, the police discovered a car key which led them to a wealthy East London grocer who had been one of the gang. He quickly informed on the rest and three of the four were arrested, including John Childs. The only one who escaped was Henry McKenny.

To help reduce his sentence the grocer told the police that McKenny, known as 'Big Harry', Childs, and a man called Terry Pinfold had for years been murdering people. John Childs, interviewed in prison, readily admitted all the murders, saying that he had only been involved because he was afraid of McKenny. But the story he told horrified the hardened police officers.

McKenny stood six feet five inches tall and weighed seventeen stones, but although a violent man, who had been offered a job by the Kray brothers, he was far from being an ignorant thug. A qualified and experienced pilot, he had also trained as a diver and had invented an air pump which was in use all over the world. But the big man liked the excitement of law breaking.

In 1974 he was in partnership with Terry Pinfold, manufacturing and selling diving equipment from a converted church hall in Ilford. In another part of the premises Terence Eve ran a successful business manufacturing soft toys. McKenny decided to take over the business and one night he, with an iron bar, and Childs, with a hammer, battered Eve to death. They removed the body to Childs's council flat in Poplar and cut it up. But an industrial mincing machine they'd bought to reduce the fragments still further jammed, so they burnt the body on the living-room fire.

At first the police simply didn't believe this could be done, but pathologist Professor James Cameron cut up the body of an eleven-stone pig and successfully burnt it on the fire, though it did take thirteen hours. The smell outside the flat during the process was hardly noticeable.

Later McKenny discovered that Robert Brown, an ex-wrestler friend of Eve's, had seen him and Childs clearing up in the church hall after Eve's murder. They killed him in January 1975 and disposed of the body in the same way, as they did with all their killings.

That same month Big Harry was paid £2,000 to kill London haulage contractor George Brett. Childs lured him to the church hall, but Brett's ten-year-old son came along for the ride. McKenny shot them both with a silenced Sten gun, the boy still holding a teddy bear.

The next contract was in July 1978, when the murderous pair were offered £4,000 – £1,500 deposit and five monthly payments of £500 – to kill Freddie Sherwood, a small-time crook who was the proprietor of a Herne Bay nursing home. He was lured to McKenny's bungalow in East London by Childs with a promise to buy his car, and shot by the big man while he was sitting at a table counting his money.

The last murder was in October of the same year and this time it was for love. Ronald Andrews was one of McKenny's best friends, but the big man was having an affair with his wife and wanted to marry her. Andrews was persuaded to go to Childs's flat, where he was killed. McKenny took his friend's car to the River Nene at Wisbech and drove it into the water to make it look like a drunken accident, the body having been swept out to sea. He escaped from the car wearing frogman's gear.

Although Harry McKenny was still at liberty when Childs made his confessions, after a three-month manhunt and following an underworld tip-off he was finally captured in Plaistow, East London.

John Childs was tried first, at the Old Bailey in December 1979, and pleaded guilty to all six murders. He was sentenced to six terms of life imprisonment. McKenny was not brought to trial until October 1980, and the trial lasted for forty days. Childs was the chief prosecution witness, but McKenny was convicted of killing only the Bretts, Sherwood and Andrews. The judge recommended that he should stay in jail for at least twenty-five years.

Terence Pinfold was convicted of the murder of Terence Eve and received life.

Charles Jenkins, twenty-three, Christopher Geraghty, twenty-one, and seventeen-year-old Terence Rolt attempted to rob a jeweller's in Charlotte Street, London, in April 1947, but when the alarm went they rushed out of the shop. A motorcyclist, Alec de Antiquis, tried to stop them and was shot in the head. The police traced them through a raincoat Jenkins discarded and all three were convicted of murder. Jenkins and Geraghty were hanged and Rolt, too young for the death penalty, was ordered to be detained during His Majesty's pleasure.

Thomas McMahon and Francis McGirl   At five to ten on the morning of Monday 27 August, 1979, a Garda (an' Irish policeman) stopped a red Ford Escort in the main street of Granard in County Longford, Eire. It was a routine tax and insurance check, but the driver was nervous; he put the car in reverse when asked to pull in to the side of the road and his hands shook so much he could hardly open the boot. The policeman was suspicious and took the driver and his passenger to the police station for further questioning.

About two hours later and more than seventy miles away in Mullaghmore Bay, County Sligo, on the north-western coast of Ireland, a small fishing boat exploded. On board the twenty-eight-foot-long *Shadow V* had been Earl Mountbatten of Burma, national war hero and the last Viceroy of India. With him were his daughters Lady Pamela and Lady Patricia, and Lady Patricia's husband Lord Brabourne, her twin fifteen-year-old sons Nicholas and Timothy, the eighty-three-year-old dowager Lady Brabourne and a local, fifteen-year-old Paul Maxwell, who acted as boat boy to Lord Mountbatten.

The Earl, his grandson Nicholas and Paul Maxwell were killed outright and all the others were injured. The next day the dowager Lady Brabourne died of her wounds in Sligo hospital.

The IRA claimed responsibility, saying they had planted a fifty-pound bomb on the vessel. The outrage was condemned all over the world and the Irish government poured every resource into tracking down the bombers. Eventually the two men questioned in Granard, the driver Francis McGirl, a twenty-four-year-old farmer, and his passenger Thomas McMahon, were charged with murder.

Their trial began in November at Dublin's Special Criminal Court before three judges, Judge Sean Fawsitt, District Justice John Garavan and the president of the court, Mr Justice Liam Hamilton. There was no jury.

The prosecution evidence was almost entirely scientific. Dr Donovon of the Irish forensic science laboratory explained that sand found on the footwear of both men could have come from the slipway at Mullaghmore harbour. Traces of nitroglycerine and ammonium nitrate had also been found on their clothing and these compounds indicated contact with the explosive gelignite.

The police also claimed that McGirl had shouted: 'I put no bomb on the boat', when he was interviewed at the police station, before it was mentioned that there had been an explosion. McGirl strenuously denied this.

Mr Justice Hamilton, giving the verdict of the judges, said that the presence of sand was not conclusive that McGirl had been at Mullaghmore. The other evidence against him was consistent with his guilt, but it might also have an innocent explanation. There was thus a doubt about his guilt and he was entitled to be found not guilty.

The case against McMahon was stronger. Green and white paint flakes taken from his boot were proved conclusively to have come from the *Shadow V* and smears of paint on his jacket had also come from the boat. The court was satisfied that he had been in contact with explosives. This evidence convinced the three judges that he, either alone or with others, had placed explosives on the boat. He was sentenced to penal servitude for life.

Later both men were acquitted on the charge of membership of the IRA after swearing on oath that they were not members.

Donald Merrett   'Rita!' cried seventeen-year-old Donald Merrett. 'Mother's shot herself!'

The maidservant followed the youth back into the sitting-room to discover Mrs Merrett lying on the floor bleeding from a wound behind her right ear. The police were called and completely accepted Merrett's explanation, not bothering to examine the gun for fingerprints or to consider why a woman would shoot herself in the middle of writing a letter.

The poor lady, who was still alive, was bundled off to the felons' ward at Edinburgh Royal Infirmary, for in March 1926, attempted suicide was a criminal offence. She lingered on for another fortnight, at one time regaining consciousness, becoming quite lucid and explaining that she had been writing when a bang went off in her head. 'Did Donald do it?' she asked. 'He's such a naughty boy.'

Soon after this she died. Then the Clydesdale Bank discovered that Donald had been forging cheques on his mother's account. Eight months later he was arrested and charged with murdering his mother and forging twenty-nine cheques.

His trial began in Edinburgh in February 1927, by which time the police had lost the letter Mrs Merrett was writing when she was shot. The defence produced an eminent psychiatrist, Dr George Robertson, to state that Mrs Merrett's brain would undoubtedly be affected by her injury and her statements should be received with great caution.

But big guns were deployed on the scientific side. Professor Harvey Littlejohn of Edinburgh University, supported by Professor Glaister, said that the lack of blackening around the wound indicated that the gun had been held more than three inches away from the skin when it was fired, making suicide extremely unlikely. But Professor Littlejohn's opinion was made to look rather less certain when he was reminded, during cross-examination by defence lawyer Craigie Aitchison, that his original idea had been that it was suicide.

Aitchison then brought on his heavyweight, Dr (later Sir) Bernard Spilsbury, the most illustrious pathologist of his day, in his first appearance ever for the defence. In his opinion, neither the site of the wound nor the direction of the bullet was inconsistent with suicide, and any blackening could well have been removed by bleeding and by washing.

The jury of fifteen took an hour to reach a verdict of not proven on the murder charge – there were five for guilty and ten for not proven – a verdict that, without giving the connotation of innocence, allows the prisoner to go free. But Donald Merrett was found guilty of forgery and sentenced to twelve months imprisonment.

When he was released he changed his name to Ronald Chesney and embarked on a life of smuggling in the Mediterranean. He served with distinction in the navy in the Second World War and afterwards continued smuggling and trading on the black market. By this time he was married, but his wife ran an old people's home in Ealing with her mother, while Chesney lived with various girlfriends in Germany.

Having settled some money on his wife years before, he realized that if she should die it would come to him, so he embarked on his second perfect murder. Using a false passport and setting up an alibi with his girlfriend in Germany, he came to London secretly and met his wife. He got her drunk, drowned her in the bath at the old people's home and made it look like an accident. But creeping downstairs to make his escape he ran into his mother-in-law, who immediately recognized him.

In a panic he killed the old lady with the coffee pot she was carrying and fled back to Germany. He knew that things had gone badly wrong; his bloody fingerprints would be on the coffee pot and elsewhere. This time he would not escape. He went into a wood on the outskirts of Cologne and shot himself.

Another man who got away with murder for a long time was Henri Désiré Landru. Arrested in Paris in 1919 on suspicion of being involved in the disappearance of two women, he tried to get rid of a notebook containing details of some 283 women the small, balding Casanova had met and defrauded over a four-year period. At his trial in November 1921, details were given of ten women and one youth whom he had murdered, though no remains were ever found. He was convicted and guillotined in February 1922. In 1968 a newspaper alleged that he had given one of his lawyers a framed drawing, on the back of which were the scribbled words: 'I did it. I burned their bodies in my kitchen oven.'

Alfred Moore　The police suspected that Alfred Moore, thirty-six, was a burglar. On the night of 14 June 1951, a team of ten policemen surrounded his home, Whinney Close Farm, at the top of a hill on the outskirts of Kirkheaton, a small town near Huddersfield. They intended to intercept him when he came home across the fields, hopefully with the proceeds of a burglary on him.

But the plan went wrong. At about two a.m. the silence of the dark night was shattered by the sound of gunfire and two policemen lay wounded on the ground. Detective Inspector Duncan Fraser was dead by the time he reached hospital, shot through the heart, and Police Constable Arthur Jagger was severely wounded with a bullet in his stomach.

The occupants of the farm were roused and Alfred Moore taken into custody. On searching the farmhouse and the surrounding fields, skeleton keys and the proceeds of several burglaries were discovered, together with rounds of 9mm ammunition which matched those taken from the shot policemen. But the murder weapon was never found.

At Huddersfield Royal Infirmary PC Jagger was in a perilous condition and an identification parade was hurriedly held at his bedside. He picked out Moore. A special court was then convened before a local magistrate and the constable gave his evidence on oath from his bed, recounting how he had seen the prisoner by torchlight coming up the hill and when he and DI Fraser had attempted to detain him they had both been shot.

Asked if he would like to ask any questions, Moore said: 'Are you sure?'

'I'm quite sure,' came the reply from the PC.

The next day Arthur Jagger died and Moore was charged with double murder.

The trial took place in December 1951 at Leeds Assizes. Moore's brother Charles gave evidence that after he had visited Whinney Close Farm his brother had walked him home and they parted at 11.20 p.m. The prosecution contended that Moore could not have reached home before the cordon had been set, at 11.45 p.m., and therefore it must have been him who was seen by Jagger at two o'clock.

Defence counsel Harry Hylton-Foster pointed out that a few minutes either way in the timings would have meant Moore could have reached home before the policemen arrived. He also showed that 9mm ammunition was one of the most common kinds. But there was little he could do about Jagger's evidence. The jury of ten men and two women took only fifty minutes to bring in a verdict of guilty and Alfred Moore was hanged in Armley jail, Leeds, on 6 February 1952.

The prosecution case rested mainly on PC Jagger's evidence, but when this was given Moore was not represented by a solicitor; it was a Sunday and the man he asked for could not be found. An experienced lawyer might have asked the policeman how much he could actually see on that dark night and by the light of a torch, when people's faces look very different. Moore lacked the expertise to make a proper challenge to a vital part of the case against him, which may have cost him his life.

Steinie Morrison   Leon Beron, a forty-seven-year-old of Russian extraction, was found dead early on the morning of New Year's Day 1911 on Clapham Common. It was believed that he had been struck down on a footpath by something like an iron bar and the body dragged on its face to some bushes.

Beron, an East End landlord, usually carried with him twenty to thirty pounds – in those days a considerable sum of money – and a gold watch. Both watch and money were missing from the body.

He also spent much of his time in a Whitechapel eating-house called the Warsaw Restaurant, which served as a kind of club to the foreign colony to which Beron belonged. Another member of the group who used to meet at the Warsaw was Steinie Morrison, twenty-nine, a tall, striking figure with a strong Jewish cast of features. He was arrested a week after the murder and his trial came on at the Old Bailey in March 1911 before Mr Justice Darling.

On the body there were two almost symmetrical cuts, one on each side of the face, which some observers claimed were deliberate and constituted the letter 'S', to indicate 'Spy'. The murder, it was suggested, had been committed by some secret society, of which there were a lot in the East End at the time. The judge was sceptical about this, though he left it up to the jury to decide.

The prosecution case, well put by Richard Muir, an able counsel with a suave manner and a melodious voice, was detailed but very circumstantial. Morrison had been seen examining Beron's watch. He had been employed as a baker on Lavender Hill, near Clapham Common, and thus knew the area. A waiter saw him at the Warsaw on New Year's Eve with a parcel, which felt like an iron bar. He had been seen walking the streets with Beron some hours before the murder took place and identified as taking a cab to Clapham Common, together with another man, at two o'clock in the morning and returning to Kennington by cab later alone.

A great deal of the evidence was of identification, and defending counsel's job was to make the jury believe the witnesses were either mistaken or telling lies. Edward Abinger was an experienced advocate, but impulsive and emotional. He took snuff continually and was given to waving about a blue silk handkerchief.

Mrs Nellie Deitch and her husband had been walking home after a party, at one o'clock in the morning, and had seen Beron, whom she knew well, with Steinie Morrison. Abinger could not move her on cross-examination and he endeavoured to discredit her, trying to show that she had kept a brothel. Mrs Deitch strongly denied this, but Abinger persisted.

Several times he was warned by Mr Justice Darling, who pointed out that the Criminal Evidence Act of 1898 protected a prisoner when giving evidence, but not if he – through his counsel – attacked the character of a witness for the prosecution. Abinger claimed to be fully aware of this.

But when he put Morrison into the witness box and Richard Muir rose to cross-examine, the question soon came: 'When were you first convicted of felony?'

In vain Abinger jumped to his feet and protested vigorously. The judge had to tell him that he had opened the door himself. And Muir went on to extract from the defendant the whole of his long record for burglary.

It undoubtedly turned the jury against Morrison. Mr Justice Darling obviously felt that the prosecution's case was not strong, and summed up in the prisoner's favour. But the jury took only thirty-five minutes to find Steinie Morrison guilty of murder. He was sentenced to death. An appeal to the Court of Criminal Appeal failed, but significantly the Home Secretary, Winston Churchill, granted a reprieve and the sentence was commuted to a life sentence.

It was no reprieve for Morrison, however. He was persistently violent in prison and was flogged, went on hunger strikes and eventually died in Parkhurst prison at the age of thirty-nine.

N

Donald Neilson The first murder occurred on the night of 15 February 1974, when a hooded man, afterwards dubbed the Black Panther, shot and killed Donald Skepper, a sub-postmaster at New Park, Harrogate. He had broken into the little grocery shop intending to rob it, and shot the proprietor during a struggle.

In the following September, Derek Astin was gunned down in his flat above a sub-post office near Accrington, Lancashire, by a masked man who had broken in during the night. And nine weeks later Sidney Grayland, whose wife Margaret ran a sub-post office at Langley in the West Midlands, was shot and killed, and his wife severely injured, after a struggle with a masked intruder.

By this time the press were calling him Public Enemy Number One, but there was worse to come. Lesley Whittle, seventeen, was abducted from her bedroom at her home in Highley, Shropshire, during the night of 13 January 1975. A ransom demand for £50,000 was left behind on Dymo tape, with instructions to wait by a phone in a Kidderminster shopping centre for details on how to deliver the money.

Things went wrong from the start. Someone tipped off the press, and the police, who had been called in, told Ronald Whittle, Lesley's brother, not to answer the phone.

Two days after the kidnapping, Gerald Smith, a security guard at the Freightliner depot in Dudley, surprised a man hanging about at night and was shot six times. He died later of his wounds. Nearby was found an abandoned car containing items connected with the Whittle kidnapping.

On 16 January Ronald Whittle, having finally received telephone instructions on how to deliver the ransom, set out with the money. He was delayed in starting by the police insisting on recording every banknote number, then he got lost, and finally arrived at his destination, Bathpool Park, near Newcastle-under-Lyme. The flashing light he had been told to look out for never materialized and he went home disappointed.

It was eventually discovered that a police car seen entering the park by the kidnapper had scared him off. Lesley was discovered seven weeks later, when the police made another and this time exhaustive search of the park. Her body was in an inspection shaft, in a drainage system, sixty-two feet below ground. She was hanging by the neck.

On 11 December, two police constables near Mansfield, Nottinghamshire, stopped a small man behaving suspiciously outside a pub. He produced a sawn-off shotgun, but after a titanic struggle, helped by two members of the public, they disarmed the suspect and took him into custody. After twelve hours of questioning he confessed that his name was Donald Neilson, he lived in Bradford and he had kidnapped Lesley Whittle.

Neilson went on trial for the murder of Lesley Whittle only, in June 1976 at Oxford Crown Court, since it was felt that no court in the Midlands could give him a fair hearing. He claimed that he had left the girl on an inspection platform halfway down the shaft, with a wire round her neck to prevent her moving about, and that she must have slipped off the platform and been hanged. But Phillip Cox QC for the prosecution said that Neilson had admitted the girl had seen his face and his intention from the beginning must have been to kill her. The jury agreed and he was convicted, but sentence was deferred until the end of his second trial.

In July, Neilson went on trial for the murder of the three men killed during the post office raids, and for the attempted murder of three people: Margaret Grayland, one of the officers who had captured him, and Gerald Smith. He could not be convicted of the murder of the Freightliner security guard, who died fourteen months after being shot, because he did not expire within a year and a day after being assaulted – the legal limit.

But Neilson was eventually found guilty of all charges and sentenced to five life terms.

Arfinn Nesset The trial opened in October 1982 in Trondheim and, taking five months, became Norway's longest trial of modern times. The defendant was forty-six-year-old Arfinn Nesset, a thin, balding man who had been the manager of the Orkdal Valley Nursing Home for the elderly in central Norway. He was accused of murdering fourteen women and eleven men, between the ages of sixty-seven and ninety-four, in the period from May 1977 to November 1980. They were all patients at the nursing home and he was alleged to have injected them with the drug Curacit, which is a derivative of curare, the poison used by some South American Indians to tip their arrows, and is also used as a muscle relaxant during operations.

The indictments represented only those murders that prosecutor state attorney Olaf Jakhelln thought that he could prove. When Nesset was first arrested he confessed that he could not remember how many people he had killed and asked for a list of all the patients who had been in his care in the three institutions he had worked at since 1962. The police subsequently investigated the deaths of some sixty-two people, but were only able to present evidence for twenty-five.

Nesset denied all the allegations when he came to court and claimed that the confessions had been obtained by undue pressure when he was depressed. The trial was thus a long exposition of circumstantial evidence. More than 150 witnesses were called, but it could not be shown that anyone had actually observed Nesset administering lethal injections, although he had been seen with elderly patients just before they died and they had been found with puncture marks on their arms. No post mortems were carried out since Curacit is so rapidly broken down in the body that it is difficult to detect after a period of time.

The police were first alerted after Nesset ordered substantial quantities of the drug, but when questioned he said that he wanted it for killing a dog.

There seemed to be no clear motive for the crimes, as there often isn't with serial killers, but four psychiatrists declared him to be sane, although he showed no remorse for what he had done.

The jury of six women and four men took three days to find the accused guilty on twenty-two counts of murder and one of attempted murder and not guilty on two other counts of murder.

Before sentence was pronounced the judges heard pleas from defence counsel Alf Nordhus, who claimed that the deaths were mercy killings. But the judges sentenced Nesset to twenty-one years imprisonment, the maximum which can be given for murder under Norwegian law, and up to ten years preventive detention.

Dorothea 'Nurse' Waddingham set up a nursing home for the elderly in Nottingham in the 1930s though she had no nursing qualifications. But when eighty-nine-year-old Mrs Baguley and her fifty-year-old daughter Ada died after leaving wills in favour of Waddingham and her assistant Ronald Sullivan she foolishly forged a letter, purportedly from Ada, asking to be cremated and requesting that her relatives not be informed of her death. Post mortems were ordered and morphine found in the bodies. 'Nurse' Waddingham and Sullivan were tried in February 1936. Sullivan was acquitted but Waddingham was convicted of murder and hanged at Birmingham in April 1936.

Dennis Nilsen 'This morning, Mr Nilsen,' said DCI Peter Jay, chief of Hornsey CID, 'we found a piece of flesh in your drains. It's been identified as part of a human body.'

'Good grief! How awful!'

'Don't mess about,' said the inspector briskly. 'Where's the rest of it?'

There was a long pause, then the tall thirty-seven-year-old man from Fraserburgh, Scotland, who occupied the top flat of a semi in Cranley Gardens, Muswell Hill, shrugged his shoulders. 'In two plastic bags in the wardrobe next door. I'll show you.'

Dennis Andrew Nilsen went for trial at the Old Bailey in October 1983, charged with six murders and two attempted murders. He had already confessed to fifteen murders of young, mostly down-and-out homosexuals he had picked up in pubs in the West End and North London over a period of four years. He took them back to his ground-floor flat in Melrose Avenue, Cricklewood, where he lived from 1975 to 1981, and when they had fallen asleep after heavy drinking he strangled them, often with a tie. He confessed to killing twelve men at Melrose Avenue, eight of whom have never been identified. When he moved to Cranley Gardens he killed a further three.

Prosecution and defence agreed that Nilsen had an abnormality of mind, but his defence counsel, Ivan Lawrence QC, contended that it was so substantial that his responsibility for the crimes was diminished and he should be convicted only of manslaughter.

Allan Green QC, who prosecuted, gave the jury details of all fifteen killings and how Nilsen had disposed of his victims. At first he had kept the bodies under the floorboards, but later he cut them up and disposed of the soft organs in dustbins or by putting them over the garden fence at the back which bordered waste land. Eventually he got rid of a number of bodies by burning them on an enormous bonfire on the waste land and placing old tyres on top to disguise the smell of burning flesh. When he moved to Cranley Gardens he hadn't the use of the garden and was reduced to keeping cut-up bodies in plastic sacks in his living-room and trying to flush away portions down the toilet, which inevitably became blocked and led to his discovery.

Three young men testified that Nilsen had tried to strangle them while they were asleep at his flat, but for some reason he had not gone on to kill, and had let them go. One even went to the police, who put it down to a homosexual lovers' quarrel and did nothing about it.

Detective Chief Superintendent Chambers read out the transcript of Nilsen's confession, which he had made at Hornsey police station, chilling the jury with details of how he had boiled the heads of several victims in a cooking pot.

The defence called two psychiatrists. One claimed that Nilsen treated people only as components of his own fantasies; the other suggested that he had paranoid and schizoid tendencies, but clashed with the judge, Mr Justice Croom-Johnson, when he suggested that because of Nilsen's lack of feeling he could not have malice aforethought, the essential prerequisite of murder. The judge suggested that he should leave the interpretation of the law to others.

In his summing up Mr Croom-Johnson claimed that evil had a place in moral philosophy and he hinted strongly to the jury that he thought Nilsen was evil and not insane. The jury had difficulty coming to a decision on whether his mental capacity was sufficiently impaired for him to be guilty only of manslaughter. Eventually, after the jury had deliberated for nearly two days, the judge said he would allow a majority decision. Dennis Nilsen was then found guilty on all six counts of murder, by a majority of ten to two, and guilty of one attempted murder, by the same majority.

He was sentenced to life imprisonment with the recommendation that he serve at least twenty-five years.

Pauline Parker and Juliet Hulme According to the crown prosecutor, Alan A. Brown, they were 'two dirty-minded little girls'; but then this was New Zealand in 1954 and lesbian relationships were viewed with something like horror.

Pauline Parker was sixteen, dark and smaller than her tall blonde friend Juliet, who was fifteen. They had met only a year earlier when Juliet Hulme and her family came to New Zealand from Liverpool and she went to school in Christchurch.

The relationship rapidly became intense and Pauline spent nearly all her spare time at Juliet's palatial home in the suburbs of Christchurch; Juliet's father was the new rector of Canterbury University College there. Both families became worried about the association and quarrels with the girls were frequent.

Eventually Dr Hulme, Juliet's father, accepted a new appointment in England and proposed that on his way back he would take Juliet to a school in South Africa. Pauline pleaded to be able to go too, but both girls' parents were adamant that they must be separated and the date for Juliet's departure was fixed at 3 July 1954.

On 22 June the girls persuaded Mrs Parker to take them on a farewell picnic in Victoria Park, Christchurch. They carried with them an unusual pink stone and a brick wrapped in a stocking. After the meal they went for a walk. Juliet went ahead and dropped the pink stone unobserved. When the other two reached the spot Pauline pointed it out to her mother and as Mrs Parker bent to pick it up Pauline swung the brick at her mother's head.

It took more than forty blows to kill the poor woman, by

which time the girls were covered in blood and their carefully prepared story, that Mrs Parker had fallen and hit her head on a brick, was plainly untrue.

They were tried for murder at the Supreme Court in Christchurch in August 1954. The defence pleaded insanity and a psychiatrist referred to the girls as suffering from *folie à deux*, a term sometimes used to describe communicated insanity, although there is no academic acceptance of the idea. There are, however, a number of examples of pairs like Leopold and Loeb (*see* p. 202), Brady and Hindley (*see* p. 38), who together have committed murder.

Both prosecution and defence made use of Pauline Parker's diary in which she discussed the plans the girls made to murder her mother.

'We have worked it out carefully,' she had written, 'and are both thrilled at the idea. Naturally we feel a trifle nervous, but the pleasure of anticipation is great.'

But the entry for 22 June was only one line: 'The Day of the Happy Event'.

Neither showed any emotion in court and the jury took only two hours to find them guilty of murder. They were sentenced to be detained during Her Majesty's pleasure, the only sentence which could be passed on persons under eighteen convicted of an offence punishable by death, and sent to prisons four hundred miles apart.

Both were model prisoners and Pauline passed her school certificate in prison. They received psychiatric treatment and both were released on parole in November 1959.

Another case of lesbian lovers has a more modern flavour. In April 1985 Christie Offord was thirty-five and Margi Dunbar twenty-nine and they lived as man and wife in an expensive house with a swimming pool in Hounslow, Middlesex. Christie went off to work each morning as a high-class prostitute in South Kensington, and Margi stayed home to look after the child she'd had by artificial insemination. But the husband-and-wife arrangement was not to Margi's liking. She complained that Christie was becoming too much like a man and even wanted a sex change operation, and all she wanted was to be a gay girl and to make love to a woman. So she left and went back to her old occupation, which was also prostitution. They argued over the custody of Margi's child. Then Christie was found beaten to death in the flat where she took her clients and Margi and two men friends were tried for her murder. She claimed that she hadn't wanted the men to kill Christie, just to hurt her. The men were sentenced to life imprisonment, but Margi had her charge reduced to manslaughter and was given seven years. After two years she appealed and the appeal court ruled that the trial judge had given incorrect advice to the jury. The conviction was therefore quashed and she was freed.

Judge Joe Peel This trial showed up the evils of the American system of plea bargaining, but demonstrated the only way to solve an unsolvable murder and to bring the main perpetrator to justice.

Sixty-six-year-old Judge Curtis Eugene Chillingworth, the senior judge in the Palm Beach district of Florida, and his wife Marjorie, disappeared from their beach cottage on the night of 14 June 1955. Blood on the steps of the cottage leading down to the beach suggested violence, but their bodies were never found.

In March 1961, five years later, former Judge Joe Peel was tried for the murder of Judge Chillingworth and his wife. According to state attorney Phil O'Connell, who had been a former prizefighter and acted with all a boxer's aggression, Peel had plenty of motive.

He had become a junior and part-time judge when he was only thirty-two, but while acting as an ordinary lawyer he had already been reprimanded once by the senior judge for representing both sides in a case, and was about to be carpeted again for informing a client that she was legally divorced when she wasn't. This second offence could have meant disbarment from practising law in Florida for life had Judge Chillingworth lived to rule on it.

Judge Peel also feared to lose his privileged position because he was heavily involved with the local makers of illegal 'moonshine' liquor and the numbers racket. His partners in these enterprises were Floyd Holzapfel and a black crook called George 'Bobby' Lincoln.

Police attention had been attracted to Holzapfel by his involvement in several other murders, including one where the victim had been dumped in the sea. Eventually he confessed to the Chillingworth killings and appeared as a prosecution witness against Peel.

He said that on the judge's instructions he and Lincoln went to the beach cottage by boat, woke Chillingworth and his wife and abducted them at gunpoint. When they were forcing the tied-up pair down the cottage stairs to the beach Mrs Chillingworth began screaming and Holzapfel clubbed her on the head, causing the blood on the steps. When they were far enough out to sea the elderly pair were pushed over the boat side with weights tied to them, and as the old man's wife entered the water he shouted to her: 'Remember I love you.'

Holzapfel faced the electric chair by admitting to first-degree murder, but Lincoln, who had committed three other murders, was offered immunity if he would testify against Peel. This caused considerable disquiet in Florida, but showed the desperation of the prosecution who had no forensic evidence against the former judge.

Lincoln went on to the witness stand to confirm Holzapfel's story, but also to claim that he played only a minor part in the Chillingworth killings.

The defence claimed that the prosecution was a plot to get rid of Peel for political purposes, it being well known that Phil O'Connell was a political boss in Palm Beach. This, in a state where judges were often elected by popular vote, was not so fantastic an idea as it seems.

But the prosecution were able to produce secretly made tape recordings of conversations between Peel and his associates which showed that he had masterminded the murder of Curtis and Marjorie Chillingworth.

The verdict was guilty of being an accessory before the fact in the Chillingworth murders, but the jury recommended mercy, which meant that Peel was spared the electric chair. He received two life sentences. Holzapfel was at first not so lucky. He was condemned to death, but reprieved at the last minute.

The aggressive O'Connell, who was disappointed that there had been no death sentences, defended the prosecution tactics. 'You can't go huntin' skunks', he claimed, 'in a tuxedo.'

Howard Wilson had served for ten years in the Glasgow police when he left to go into business. On the last day of 1969, together with two other men, he robbed a bank. They took the proceeds back to Wilson's flat in a car, but were seen unloading heavy suitcases by a police inspector, who recognized Wilson. The inspector, with a sergeant and three constables, entered the flat. Wilson produced a gun and fired, killing two policemen. He was overpowered and at his trial admitted full responsibility. In Scots law if the shots had been fired during the robbery all three would have been guilty of murder as they were acting in concert, but at the flat it was considered that Wilson had been acting on his own. He was convicted of murder and received a life sentence. His associates were convicted only of robbery.

Dr Marcel Petiot It was 11 March 1944, and the Germans still occupied Paris. Neighbours in the rue Le Sueur didn't really like calling the police, even though they were French police. The Germans might become involved. Worse still they might find themselves under investigation by the Gestapo. But the black smoke which had been pouring out of the chimney of number

21 for five days, choking the street and causing an appalling smell, was too much. Eventually someone reported it.

The police discovered that the owner of the building was a Dr Marcel Petiot and rang him to come and open up. When he didn't appear they broke in and discovered a stove in the basement burning what looked like a human body. Parts of other bodies including skeletons were strewn about the basement floor.

While this was going on a middle-aged man with piercing eyes rode up on a bicycle and took the head of the police detachment on one side. After asking if the officer was a true Frenchman he said that he was a member of the Resistance. The bodies, he explained, were traitors and Germans. The policeman advised him to make his escape quickly.

It took another seven months for the police to catch up with Petiot. During that time the Allies had invaded France, Paris had been liberated and Parisians set about dealing with collaborators. Active in the capital was the Resistance, known as the FFI (Force Française de l'Interieur), and when the police guessed that Petiot might have joined them under a false name they kept watch. He was soon recognized and arrested at a metro station.

Petiot's trial began at the Paris Palais de Justice in March 1946. He was charged with the murder of twenty-seven people. He admitted some of the killings, but said that he had been a member of the Resistance and had only used the house to dispose of the bodies of spies, traitors and occasionally Germans whom the Resistance had got rid of.

He pointed out that he himself had been arrested by the Gestapo in 1943, suspected of helping people to flee from occupied France, and had been held, interrogated and tortured for nearly eight months before being released.

Many of the bodies, he claimed, had been subsequently dumped there by the Resistance or the Germans themselves to incriminate him.

It was a persuasive story. But the prosecution had a different version. Petiot, they said, had only pretended to run an escape route. He had charged prospective clients 25,000 francs to get them out of the country, then allowed them to take large sums of money sewn into their clothes. After meeting them at a barber's shop he took them to 21 rue Le Sueur and there killed them, possibly by giving them poison in the guise of necessary inoculations, and stole their money.

The prosecution took the jury to 21 rue Le Sueur and showed them the triangular room which had been built on the back of another, furnished as a doctor's consulting room. The triangular room had only one door which was soundproofed. What looked like another door was in fact false; beyond it was a brick wall. The room had iron rings secured to one wall and a spyhole in another, so that a viewer could observe occupants inside.

Plainly it was the death room in which prisoners, possibly secured to the iron rings, would be left to die, while their death throes were watched from outside. This could only be the work of a monster who enjoyed seeing people suffer. The jury were also shown the forty-five suitcases containing assorted clothing which Petiot had collected from his victims and it became obvious that he had additionally killed for greed.

The jury took only three hours to convict Petiot on twenty-five of the twenty-seven counts of murder. He was guillotined on 25 May 1946, at Santé prison in Paris.

Eugen Weidmann was a German who led a gang in Paris in the 1930s. In six months they robbed and murdered six people, mostly by shooting them in the back of the neck. But a visiting card Weidmann dropped near the body of an estate agent he had murdered eventually led to his discovery. He was tried at Versailles in March 1939, together with three accomplices. He and another man, Roger Million, were condemned to death, the other two were acquitted. Million was reprieved, but Weidmann was guillotined on 18 May 1939 before a noisy crowd of thousands. The French president was so appalled that he abolished public executions.

Colin Pitchfork This was the first murder trial in which evidence of genetic fingerprinting was allowed, but in this case it turned out to be of more use in the investigation.

It began on 22 November 1983, when the body of fifteen-year-old Lynda Mann was found just off a path which ran beside the grounds of Carlton Hayes psychiatric hospital, between the villages of Narborough and Enderby, near the M1 motorway, just outside Leicester.

She had been raped and strangled, and from the high sperm count in the semen found on her the pathologist deduced that the murderer must have been a male between thirteen and thirty-four. But although appeals for information from the public were broadcast widely and the police interviewed literally thousands of people, they could not find the murderer.

Two-and-a-half years later, on 3 August 1986, the body of another fifteen-year-old, Dawn Ashworth, was discovered near a footpath on the other side of the hospital. She too had been raped and strangled.

This time, however, the police interviewed a seventeen-year-old kitchen porter at the hospital and after making a series of rambling statements he finally confessed and was charged with the murder of Dawn Ashworth. But the young man proved to be very fortunate.

Dr Alec Jeffreys at Leicester University had recently developed a technique by which DNA, extracted from body fluids or even the roots of hair, could be matched to an individual like a fingerprint. When semen from the young man was compared with samples of semen taken from Dawn's body they did not match and he was released.

Using the same technique it was shown that one man had murdered both Dawn Ashworth and Lynda Mann. The police then decided on a bold move. They would genetically fingerprint every young male in the area, and a campaign was mounted asking men to come in and give blood samples. The police estimated they would need to test nearly five thousand men. The cost was astronomical and the testing took months.

By August 1987 the project had nearly run out of steam. Almost all the men had been tested and no positive match had been obtained. The Home Office had warned the Leicestershire constabulary that the enquiry could not continue indefinitely. The squad had been reduced in numbers and morale was low.

Then Jackie Foggin, the young manageress of one of the Hampshire Bakery's shops in Leicester, was having a drink with other employees of the company when one, Ian Kelly, mentioned that he had taken the DNA blood test for a fellow bakery worker, Colin Pitchfork. Jackie reported the conversation to the police and twenty-seven-year-old Colin Pitchfork, who lived close to the hospital, was interviewed.

He immediately confessed to both murders. But what was more important, his DNA matched that found on the bodies of the two girls. His trial at Castle Court, Leicester, in September 1987, lasted only one day. He pleaded guilty, which is very unusual in a murder trial. Admitting the two murders, he said that he had only wanted to expose himself to the girls, having a history of this, and assaulted them only when they ran away into the narrow pathways, thus cutting off his escape route. He also pleaded guilty to the rape charges. Colin Pitchfork was sentenced to life terms for the murders and ten years each for the rapes.

Ian Kelly was convicted of conspiracy to pervert the course of justice and given an eighteen-month jail sentence, suspended for two years.

When, in February 1989, Ian Simms went on trial for murder, the significant forensic evidence was again genetic fingerprinting, but with a difference.

Pretty twenty-two-year-old Helen McCourt disappeared on her way from work in Liverpool to her home in the village of Billinge, near St Helens, on 9 February 1988. She had to pass a pub in the village called the George and Dragon, and a witness reported hearing a scream coming from the pub about ten minutes after Helen's bus would have dropped her off. The publican, Ian Simms, denied involvement, but was known to be friendly with Helen. Then most of her clothes were discovered in a plastic bin liner on a river bank near Manchester. Not far away were some clothes, including jeans, belonging to Simms which were heavily bloodstained.

At his trial in Liverpool Crown Court, forensic scientists claimed that by examining DNA from Helen's father and mother they were able to obtain a match with blood on Simms's jeans. It was 126,000 times more likely to have come from an offspring of Mr and Mrs McCourt than from a member of the public.

Ian Simms was convicted of murder and sentenced to life imprisonment. Helen McCourt's body has never been found.

Guenther Podola   On 13 July 1959 a man rang Mrs Verne Schiffman, an American model in London on holiday, at her rented flat in South Kensington. She was expecting the call. A few days earlier her flat had been burgled, and the burglar had written asking for $500 for the return of compromising documents he said were in his possession. She contacted the police who arranged to have her phone tapped and when the man rang she had instructions to keep him talking while the call was traced.

This resulted in two officers, Detective Sergeants Purdy and Sandford, racing round from Chelsea police station to South Kensington underground station, where the call had come from. They arrested a man in the act of calling Mrs Schiffman, but he struggled free, ran down the street and disappeared into the foyer of a block of flats in Onslow Square. He was soon recaptured inside, but after being made to sit on a marble windowledge, jumped down while Sergeant Purdy's attention was momentarily distracted, produced a gun and shot the officer through the heart. He then made his escape.

He was quickly identified, through a pocketbook he left behind and fingerprints on the window sill, as Guenther Podola, a thirty-year-old German, with a record of burglary and theft in Canada. Following a tip-off the police raided a hotel in Queen's Gate, Kensington, and after a struggle took him into custody.

At Chelsea police station he seemed dazed and unable to speak and after seven hours was taken to St Stephen's Hospital where he slowly regained the power of speech. After tests the doctors assumed he must be suffering from concussion and retrograde amnesia since he could not remember the events up to his admission to hospital. By 14 August, at the magistrates court in Fulham, where he was committed for trial on a charge of murder, he still claimed to be unable to remember anything of his past life except for a few 'memory windows'. His solicitor said that he had been unable to take any instructions from his client at all.

This state of affairs continued at his trial at the Old Bailey in September 1959. His counsel, Frederick Lawton QC, rose at the beginning to say that he had no notion of what his client's defence was since he could remember nothing. The judge, Mr Justice Edmund Davies, then decided that it would be up to the defence to prove to the jury that Podola's loss of memory was genuine; not to the usual standard of proof, 'beyond a reasonable doubt', but only to the lesser standard of the 'balance of probability'. If that were done, he would decide if it debarred Podola from being tried for Purdy's murder; and that being so, Podola would be held in custody 'during Her Majesty's pleasure'. This had never before occurred in an English murder trial.

Frederick Lawton brought forward four doctors who claimed that Podola's loss of memory was not faked. The prosecution, in the hands of Maxwell Turner QC, vigorously contested this, bringing their own two medical experts to testify that Podola's amnesia was not genuine. In addition the prosecution produced a letter which Podola had written from prison to a friend.

'Dear Ron' (Podola wrote), 'Thank you for your card. I was very pleasantly surprised to hear from you. How are you keeping yourself these days, old boy?' And after asking his friend to bring in magazines, etc., he concludes: 'It sure was nice to hear from you, Ron. Cordially yours, Mike' (Podola's alias).

Confronted in court by his erstwhile friend, Podola claimed that he did not know the man. However, the jury plainly did not believe him and their verdict was that Podola's amnesia was bogus.

The trial for murder then proceeded with a fresh jury, but the same judge and counsel. The result was a foregone conclusion. Detective Sergeant Sandford had seen Podola shoot his colleague at point-blank range and his fingerprints proved he was there. Podola declined to give evidence on oath as this would have meant exposing himself to cross-examination. Instead he chose to make an unsworn statement from the dock and spoke in a guttural German-American accent saying that he understood the accusations, but had no memory of the events to which they referred. The jury took only half an hour to find him guilty and he was sentenced to death.

He might still have cheated the hangman and gained a reprieve, for just before he was due to be executed he miraculously regained his memory. But instead of saying that the shooting was accidental he wrote to his solicitor and his friend Ron trying to establish an alibi and claiming that he wasn't even present at the shooting. It was a futile effort and he was executed on 5 November 1959, the last man to suffer the death penalty at Wandsworth prison for killing a policeman.

Peter Queen Is it possible for a woman to tie a rope around her neck and strangle herself? This is what the jury had to decide in a trial which began in January 1932 at the High Court of Judiciary in Glasgow. Was it suicide or murder?

Peter Queen had rushed into Partick police station, Glasgow, at three a.m. on 31 November 1931 and told the police to go to his flat on Dumbarton Road, where he thought his wife was dead. He next claimed that he said: 'Don't think I have killed her.' Two police officers later reported that he said: 'I think I have killed her.'

Twenty-eight-year-old Chrissie Gall, who was Queen's common-law wife, lay in bed in her nightclothes with no sign of a struggle on the bed or in the room. A piece of clothesline was knotted tightly round her neck. Death, the pathologist reported, was due to strangulation. Also in the bed, propped up on the next pillow, was a bottle of beer.

Chrissie Gall had met Peter Queen five years before when she had been a nursemaid to his father's young children by a second marriage. Queen was three years older than her and married, but separated from his wife who was in a home for alcoholics. They fell in love and eventually she went to live with him, but became very depressed because they were 'living in sin', drank heavily, and had several times threatened to commit suicide.

An impressive array of medical talent appeared at the trial. Bernard (later Sir Bernard) Spilsbury, then at the height of his powers, appeared for the defence and said categorically that the death was suicide. John Glaister, Professor of Forensic Medicine at Glasgow University and a very eminent pathologist, was just as sure that it was murder. The Professor of Forensic Medicine at Edinburgh University, Sydney (afterwards Sir Sydney) Smith, appeared for the defence, but was not so certain as Spilsbury, though he was inclined to believe it was suicide.

The judge, Lord Alness, perhaps feeling that the medical heavyweights cancelled each other out, directed the jury's attention to the general evidence, including the behaviour of Peter Queen.

By his own account, on finding Chrissie he had made no attempt to loosen the ligature, revive her or call a doctor, but had rushed straight round to the police station and told them that he had not killed her. But he had no discernible motive and all the people who knew them said he was always loving and kind to Chrissie.

The jury took two hours to find Peter Queen guilty of murder, but made a strong recommendation for mercy. He was sentenced to death. An appeal failed but the Secretary of State for Scotland commuted the sentence to life imprisonment. He was eventually released and died in 1958.

In his book *Mostly Murder*, Sir Sydney Smith quotes the case of a woman in Westcliff-on-Sea, who was found dead in bed in a locked room with several scarves tied round her neck and a small handkerchief stuffed into her mouth. She had died from strangulation and smothering. She had a history of suicide attempts and was known to be depressed over the death of her mother. Plainly she had killed herself and Smith wonders what would have happened if the case, which happened only a year after the trial, had become known to the jury.

Florence Ransom During this trial the jury were allowed to go home at night instead of being put up in a hotel, the first time this had happened in recent times, because the trial was held at the Old Bailey in November 1940 and German air-raids were nightly expected over the city. Presumably the authorities wanted to avoid the risk of one bomb wiping out the jury. Spotters on the roof of the building kept watch during the day for enemy planes. The tragedy which had occurred in a sleepy orchard in Matfield, Kent, that hot summer, however, had nothing to do with the war.

In the evening of 9 July, the bodies of three women were found in various places in the garden and orchard of a cottage called 'Crittenden'. Mrs Dorothy Fisher was forty-eight, her daughter Freda twenty and the housekeeper Charlotte Saunders was forty-seven. All three had been shot with a sporting gun, each more than once and Freda three times. Windows and doors in the cottage were open and inside it looked as if there had been a burglary. But a pile of smashed crockery in the kitchen, when painstakingly put together by the police, revealed that a visitor had taken tea there that afternoon. And a woman's glove was found in the orchard.

Mr Fisher did not live with his wife. He was the editor of a motoring magazine with offices in London and lived on a farm in Oxfordshire with a lady who sometimes called herself Mrs Fisher, but was also known as Mrs Ransom. However, it seemed an amicable arrangement for all concerned; the two parts of the family frequently visited each other and appeared to be on good terms.

Nevertheless the attractive red-haired Mrs Ransom was put on trial for the murder of Mrs Fisher.

Four witnesses had seen a red-haired woman wearing trousers – an unusual sight in those days – and carrying a parcel which might well have been a shotgun, in Matfield on the afternoon of the murder. Two had given her a lift to Tonbridge railway station and a ticket collector there remembered a woman with a parcel enquiring about trains to London. All these identified the woman as Mrs Ransom.

Her brother, who worked on the farm, gave evidence that she had borrowed a shotgun the day before the murder, after asking him to show her how it worked. She also took about a dozen cartridges. Although she returned the gun the day following the murder she brought back none of the cartridges.

Mrs Ransom went into the witness box to claim that she knew nothing about the crime, but she did not have an alibi and nobody had seen her on the farm that day. The prosecution claimed that there was evidence of a meeting a few days before the crime at Crittenden between Mrs Ransom and Mr and Mrs Fisher at which Mrs Fisher flatly refused to agree to a divorce.

The jury took only forty-seven minutes to find Mrs Ransom guilty of murder. When the judge put on the black cap for the death sentence she collapsed.

But she didn't hang. Although her appeal was dismissed she was certified insane and confined at Broadmoor Asylum.

In March 1948, Broadmoor inmates produced a play called *The Earl and the Girl*. The part of Daphne Brent was played by Mrs Florence Ransom.

Winnie Ruth Judd went to Los Angeles by train on 18 October 1931 with two trunks, one of which dripped a dark red liquid. Station staff found they contained the bodies of two young women she had previously lived with in Phoenix, Arizona, one of them cut up into pieces. At her trial in January 1932, she claimed the girls were shot accidentally and a businessman friend helped her cut up one of the bodies. She was found guilty and sentenced to death. The businessman had the charges against him dismissed. Then Judd was granted a retrial. This time she was found insane and confined to an asylum. She absconded seven times, once for six years, before being paroled in 1971.

Alma Rattenbury and George Stoner   The trial of Mrs Rattenbury and Stoner for the murder of her husband Francis was similar to the earlier trial of Thompson and Bywaters (*see* p. 310). Each pair were lovers and the male partner had killed the woman's husband. Both trials took place in the same room at the Old Bailey, one in 1928, the other in 1935. Travers (later Sir Travers) Humphreys who prosecuted Edith Thompson and Frederick Bywaters in 1928 and secured guilty verdicts on both, was in 1935 the judge in the trial of Rattenbury and Stoner. But times had changed. Over the years public feeling had been growing that Edith Thompson should not have been hanged, and Mr Justice Humphreys himself made a significant contribution to Alma Rattenbury's fate . . .

Francis Rattenbury was an eminent architect in Canada when he met Alma, a noted musician and composer. Both were already married; Alma had been married twice before, and whereas Francis was sixty, Alma was only thirty-one. They eventually married in 1928, but the scandal forced them to leave Canada and they went to live in Bournemouth. After their son John was born sexual relations between them virtually ended.

In September 1934, seventeen-year-old George Stoner was engaged by Alma as a handyman/chauffeur. They soon became lovers. George was given a room in the Villa Madeira, where the Rattenburys now lived, but spent many nights in Alma's bed, since she had a separate room to her husband. Mrs Rattenbury became besotted with Stoner, and in late March 1935 she took him with her to London where she bought him expensive suits and silk pyjamas. When they returned Stoner's head was completely turned.

The Rattenburys decided to go away for a few days to stay with a friend of Francis. Stoner became violently jealous because he thought Alma and Francis would be sleeping together.

On the afternoon of Sunday 24 March he borrowed a mallet from his grandparents, and when he slipped into Alma's bed that night he told her she wouldn't be going away the next day as he'd hit Francis with it. Alma rushed downstairs to find Francis with severe head wounds, slumped in a chair. She became hysterical and screamed for her companion-help, Miss Irene Riggs, who also lived at the Villa Madeira. Miss Riggs phoned for Dr O'Connell who took Francis to hospital, where it became obvious that the injuries could not have been self-inflicted. The police were called.

Later Dr O'Connell returned to the Villa Madeira to find the lights all on, a gramophone playing and Mrs Rattenbury very drunk indeed. The police were there in force and Alma was explaining to them that she had killed her husband with a mallet. The doctor finally got her to bed and gave her an injection of morphine.

Next morning when she awoke Inspector Carter was in her room and she again said that she had killed Francis. She was taken to the police station where she was charged with murder and made a statement admitting it. She was transferred to Holloway prison in London.

Stoner visited her there and while he was away Miss Riggs got in touch with Dr O'Connell to explain that Stoner had confessed to her that he had killed Mr Rattenbury. The doctor called the police and Stoner was arrested when he returned. He immediately admitted hitting Francis with the mallet, saying that Alma had had nothing to do with it.

Nevertheless, they were tried together for murder in May 1935. During Inspector Carter's evidence Mr Justice Humphreys asked to see his notebook. After inspecting it he pointed out that the inspector had made notes of two statements by Mrs Rattenbury admitting the killing, one when she first woke up and the other two hours later. The inspector said that he had not mentioned the first because he felt Mrs Rattenbury might then still have been under the influence of the morphine.

But the judge pointed out to the jury that the two statements were virtually identical; if the first was considered to be made under the influence of the drug then so must the second. The jury took the hint and brought in a verdict of not guilty.

Stoner did not go into the witness box. Through his counsel he claimed not to have meant to kill Rattenbury and to have been under the influence of cocaine. But he was found guilty of murder and sentenced to death.

Alma had already decided that should Stoner be convicted and not her, she would commit suicide. Three days after he was sentenced she stabbed herself to death.

Stoner was reprieved and the sentence commuted to life imprisonment.

Horace Rayner   On the morning of 24 January 1907, the door of William Whiteley's office was flung open and the seventy-five-year-old businessman came rushing out.

'James!' he shouted to one of the clerks in the outer office. 'Fetch a policeman, quick!'

A young man had followed him out of the office and the older man turned to him. 'Not this time, sir. Not this time.'

The young man stepped forward and put out his hand in a friendly way. Whiteley ignored it. 'I have sent for a policeman,' he warned.

The other's face contorted. 'Then you're a dead man!' he shouted.

He reached into his breast pocket and drew a gun. Pointing

it at Whiteley's head he fired. Then he turned the gun on himself and pulled the trigger.

Both men fell to the ground. The older man was found to be dead, but the younger survived. The bullet had entered his right cheek and exited by his nose, damaging his nose and destroying his right eye in its progress. As he was being taken to hospital he muttered: 'My name is Cecil Whiteley. I am the son of Mr William Whiteley.'

The young man was patched up, fitted with a glass eye, and stood trial for the murder of William Whiteley at the Old Bailey in March 1907, under the name by which he normally went – Horace Rayner.

The trial created a sensation because Mr Whiteley was the famous founder of Whiteley's, the largest of London's department stores. He called himself 'The Universal Provider' and claimed, as Harrods was to do later, to sell everything. A pillar of Victorian rectitude and hypocrisy, he was always ready to talk to journalists about his own success and the virtues of hard work, honesty and uprightness.

Yet it was the newspapers who revealed the true nature of the man, in the weeks leading up to the trial, when they picked up on and investigated Rayner's statement that he was the dead man's son.

William Whiteley married one of the first two lady assistants he employed in his original small shop. As his business expanded he had a succession of mistresses drawn from his shop-workers. One of these was Louisa Turner. She had a younger sister, Emily, and soon the two girls began to make a foursome with Whiteley and his friend George Rayner, going to the races with them and spending weekends at Brighton.

In 1879 Emily bore a child, whom she called Horace, and although Rayner was living with her at the time he was convinced that the child was not his. Nevertheless he supported the boy and allowed him to use his name. In 1888 Rayner and Whiteley fell out, the entrepreneur accusing his friend of having an affair with Louisa and Rayner replying by asserting that Whiteley was the father of Horace. The boy also seems to have heard this from his mother.

Horace Rayner was twenty-seven when he eventually went to see Whiteley. He was married and his wife was expecting their third child. Having been out of work for a long time he had pawned nearly everything they possessed. Rayner had told his landlord that he was at the end of his tether.

The jury heard him describe how he had secured an audience with Whiteley by pretending to have a message from the shop owner's solicitor. Once in the office he told Whiteley that he believed he was his father. The older man made no comment and merely asked what he wanted. Rayner then poured out his troubles, finishing by saying that he could not get a job. Whiteley replied to this by asking if he would like to go abroad. The young man perked up, thinking help was at hand, and said he would be delighted to go abroad. Whiteley then advised him to go to the Salvation Army for assistance.

This so incensed Rayner that he took out a revolver and threatened to commit suicide. Whiteley told him not to be silly and he put it back in his pocket. Then, while Whiteley sat opposite, he wrote the following in a notebook:

> To whom it may concern – William Whiteley is my father.
> He has brought upon himself and me a double fatality
> by reason of his own refusal of a request perfectly
> reasonable.
>
> – R. I. P.

While he was writing this Whiteley got up and left the room.

The prosecuting counsel was Mr (later Sir) Richard Muir who had a reputation as a brilliant lawyer and ruthless cross-examiner. Yet he did not cross-examine Rayner at all. Perhaps he felt the case against the defendant was so strong he didn't need to, or perhaps he didn't want to open the can of worms which the hidden background of the famous entrepreneur undoubtedly was.

The only defence Rayner really had was that of insanity and the Lord Chief Justice, Lord Alverstone, who presided, agreed with the prosecution that there was no evidence of that. The jury required only ten minutes to bring in a verdict of guilty. The judge then took obvious pleasure in telling Rayner that he could not hold out the slightest hope that the sentence of death would not be carried out.

But he was wrong. Sympathy for the condemned man grew rapidly and a petition containing 200,000 signatures was handed to the Home Secretary. He reprieved Rayner and commuted the sentence to twenty years.

It is said that Richard Muir was pleased, but Lord Alverstone could never understand why the death sentence had not been carried out. The unhappy young man, who obtained the maximum remission and served only twelve years, tried to commit suicide while in prison, and on his release lived only another two years.

Melvin Rees On 15 June 1955, sixteen-year-old Nancy Shomette and her fourteen-year-old friend Ann Ryan were found dead in a park near their home in Lewisville, just outside Washington DC, USA. Neither had been raped, but both had been gunned down with a 0.22 Marlin rifle and Nancy had been shot repeatedly in the stomach and breasts. Clearly it was some kind of sex crime.

Although half the resources of the local police department were deployed on the case, they had no more clues at the end of the investigation than they had at the beginning.

A year later, two girls were given a lift by a young man in a blue Ford car near Beltsville, again on the outskirts of Washington. About a week later one of the girls, sixteen-year-old Shelby Venable, was found floating in the Potomac River. She was naked and had been raped, sexually mutilated and strangled. The other, Mary Fellers, who was eighteen, was found after another week in Catoctin Creek, Virginia. She too had been sexually abused and strangled.

Once again the police, from two states this time, had few clues to work on and the investigation gradually came to a halt.

In June 1957, Master Sergeant Roy Hudson gave a lift to thirty-four-year-old Margaret Harold from the army camp at Fort Meade, Maryland, where they both worked. They stopped to talk near an old abandoned farm cottage about ten miles west of Annapolis. After some time they were approached by a dark-haired young man with scruffy jeans who produced a gun and got into the back of the car. He tried to fondle Margaret Harold and when she resisted shot her in the back of the head. This gave the sergeant time to roll out of the car. He was chased and shot at, but managed to get away and give the alarm.

The police found a basement room in the derelict cottage which had a wall covered with pornographic pictures, but apart from this there was little evidence as to who the gunman was.

The killer did not strike for another eighteen months. Then in January 1959, Carroll Jackson, a twenty-nine-year-old sales-man, his wife Millie and their daughters, five-year-old Susan and eighteen-month-old Janet, vanished. Their empty car was found parked on a lonely road some fifteen miles from their home at Apple Grove, Virginia. It appeared to have been forced off the road and the family abducted. Two months later the body of Carroll Jackson was found forty miles away in a shallow grave. He had been beaten, then shot. The baby lay beneath him. She had suffocated under the weight of her father's body.

About three weeks later Millie Jackson was found buried, with her daughter Susan, in some woods quite close to where Margaret Harold had been murdered. Indeed the basement room of the old farm cottage looked as if it had been the place where Mrs Jackson was sexually tortured before being beaten to death with a gun. The child had been despatched with a blow to the back of the head. Once again there was not the slightest indication as to the identity of the killer.

A year later, Glen Moser, who had once studied at the University of Maryland, reported to the FBI in Virginia that he was suspicious of his friend Melvin Rees, who had been a fellow student, was now a musician, and most important of all a Benzedrene addict.

Rees had disappeared, but in his parents' house in a northern suburb of Washington, where he had lived, the FBI discovered hidden in an accordion case a bone-handled 0.38 pistol and a diary. The diary contained graphic descriptions of the abduction and killing of the Jacksons, the murder of Margaret Harold and the rape and murder of Mary Fellers and Shelby Venable. But it also described the murders of many more – murders for which others had been convicted. Clearly Melvin Rees could not possibly have done them all. Did that mean that the document was all imagination?

The FBI eventually tracked down Rees to West Memphis, where he was working as a piano salesman, teaching music and playing in a local jazz band. Master Sergeant Hudson was brought to the city and he identified the musician as the man who had shot Margaret Harold.

Since Millie Jackson had been murdered in Maryland, Rees was tried for her murder in January 1961 in Baltimore, Maryland. The evidence was circumstantial. The prosecution attempted to prove that the gun found at the musician's parents' home was the one used on Mrs Jackson. There were traces of blood on it, but the amounts were too small to determine the blood group.

The diary too was inaccurate as to details, Melvin Rees having written of hanging the woman, when she was actually beaten to death.

The musician also had a good reputation as a teacher of music and said that on the night the Jacksons were abducted he was playing in a band, though other members could not be certain he was there, after a two-year interval.

The judge did allow evidence from the murder of Carroll Jackson to be used in the Millie Jackson trial and the prosecution produced its star witness.

Near where Carroll Jackson's body had been found, the FBI discovered some discarded brown plastic butt pieces which had come from the grip of a handgun. An expert at the FBI laboratory had examined these and was able to show, from microscopic examination, that they had originally come from Melvin Rees's 0.38. This placed him firmly at the spot where the salesman had been murdered, and the jury of eleven men and one woman had no difficulty convicting him of the murder of Mrs Jackson. He was sentenced to life imprisonment. In Maryland no one had been executed since 1921.

But the murder of Carroll Jackson had taken place in Virginia and Rees was accordingly extradited to stand trial at Spotsylvania, Virginia, in September 1961. The trial was largely a re-run of the previous one. He was found guilty and, since Virginia had the death penalty, executed.

Richard Robles/George Whitmore   This case, for there was more to it than just a trial, resulted in an important decision of the American Supreme Court, spawned a major film and the TV series Kojac, episodes of which can still be seen on British TV, and, in keeping with its sensational outcome, began with a murder which shocked New York.

On a hot August day in 1963 the bodies of two young women were found in their apartment in a select part of Manhattan. Janice Wylie, a pretty blonde twenty-one-year-old, was the niece of bestselling novelist Philip Wylie. She was naked. Emily Hoffert, her flatmate, was fully dressed. The girls had been tied together with strips cut from a bedsheet and their bodies horribly mutilated with stab wounds and beaten with Coca-Cola bottles.

The Manhattan police interviewed thousands of people, one theory being that the murderer was known to the two girls, but were not able to find the killer.

The following April a forty-six-year-old black cleaning woman, Minnie Edmonds, was stabbed to death in what looked like an attempt at rape in an alley in Brooklyn. About a week later, and not very far away, twenty-year-old Elba Borrero was attacked while walking home late one night. A young black man grabbed her bag and attempted to rape her, but was interrupted by Patrolman Isola, who fired at him as he made his escape.

Later that night Isola saw a young black man huddling for warmth in the doorway of a laundromat only a block from where the woman had been attacked. George Whitmore was twenty, not very bright, had trouble reading and writing and didn't have a job, but had never been in trouble with the police. Questioned later at a police station in Brooklyn he was soon persuaded to confess to the attempted rape, then to the murder of Minnie Edmonds.

While his pockets were being turned out, a detective noticed a photograph of two white girls sitting in a convertible. The one in the back seat was blonde and the detective, who had worked on the Wylie/Hoffert murder, identified her as Janice Wylie. Although George Whitmore initially said that he had picked up the picture from a rubbish dump near his home, in no time at all he had confessed to the murder of the two girls in Manhattan.

But Manhattan has a separate police force from Brooklyn and a different district attorney, and an assistant DA in Manhattan couldn't quite believe the sixty-one-page confession of George Whitmore. It was too close to what the police knew of the crime and contained nothing that the police did not know. Patient investigation established that the girl in the photograph was not Janice Wylie, but a girl from Whitmore's home town of Wildwood, New Jersey. And witnesses placed Whitmore in Wildwood on the day of the Wylie/Hoffert murders.

In October 1964, a New York drug dealer, Nathan Delany, who had been arrested for murder, struck a deal with the police. He told them that a twenty-two-year-old drug addict and ex-convict, Richard Robles, had come to his house on the day of the murders covered in blood and confessed that he'd 'iced two dames'.

Robles vehemently denied the murders, but due to Delany's evidence and taped conversations he had with Robles, the ex-convict was finally brought to trial in October 1965 and convicted of the murders. The death penalty had been suspended in New York State, largely due to the Whitmore case, and Robles was sent to prison for life. It will be 2019 before he is eligible for parole.

In June 1966 the Supreme Court of the United States ruled that the Fifth Amendment's privilege against self-incrimination became effective the moment a person was taken into custody. The suspect must be informed of his constitutional rights: to remain silent, to have a lawyer and be provided with one if he can't afford one. And the court cited the Whitmore case as a flagrant example of psychological intimidation.

In another case the British police came in for public criticism, this time unjustly. It occurred in Abertillery in 1921. Fifteen-year-old Harold Jones was accused of the murder during an attempted rape of an eight-year-old girl. But the Scotland Yard detective in charge of the case so offended local sensibilities by his high-handed manner, that at Jones's trial several people came forward to give him an alibi. He was acquitted. Fourteen days later eleven-year-old Florence Little's body was found in the attic of his home. He confessed, and also confessed to the earlier murder. His lawyer rushed to get the trial on before Jones's sixteenth birthday, to save him from the death penalty. He was sentenced to be detained during His Majesty's pleasure.

Marthinus Rossouw   Did a man plan his own murder? That was the question for the jury when twenty-three-year-old Marthinus Rossouw stood before them in the High Court in Cape Town in September 1961. If it was true it certainly was a crazy scheme. But then the man who allegedly hatched it was a man out of the ordinary.

In the first place he was a baron: Baron Dietrich Joachim Gunther von Schauroth, usually called Dieter, whose father had been a German aristocrat who had settled in south-west Africa before the First World War. Unfortunately he was as unlike his tall, energetic, resourceful father as it was possible to be. Short, and with no great intellectual ability or industry, he had a number of jobs and enterprises and failed in nearly all of them. Nevertheless he loved spending money and pretending to be a rich man which, at the end, he was not.

His younger brother Udo was more like their father. Tall, he took a science degree at university, became a successful surveyor, married a girl with wealthy parents, and bought his own farm. When the old baron died, in March 1958, he split the land between his two sons, giving the larger section, including the ancestral home, to Udo, with the proviso that should either sell his land it first had to be offered within the family at a low price. This effectively meant that Dieter could not realize on his own land. To cap it all, in May 1959 he married a girl from the wrong side of the tracks.

However, they seemed to be very much in love and soon produced their firstborn. In December 1959 Dieter began taking out large insurance policies on his own life and by March 1961 had made a will disposing of over £200,000 in insurance, several million pounds at today's prices, and was paying nearly £2,000 per year in premiums, which it was said he could not afford. Just before he died he took out a short-term life policy for £70,000.

In January 1961 Dieter met Marthinus Rossouw, a shady character who was a poorly paid railway worker, but was supposed to have contacts with black diggers illegally selling diamonds. He was greatly taken with the flamboyant Dieter and apparently the two became firm friends. According to Marthinus, at one stage his friend asked him if he would murder someone and the railway worker, assuming it was a joke, said yes.

On the night of Friday 24 March, again according to Marthinus, they met and drove north out of Cape Town, stopping at several bars on the way. But Dieter insisted they enter each separately and pretend they didn't know each other. When they had gone about sixteen miles they turned into an abandoned road and Dieter, handing Marthinus a gun, asked his friend to shoot him in the back of the neck. He gave the railway worker a post-dated cheque with a note saying it was for 'services rendered' and told him his bank manager would give him £5,000.

Dieter's body was found the next morning and Marthinus, having been seen with Dieter the previous night, was soon picked up. He eventually told the whole story and made a signed statement before a magistrate. He also showed the police where he had thrown the gun into the sea. It was recovered and matched to the bullets taken from Dieter.

At the trial, Judge-President Andries Beyers instructed the jury that since Marthinus had admitted he deliberately killed Dieter, they were obliged to return a verdict of guilty of murder. Under South African law they could, however, if they wished, find 'extenuating circumstances', which might tend to diminish morally, but not legally, the prisoner's guilt. The judge might then not apply the death sentence, although he could ignore the jury's findings if he chose.

The prosecution case was to suggest that there were no extenuating circumstances. The body had been found on its back and the pattern of bloodstains on the face suggested it had been turned over soon after the shooting. The pockets were empty, but two witnesses from the bars the pair had visited claimed that they saw a wad of money in Dieter's pocket. The suggestion was that Marthinus had deliberately killed Dieter to rob him.

The jury had to decide whether the story of one man asking another to shoot him was true. They decided it was not and were thus unable to find any extenuating circumstances. Marthinus Rossouw was sentenced to death and was hanged on 19 June 1962.

Authorities who have since studied the case, detailed in Henry John May's book, have given their opinion that there was compelling evidence that Dieter von Schauroth had indeed conspired to have Marthinus murder him. And May's book is called *Murder by Consent*.

Walter Rowland At 11 a.m. on Sunday 20 October, 1946, Olive Balchin, a prostitute, was found dead on a bombsite near the centre of Manchester. She had been killed by blows to the head and face from a hammer, which was found near the body.

It was a special kind known as a leather dresser's hammer and it was recognized, from a picture inserted in the local newspaper, by the shopkeeper who had sold it to a man on the very Saturday of the murder. He described him as wearing a dark suit and a fawn raincoat.

A waitress in a café near the site of the murder told police she saw a man come in with two women at 10.30 to 11 p.m. on the Saturday night. She identified one of the women as Olive Balchin. About midnight the same night a publican out walking his dog said he saw the prostitute and a man quarrelling near the bombsite. He said the man was wearing a dark suit.

Further enquiries by the police led them to Walter Rowland. During questioning he admitted that he knew Olive Balchin, had met her on the Friday and had promised to meet her the next night. He had also begun treatment for venereal disease that day and suspected Olive of having given it to him. 'If I had been sure it was her,' he said, 'I would have strangled her.'

At an identification parade the shopkeeper picked out Rowland immediately as the man who had bought the hammer, and the waitress also identified him, though with some hesitation. The publican said Rowland was the man he had seen with Olive Balchin on the night of the murder.

Rowland's story was that he had been at his parents' home in New Mills until he boarded a bus to Manchester at 9.30 p.m. He got off at Stockport and had a drink in the Wellington Hotel. While he was there at about 10.30 he saw two policemen.

It was afterwards confirmed that two policemen did walk through the bar at about this time, though neither remembered seeing Rowland. This evidence conflicted with that of the waitress who said she saw him at 10.30 to 11, for Stockport is some seven miles from the centre of Manchester and he would have had considerable difficulty getting there for that time.

Rowland's trial opened in December 1946 at the Manchester Assizes. His admissions to the police that he thought Olive Balchin had given him VD went heavily against him as did the identifications by the three witnesses. The jury took only two hours to find him guilty and he was sentenced to death.

But no blood was discovered on his suit and it was the only one he had. It was suggested that he wore a fawn mac and afterwards discarded it, but the man seen by the publican at midnight wasn't wearing a mac. Besides, the three witnesses who identified Rowland all gave different descriptions of the man they'd seen: one said he was thin and dark, another that he had a round face and dark hair and the other that he had black hair. Rowland's hair was fair.

As Rowland's submission to the Court of Criminal Appeal was being prepared, David Ware made a detailed confession to the crime. A prisoner in Walton jail at the time, he had been diagnosed as a manic-depressive in 1943. His confession, however, was not allowed as evidence in the appeal, which was subsequently dismissed, though the court suggested that the Home Secretary order an inquiry.

On 21 February 1947, J. C. Jolly KC was asked to conduct an inquiry and given six days to do it, since Rowland was due to be hanged on 27 February. During the investigation Ware withdrew his confession and Mr Jolly reported that no miscarriage of justice had occurred in Rowland's conviction. The condemned man was executed two days later.

Some observers have pointed out that Rowland was already a convicted murderer. In 1934 he received a life sentence for strangling his baby daughter. The jury recommended mercy and he was released in 1942.

Four years after Rowland's execution Ware bought a hammer and attacked a woman on the Downs near Bristol in precisely the same manner that Olive Balchin was killed. The woman luckily survived. Ware was found to be insane and sent to Broadmoor.

Robert Wood, an artist, was tried at the Old Bailey in December 1907 for the murder of prostitute Phyllis Dimmock, in Camden Town. He was defended by the redoubtable Edward Marshall Hall. Wood had asked his girlfriend to give him a false alibi and tried to persuade witnesses, who recognized his handwriting on a postcard sent to Phyllis, not to come forward. But Marshall Hall dealt severely with several witness identifications and made a powerful and persuasive speech to the jury. His client was found not guilty.

S

Nicola Sacco and Bartolomeo Vanzetti This American trial, or rather trials, for there were two, caused political reactions, most of them adverse, in almost every large city in the world. American embassies were attacked and bombs were thrown at the house of the judge in charge.

The case began on the morning of Christmas Eve 1919, in Bridgewater, a small manufacturing town some thirty miles south of Boston, Massachusetts. A lorry carrying the wages of a shoe-making firm was fired on by some foreign-looking men, one with a shotgun. When the lorry occupants returned fire the assailants escaped in a car, leaving behind a cartridge case.

On 15 April 1920, two employees of the Slater & Morrill Shoe Factory, Parmenter and Berardelli, were carrying boxes containing money across the street in South Braintree, a neighbouring town, when two men gunned them down and escaped in a car with the boxes. Berardelli was shot four times on the spot and the autopsy produced four 0.32 calibre bullets. Parmenter was killed running away.

Two Italian emigrants were later arrested on a tram near Bridgewater. Twenty-nine-year-old Nicola Sacco was carrying a 0.32 Colt Automatic and thirty-two-year-old Bartolomeo Vanzetti had a 0.38 calibre revolver and shotgun cases in his pockets. Both had anarchist literature on them.

At that time in America many people were bitterly hostile to 'radicals', who included socialists, communists and anarchists, and many foreign nationals accused of being radicals had been deported.

Sacco, who worked in a shoe factory, had an unbreakable alibi from his employer for the day of the Bridgewater attack, but Vanzetti, who was a self-employed fish peddler, did not. He was tried for assault in Plymouth in June 1920 before Judge Webster Thayer.

There was little against him. Cartridges found in his pocket were said to be similar to those found after the attack. Five witnesses said they recognized him, but descriptions they'd previously given did not tally. Vanzetti produced sixteen witnesses to say he was selling them fish at the time of the assault, but District Attorney Katzmann dismissed this as an attempt by the Italian community to shield one of their own. Vanzetti was convicted and sentenced to serve twelve to fifteen years in jail.

This was followed by the trial of Sacco and Vanzetti in May 1921, at Dedham, ten miles outside Boston, for the murder of Berardelli and Parmenter. Katzmann, who again prosecuted, produced witnesses who swore the prisoners were at the scene of the crime, even though there had been no proper identification parades. The pair were simply placed before witnesses who were then asked if these were the men.

The prosecution produced two experts who claimed that at least one of the bullets taken from Berardelli's body had been fired from Sacco's gun. But such was the primitive state of the science of ballistics at the time that the defence was able to produce two equally eminent authorities who claimed that it had not.

Politics soon came into the trial. Katzmann cross-examined Vanzetti on a speech he had been due to make to returning soldiers on workers' rights, and pilloried Sacco because he had gone to Mexico during the First World War to avoid enlisting in the American armed services.

The jury were out for nearly five hours, but they returned with a verdict of guilty against both men. Judge Thayer said he would pass sentence at a later date.

Then began the first of six appeals for a retrial. Most of them went to Judge Thayer. The last one went to the Massachusetts Supreme Court, in April 1927, but this too was rejected. Four days later Sacco and Vanzetti were sentenced to death.

A final appeal was made to Governor Fuller, who appointed a three-man commission, headed by the president of Harvard University, to examine the case. This was completed in August and on the basis of the report the governor refused to order a retrial. Sacco and Vanzetti were executed in Charleston state prison on 23 August 1927.

But the controversy continued. At least twelve books have been written about the case, most of them considering that the trials and executions were travesties of justice. On 19 July 1977, fifty years later, Governor Dukakis of Massachusetts made a proclamation including the words: 'any stigma and disgrace should be forever removed from the names of Nicola Sacco and Bartolomeo Vanzetti'.

Michael Sams Michael Sams was a strategist but not a tactician; a brilliant planner, but not a man of action. When his plans went wrong and he saw his face on Crimewatch UK he was unable to do anything except sit around waiting for the police to arrive.

For some years he had pondered the possibilities of obtaining a large sum of money by kidnapping or extortion, and according to his own account had made several abortive attempts. The first that the police knew about it was when Julie Dart, a pretty eighteen-year-old who, unbeknown to her family, was working as a prostitute in the Chapeltown area of Leeds, disappeared on 9 July 1991. The West Yorkshire police soon received a ransom note for £145,000 with the warning that if it was not paid the hostage would die.

Julie's naked body was found in a field near the village of Easton, not far from Grantham, Lincolnshire, on 19 July. She had been hit on the back of the head and strangled.

But even after this Sams continued to send the police letters and notes in what seemed to be a bizarre game reminiscent of the phoney tape in the Yorkshire Ripper case. Most of the letters were ill-written and full of spelling errors and contained additional demands for money with threats that he would kidnap other prostitutes.

This culminated in a letter to the senior executive of British Rail, threatening to derail a high-speed express unless £200,000 was paid. But the attempt at blackmail came to an end when a large piece of sandstone was found on the track below a bridge near the village of Millmeece, Staffordshire. It had plainly been intended to hang from the bridge to damage the electrical pick-up of a train, but had failed to work properly.

On Wednesday 22 January, 1992, Stephanie Slater, a twenty-five-year-old estate agent, was kidnapped when showing a client, who was Sams, round a property in Turnberry Road, Birmingham. The next day a letter was received at Shipways, the branch estate agency where she worked, demanding £175,000. This was followed by tape-recorded messages made by Stephanie while in captivity and played over the phone.

Shipways were a fairly large firm, owning sixty branches, and they agreed to pay the ransom. Sams nominated Kevin Watts, manager of the branch where Stephanie worked, as courier for the money and on the following Tuesday Kevin received a telephone call from him to confirm instructions for delivering the money. It was Sams's first mistake . . .

The next day Kevin was led from call box to call box starting from Glossop, in Derbyshire, across the Pennines towards Penistone and eventually to a narrow lane near Oxspring. He was carrying the money in a bag fitted with a bug so the West Midlands police could follow it, and he was accompanied by police cars, in front and behind, at discreet distances. He kept in touch with them by a phone in his car.

But near Oxspring he lost contact with the police and, follow-

ing instructions he found at the side of the road, emptied the
money into another bag he found on top of the stone side of a
bridge. It was then pulled off by a rope attached to it and hanging
down over the bridge. Sams, standing below, in a track which
had once been a railway line, retrieved the money and made his
getaway on a motorcycle. The thousand police officers who had
been deployed in the operation to catch him were left literally
holding the empty bag.

But it was good news for Stephanie. She had been concealed
in Sams's workshop in Newark, Nottinghamshire. Forced to sleep
at night squeezed into a wooden coffin inside a wheely bin and
hardly able to move, she was mostly tied up during the day,
and blindfolded all the time. She suffered from the bitter cold and
had been in constant fear for her life. But the next day Sams
dropped her off near her home in Great Barr, Birmingham.

His red Mini was seen by a man who lived near Stephanie.
This, together with recordings of his voice police had made from
his telephone calls, and the artist-drawn likeness they were able
to produce from the descriptions given by Stephanie, provided
the clues which were to trap him.

They were presented on a BBC Crimewatch UK programme
on 20 February and Michael Sams's first wife recognized
his voice and his likeness. He was soon arrested and promptly
admitted kidnapping Stephanie, but denied murdering Julie
Dart.

He was charged with the murder of Julie Dart and with
kidnapping her, the attempted blackmailing of the West Yorkshire
police and British Rail. The trial began in June 1993 in the
Crown Court building in Nottingham. Sams had already pleaded
guilty to kidnapping Stephanie Slater, imprisoning her and blackmailing her employers.

In his evidence he claimed that Julie Dart had been kidnapped and murdered by a friend of his, whom he refused to
name. He explained the fact that letters he had written in

connection with the Stephanie Slater kidnap were very similar to ones received by the police in the Dart case by saying that he had written the Dart letters at the bidding of his friend.

But he could not explain why carpet fibres found on the material used to cover the body of Julie Dart and pieces of rope used to secure it were identical to fibres and rope found in his workshop. And discs taken from his computer contained information which he had erased in the normal way, but which computer experts were able to recover and clearly related to timetables he had devised for the Dart kidnapping and the black-mail of British Rail.

The jury of eight women and four men, after a three-and-a-half-hour retirement, brought in guilty verdicts on all counts. Michael Sams was given life imprisonment sentences for the murder of Julie Dart, the kidnappings and the unlawful imprison-ment of Stephanie Slater and the judge awarded ten-year sen-tences for each of the blackmails.

On the fourth day of his prison sentence Sams admitted to the murder of Julie Dart.

John Seadlund was an even more callous kidnapper. Together with an associate, James Gray, he snatched a wealthy Chicago businessman in September 1937. He was soon identified by fingerprints on the ransom note and traced to the race track at Los Angeles where he was arrested. He then admitted he had shot the businessman and also his partner Gray and led the police to where they were buried. He subsequently went to the electric chair.

August Sangret Dr Keith Simpson lifted the cardboard con-tainer onto the edge of the witness box and raised the lid. With something of a flourish he took out a human skull and showed it to the jury. It was the first time this had ever happened in an English trial.

The trial was held at Kingston Assizes in February 1943, and the skull belonged to a girl who had died when she was nineteen. Her body had been found the previous October buried in a shallow grave on Hankley Common, near Godalming, Surrey, which at the time was used for army training.

The skull had been shattered by a massive blow into thirty-eight pieces and most of the soft parts of the body eaten away by maggots or vermin. It was carefully raised from the ground and taken to Guy's Hospital in London, where Dr Simpson, who was the Home Office pathologist, worked. Simpson and Dr Eric Gardner, consultant pathologist at Weybridge Hospital, worked long and hard to reconstruct the skull from the pieces. Eventually they succeeded, only to discover a gaping hole at the back. This was explained when a heavy stake of birchwood was found near where the body had been discovered, with hairs crushed into the bark. The skull and parts of the arms and hands also showed curious puncture wounds caused, the pathologists surmised, by a blade with a kind of hook at the end.

The police made a careful search of the common and discovered the girl's shoes and a bag containing her identity card and a rosary. Her name was Joan Pearl Wolfe and she was known to the police as one of a number of girls who hung round the army camps which surrounded the common. She had been associating with a Canadian private called August Sangret. Subsequently the police found a letter she had written telling him she was pregnant and hoping he would marry her.

Enquiries at the Canadian Army camp established that Sangret, who was half French-Canadian and half Cree Indian, had been living with her in various 'wigwams' which he had built on the common. He was kept in the camp guardroom while he waited to be interviewed by Chief Inspector Greeno of Scotland Yard, who took him to a local police station where he made a long statement about his association with Pearl. He denied having killed her or seeing her after 14 September, but in December he was charged with her murder.

The prosecution were able to produce the carefully reconstructed skull and the piece of birchwood which fitted almost exactly into the hole at the back. Also shown was a black-handled clasp knife, the end of whose blade had been filed into a kind of hook.

This had been discovered stuffed into the wastepipe of the washroom just behind the guardroom where Sangret had awaited CI Greeno, and it did not come to light for several weeks. When it was found, several soldiers were able to testify that they had seen Sangret with it. Dr Simpson showed that it fitted exactly into the holes in the skull, and was responsible for the puncture marks in the arms and hands in which muscles and tendons had been hooked out by blows from the beak-shaped blade.

Eric Neve KC for the prosecution was able to reconstruct the murder. He suggested that Sangret and Wolf had a row in their wigwam, possibly over the Canadian's refusal to marry her, since it was known that he had another girlfriend in Glasgow. He began stabbing Pearl with the knife, but the head wounds, although painful and frightening, would not be enough to cause unconsciousness and she must have rushed out of the wigwam in terror and fled across the common, with Sangret in pursuit. She could have fallen over one of the many trip wires with which the common abounded and sprawled on her face. Sangret could have picked up the birch stake and killed her with one tremendous blow to the back of the head.

The jury returned a verdict of guilty inside two hours, but made a strong recommendation for mercy. This was ignored by the Home Secretary and August Sangret was hanged at Wandsworth jail on 29 April 1943.

Dr Simpson, being a Home Office pathologist, conducted the post mortem on the hanged man. On his strong, bronzed arm, the pathologist remembers seeing the tattooed name 'Pearl'.

A girl was found shot by a railway line near Pretoria, South Africa. She also had been pregnant. One of the detectives sent to investigate the crime, Sergeant Jacobus Coetzee, was afterwards linked to the girl. Several people had seen them together in compromising situations and he had written to her arranging a meeting just before she died. Ammunition of the type used to kill her was found in his possession and there was blood on his trousers. He was found guilty of murder and sentenced to life imprisonment.

Dr Samuel Sheppard   Judge Carl Weinman of the US District Court described the trial as a mockery of justice. 'If ever there was a trial by newspaper,' he said, 'this was it.'

In the early hours of Sunday 4 July, 1954, the body of Marilyn Sheppard was found in her bedroom with severe head injuries. She had lived in an expensive house in the small town of Bay Village on the shores of Lake Erie, just outside Cleveland, Ohio. Downstairs her husband, thirty-one-year-old Dr Sam Sheppard, had face and neck injuries. He said that he had fallen asleep on the couch after his wife had gone to bed. Woken by her screams, he rushed upstairs and grappled with a shadowy figure and was knocked unconscious from behind. Coming to, he chased someone he didn't recognize out of the house to the beach and was again rendered insensible by a blow.

It was an incredible story, since no one had heard the Sheppard dog bark and his seven-year-old son, asleep in another room, had not woken up. Many locals disbelieved him, but the Sheppard family – father and two elder brothers, who were all doctors – were influential in the area and for a time it looked as if the police were not going to charge Dr Sam. The *Cleveland Press* mounted a vicious campaign against him and eventually he was brought to trial.

It began in Cleveland in October 1954. The prosecution produced a witness who said she had been Sheppard's lover, and he had told her he was thinking of getting a divorce. This supplied a motive as well as making the doctor guilty of adultery, a very serious affair in those days. Dr Gerber, the local coroner, testified that he had found the imprint of a surgical instrument outlined in blood on the bedclothes below Marilyn's head. Dr Sheppard was a surgeon.

The jury deliberated for more than five days, but eventually brought in a verdict of guilty of second-degree murder, that is killing without premeditation. He was sentenced to life imprisonment.

Soon after he went to prison his lawyer hired Dr Paul Leland Kirk, one of the country's leading forensic scientists, to re-examine the murder room, which had been left untouched since the crime. He found blood which did not belong to either Sheppard, his wife or his son, and fragments of Marilyn's teeth on the carpet indicated she had bitten someone severely during the attack. Sheppard had no bite marks on him, and though all four walls of the bedroom were splashed with blood, the only blood found on Sheppard was a small amount on his knee. The pattern of blood splashes, claimed Dr Kirk, indicated a left-handed assailant. Dr Sheppard was right-handed.

However, the Ohio appeal courts refused to grant a retrial and even the US Supreme Court, for technical reasons, would not review the case. Erle Stanley Gardner, one of America's most famous crime fiction writers, the author of the 'Perry Mason' books, took up the case on Sheppard's behalf, but was unable to make any headway. Then Dr Sheppard's lawyer died at the age of seventy-five and a new young lawyer appeared on the scene.

F. Lee Bailey was to become one of America's most famous defenders, but it took him until April 1963, nearly nine years after Sheppard had been convicted, to get the US District Court, a federal not a state court, to reopen the case.

The court ordered Dr Sheppard to be released. But it was not until October 1966 that a new trial began, by which time the rigid moral code of the 1950s had relaxed. Dr Sheppard's former lover, now married and with a family, refused anyway to come to court.

Dr Kirk gave evidence explaining his theory that Dr Sheppard was innocent and Lee Bailey subjected Dr Gerber to severe cross-examination. At one point he asked him what surgical instrument had made the impression he reported seeing on the bedclothes.

'I'm not sure,' replied Gerber, who had to admit that he had never seen such an instrument in any hospital or even in any medical supply catalogue.

The jury returned a verdict of not guilty.

But it was not all plain sailing for Sheppard. There were still a great many people in the Cleveland area who thought he had killed his wife. He had difficulty getting his medical licence back in Ohio and, when he did, had to resign after a year when a malpractice claim was made against the hospital which employed him. He had married a wealthy German socialite, who had become interested in his case, as soon as he was released from prison, but they were divorced at about the same time as he lost his job. He took up wrestling, which he had been keen on at college, but he couldn't keep off the booze. In April 1970 he died of liver failure.

O. J. Simpson If the Dr Sheppard case was a trial by newspaper, this was a trial by television. All three major networks in the US televised every day of the proceedings and such was the publicity generated that witnesses were selling their stories to the newspapers or television before they even went into court. Judge Lance Ito had to sequester the jury, so that they could not see the media coverage. Even the Los Angeles district attorney was so put out by the circus that he suggested that this might be the last time television cameras were allowed into a courtroom there.

It was during the night of Sunday, 12 June 1994, that a dog

howling in the street in the up-market suburb of Brentwood, Los Angeles, led to the discovery of two bodies on the narrow paved path leading to a house. One was that of a young white man whose neck had been slashed and who had been stabbed several times, though it looked as if he had made desperate attempts to defend himself. Documents in his pockets identified him as Ron Goldman, who worked at a local restaurant. The other was that of a blonde lady, in her nightdress, who also had had her throat cut and who had been savagely knifed. She had been the owner of the house, thirty-five-year-old Nicole Brown Simpson, the ex-wife of O. J. Simpson.

Forty-six-year-old Simpson is a former American football star who had leading roles in *The Naked Gun* films and recently starred in American TV adverts for Hertz hire cars. Contacted in Chicago, where he had flown on the night of the murder, he returned to Los Angeles to be interviewed by the police. After a search of his mansion, two miles away from the Brentwood address of Nicole Brown, an arrest warrant was issued against him. He then disappeared, but was subsequently apprehended after a televised slow-motion car chase in the city, which was reportedly watched by ninety-five million people.

His trial opened on 23 January 1995. The prosecution, which included white Marcia Clark and a young black lawyer, Christopher Darden, reported that Simpson had been charged in 1989 with beating his wife and sentenced to 100 hours of community service. Witnesses said that rows between the two were frequent and several times she appeared with bruises on her face, but refused to call the police. They were divorced in 1992. But neighbours testified that he was often outside the Brentwood house, ranting and raving and on 23 October 1993, seven months before the murder, the police recorded a frantic telephone call from Nicole saying that O.J. had just broken down her back door.

But the prosecution were convinced that their trump card

was the DNA evidence. Dr Robin Cotton, the woman director of a Maryland DNA laboratory, told the court that the ex-football player's genetic profile matched that of blood spots taken from the path at the scene of the murder. In addition, blood found on one of O.J.'s socks in his bedroom the day after the murder and on a leather glove discovered outside his house had the same DNA profile as Nicole Brown. A sample taken from one of Ron Goldman's boots contained blood from Simpson himself and his ex-wife.

The celebrity was defended by a dozen formidable lawyers including the black lawyer Johnnie Cochran who had successfully defended Michael Jackson the previous year, F. Lee Bailey, of Dr Sheppard (*see* p. 289) and Dr Coppolino (*see* p. 66) fame and Alan Dershowitz who won an appeal on behalf of Von Bülow (*see* p. 316). They pointed out that the murderer must have been covered in blood, but no blood-stained clothes had been associated with Simpson, apart from the sock and the glove, and they poured scorn on the methods of collection of blood and samples for DNA analysis, saying that police mishandling rendered the results meaningless. They also raised the spectre of a conspiracy by a racially motivated Los Angeles police department to convict a black man who had had the temerity to marry a white woman.

And while the lawyers battled in court, behind the scenes another drama unfolded. The original jury had consisted of seven blacks, four whites and one Hispanic. Another twelve had been picked as 'alternates' to replace any of the original jury who had to retire for reasons of ill-health, family commitments or who were dismissed for offences such as talking to outsiders. Both sets listened to all the evidence presented to the jury in court. But possibly because of the interminable supervision – they even had to go on carefully conducted and monitored shopping trips – and the close proximity to each other, tensions developed. By 7 June ten jurors had been dismissed or retired. The trial still goes on (August 1995) and there seems no likelihood of an early resolution.

Oscar Slater On the evening of 21 December 1908, the occupants of a flat at 14 Queen's Terrace, Glasgow, heard banging from above, which was the apartment of eighty-two-year-old Miss Marion Gilchrist. Arthur Adams went upstairs to investigate and was followed by the old lady's young servant, Helen Lambie, who had been sent out to buy a paper. Helen unlocked the double-locked door and went inside.

As she did so a man passed her coming out, and he was also seen by Adams who was still standing in the doorway. Neither made any move to stop him, but a few minutes later Lambie discovered the battered body of her mistress in the dining-room.

Two days later Mary Barrowman, a fourteen-year-old messenger girl, told the police that as she was passing the house that night a man rushed out, almost knocking her down, and raced by her up the street. But the girls' descriptions of the man did not tally with each other at all.

Helen Lambie reported that a diamond crescent brooch had been stolen from the flat and the police assumed that robbery was the motive for the murder. When a man was reported as trying to sell a pawn ticket for such a brooch they pounced.

Unfortunately the man, a German Jew who called himself Oscar Slater and had run gambling clubs in the city, had boarded a steamship for New York. The Glasgow police cabled New York and Slater was arrested on arrival. In vain did he show that his passage had been booked weeks before the murder, and the brooch had been pawned since the middle of November. Adams, Lambie and Barrowman were taken to New York to assist in extradition proceedings. Shown pictures of Slater before they sailed, they were 'accidentally' confronted with him – between two guards and in handcuffs – in a courtroom corridor. Even then only Barrowman claimed Slater was the man she had seen. Adams and Lambie were not sure.

Slater's lawyers were convinced that the extradition proceedings would fail, but against their advice he elected to go back to Scotland and face trial.

It took place in May 1909 in Edinburgh. This time both Lambie and Barrowman said that Slater was the man they'd seen, though Adams wasn't positive. The judge, Lord Guthrie, summed up against the prisoner, saying of his character that 'he had maintained himself by the ruin of men and women . . . and had not the presumption of innocence an ordinary man might have'. The jury of fifteen voted nine for conviction, five for not proven and one for not guilty. Slater was found guilty and sentenced to death.

A storm of protest immediately arose and a petition containing 20,000 signatures was presented to the Scottish Secretary, who commuted the sentence to life imprisonment.

Then began a long fight to get Slater released, led by such figures as Sir Arthur Conan Doyle, creator of Sherlock Holmes, who wrote a pamphlet on the case, Sir Edward Marshall Hall, and many newspapers. But it was not until 1914 that anything further happened. Then a police officer, Detective Lieutenant John Trench, who had worked on the murder, revealed his misgivings about the conviction to a Glasgow lawyer and the Secretary of State for Scotland was informed. A secret inquiry was made into the case, in which neither Slater nor his lawyers were represented and the predictable result was that the Scottish Secretary felt the conviction ought to stand.

Trench was then dismissed the service for revealing police business and he and the lawyer were arrested and charged with receiving stolen goods. They were tried, but acquitted.

Slater's supporters worked on tirelessly, but the Scottish Secretary did nothing more until the publication in 1927 of a book: *The Truth About Oscar Slater* by William Park, by which time Slater had served eighteen years. In the book Park revealed that Trench had said that when Helen Lambie was first interviewed she said that she thought she knew the man and named him as a relative of Miss Gilchrist, but the police convinced her she was mistaken. Mary Barrowman subsequently claimed that she was bullied into saying that Slater was the man and drilled every day for a fortnight in the Procurator Fiscal's office before she gave her evidence in court.

Slater was released from prison in November 1927, but it took an act of parliament for his case to be referred to the newly constituted Scottish Court of Criminal Appeal. This concluded that the judge at Slater's trial had gravely erred in his charge to the jury and the verdict was quashed. Oscar Slater received £6,000 in compensation.

He died in 1948, outliving the judge, counsel and most of the jury. But who actually murdered Miss Gilchrist remains a mystery to this day.

Pamela Smart   The trial began in the town of Exeter, New Hampshire, a small state on the north-eastern seaboard of America, in February 1991. Twenty-four-year-old Pamela Smart was accused of conspiracy to commit murder, being an accomplice to first-degree murder, and witness tampering.

Pamela, a beautiful former college cheerleader with a BA degree in communications from Florida State University, was a media services director for the school board at Hampton, a town near the coast. The prosecution claimed that Pamela had persuaded a student of hers, Billy Flynn, by lies, sex and promises of money, to kill her twenty-six-year-old husband Gregg to whom she had only been married for a little under two years.

Sixteen-year-old Billy Flynn described how Pam had first seduced him, taking him up to her bedroom when her husband was away, appearing from the bathroom in a specially bought negligé, and then slowly stripping to the music of a Van Halen CD. Later she had explained that Gregg must be killed because if she divorced him she would lose her furniture and her dog. Eventually Billy agreed and Pamela gave him instructions on how to do it.

On the night of 1 May 1990, Billy and his friend Pete entered the Smart residence, in the nearby town of Derry, through a door Pamela had left open for them. She was away at a school board meeting and when Gregg came home Billy shot him through the head and the two boys left taking valuables with them as Pamela had suggested, to make it look like a burglary which had gone wrong. They were picked up in a car outside the house by another friend, 'JR'.

But too many youngsters knew about the plot and the murder, and talked about it, and word got back to the police, who arrested the three youths.

Soon after their arrest another teenager came forward. Sixteen-year-old Cecilia Pierce had been Pamela's part-time secretary and knew all about the plot from the beginning. She had even made suggestions as to how the boys could get hold of a gun. When she confessed, the police persuaded her to wear a concealed microphone and to try to get Pamela to talk about the murder and the plot, and they also taped telephone conversations between the two.

Billy, Pete and JR confessed to the murder and were allowed to plead guilty to second-degree murder, which let them off the death penalty, provided they agreed to testify against Pamela. Billy and Pete then received sentences which would effectively keep them in prison for twenty-eight years each and JR received eighteen years.

Pamela's defence attorney contended that Billy, Pete and JR had plotted and committed the murder entirely without her knowledge, because of Billy's infatuation and his jealousy of Gregg. Pamela also testified in court that in the tapes she was pretending to know more than she actually did because she was trying to find out who had killed her husband.

Under cross-examination she was easily a match for prosecutor Paul Maggiotto. Remaining cool and calm she evaded all the traps he set for her and the papers called her 'the ice maiden'.

But it was her undoing. In an interview in the Boston *Globe* after the trial one of the jury, of seven women and five men, said that her inability to show emotion in court made him think of a schizophrenic. There had been no serious dissension as to her guilt. The jury had listened to the tapes over and over again. On them she never admitted her guilt, but her statements and the tone of her voice, when she didn't know anyone else was listening, helped to convince the jury she was guilty.

She was convicted of all three felonies and the sentence for the most serious, being an accomplice, was mandatory – imprisonment for the rest of her life without the possibility of parole.

Twenty-eight-year-old mother of six, Joyce Turner, enlisting the aid of next-door neighbour Mrs Audrey Noakes and waitress friend Clestell Gay, shot her husband while he was asleep in bed, in June 1956. The gun was eventually traced to Clestell and through Mrs Noakes back to Joyce Turner. They were tried separately and each sentenced to life imprisonment. Joyce Turner remarked: 'He always said he wanted to die in bed.'

Ruth Snyder and Judd Gray　It is difficult now to understand why this trial had the sensational publicity it did. It was front-page news for nearly all the major newspapers in America for the whole of the trial and for a while afterwards, yet the crime was a banal domestic tragedy, perpetrated with callousness and such incompetence that the murderers were under lock and key in a matter of days.

The reason for the case's popularity must lie with the characters involved. The idea of a passionate sexual relationship in which a strong, determined woman dominated a weak man and eventually persuaded him to help her murder her husband, was not such a common one in New York in 1927 as it would be today.

The trial began at the Supreme County Court, Long Island City, in April 1927. The prosecution told the jury that housewife Ruth Snyder, twenty-eight and blonde, met thirty-one-year-old Judd Gray, a married corset salesman, in New York in June 1925 and they soon became lovers. In November she tricked her husband into signing forms for several large insurance policies on his life. Eighteen months after that, Ruth left open the door of her home in the Queens district of New York, so that Judd could gain entrance while she, her husband and daughter were at a party, and await their return.

When her husband was safely asleep the pair attacked him with chloroform and a five-pound window-sash weight, finally strangling him with picture wire. The story she told of being attacked and knocked out by an intruder was not believed for a minute and eventually she confessed. She claimed that though she had helped plan the murder, Gray had committed it, carrying on even when she tried to stop him.

Gray was arrested and he too confessed. But he said that Ruth had taken an active part in the murder; that it had been her idea right from the start to persuade him to help her kill her husband.

This was the crux of the trial. Which version would the jury believe? Both sets of defence attorneys tried to get a separate trial for their client, but Judge Townsend Scudder refused and they were tried together.

Ruth now changed her story, blaming Judd for the entire planning and execution of the murder and claiming that he did it for the insurance money which she would have had to give him because he held her guilt over her. But she was unimpressive in the witness box: she was forced on cross-examination into a number of damaging admissions and she came over as being far too unemotional to convince the jury that her story was true. In fact the press called her 'The Granite Woman'.

Judd Gray was dubbed 'The Putty Man' and admitted everything, even to the setting up of an alibi, which gave ample evidence of a premeditated crime and thus would lead directly to the electric chair.

The jury took less than two hours to find the defendants guilty of first-degree murder and both were sentenced to death. On 12 January 1928 they died in the electric chair.

Charlotte Bryant provided a variation on the theme. She killed her husband, this time with arsenic, in pursuit of an itinerant gipsy with whom she had fallen in love. She was tried at Dorchester in May 1936. Traces of arsenic were found in her pockets and a tin containing the poison on a rubbish tip behind her cottage. She was hanged at Exeter prison on 15 July 1936.

Richard Speck   'I'm not going to hurt you,' said the tall young man who had appeared at Miss Amurao's bedroom door, waving a gun and a knife, 'but I need your money to get to New Orleans.'

It was about eleven o'clock at night on 13 July 1966. Cora-zon Amurao was a Filipino nurse working at the South Chicago Community Hospital and her bedroom was in a small townhouse, owned by the hospital, which she shared with seven other nurses, two of whom were Filipinos like herself. The intruder, who smelled strongly of alcohol, collected all the nurses in the house, most of whom were students, and forced them into the large bedroom upstairs at the back.

He told them he only wanted money, and when he had collected the contents of their purses he made them lie on the floor and tied their hands and feet with strips cut from sheets. But he would not leave and seemed to become increasingly agitated.

Eventually he untied the feet of one girl, took her into another bedroom and stabbed her in the neck with the knife, stifling her screams with a strip of sheet which he then used to strangle her.

Soon after this another two nurses arrived, one of whom was to stay the night as a guest of the other. The man intercepted them coming in and stabbed them both to death in another bedroom. One fought back courageously and received eighteen separate stab wounds before she died.

By now the tied-up girls in the large bedroom were terrified and tried to hide themselves under beds, but the man came back and searched them out, dragging them off one by one.

All except Miss Amurao. A tiny lady, she was able to roll under a bed. She was not discovered and heard and saw her friends being taken away. The last one was Gloria Davy, who it was discovered afterwards bore a striking resemblance to the murderer's divorced wife. Corazon saw the killer pull off Gloria's jeans and afterwards heard the sound of bedsprings rhythmically creaking. When she looked out again the room was empty.

Eventually the nurse crawled out and in a highly hysterical state raised the alarm. The police found the bodies of eight girls, three in each of two bedrooms, one in the bathroom and one downstairs in the lounge. Only Gloria Davy had been sexually assaulted.

It was the worst mass killing in Chicago history, exceeding even the infamous St Valentine's Day Massacre in the number of people killed, and it shocked the whole city.

Bloody fingerprints identified the killer as Richard Speck, a twenty-three-year-old seaman from Texas, with many convictions and a history of alcohol and drug abuse. He had a number of tattoos. One on his arm read: 'Born To Raise Hell'. When he heard the police were looking for him he tried to commit suicide by cutting his wrists, but was recognized in hospital and arrested.

The trial had to be held in Peoria, a town 150 miles to the south-west, because of fears that Speck might be lynched or attacked in court, and he was always under heavy police guard. It began in February 1967.

Corazon Amurao identified Speck as the intruder, and prosecutor Assistant State Attorney William Martin led her gently through her account of that harrowing night. He moved a small wooden figure for each victim, as the nurse mentioned her, to the room where the body had been found, in an elaborate model of the whole house. For the jury it was devastating.

Speck's only defence, from the moment he was arrested, was that he couldn't remember anything of that night. It served him no better than it had Guenther Podola at the Old Bailey seven years before (see p. 258). Richard Speck was pronounced guilty and sentenced to die in the electric chair. The US Supreme Court suspended the death penalty before the sentence could be carried out, so Speck was given 400 to 1,200 years at the state penitentiary, the longest jail term ever given up to that time. But it was all a trifle academic as Richard Speck died of a heart attack in prison in 1991.

Another incredible mass murder took place at the Shiinamachi branch of the Imperial Bank of Tokyo on 26 January 1948, while Japan was occupied by American forces. A man claiming to be from the Disinfectant Corps gave the staff medicine containing cyanide and, when they collapsed, walked off with 180,000 yen. Twelve died and four recovered in hospital. Sadamichi Hirasawa was eventually tried for the murders in December. After retracting a confession and pleading partial insanity he was found guilty and spent the rest of his life in prison, dying in 1987.

George Stephenson and the Daly Brothers The trial of Stephenson and the two Daly brothers took place in Winchester in October 1987. All three pleaded not guilty to five counts of murder. In addition Stephenson and George Daly pleaded not guilty to rape, but the younger Daly, John, pleaded guilty to rape and robbery.

David Elfer QC, prosecuting, said that on the evening of 1 September there were five people in Burgate House, a six-bedroomed mansion near Fordingbridge in the New Forest. Joseph Cleaver was a wealthy retired publisher, and he, his invalid wife Hilda, their son Tom and his wife Wendy were sitting down to a dinner served by the elderly housekeeper, Margaret Murphy.

Three masked men burst in, armed with pickaxe handles and a shotgun, and robbed the men of their cash and the women of their jewellery. They then took everybody upstairs to a large bedroom and tied them up, the invalid Hilda being secured to her wheelchair.

The burglars ransacked the house, stealing guns, liquor and other property, but failing to find a safe. Back upstairs they took Wendy Cleaver into another bedroom where they raped her, then strangled her with a length of black cloth. The other victims were doused with petrol which was also poured over furniture and furnishings and as the men left one threw a firelighter into the bedroom.

The bodies were discovered the next day. The police, searching Joseph Cleaver's correspondence, discovered that he had appointed a couple, George and Fiona Stephenson, as live-in cook and handyman a few weeks before. Enquiries established that they hadn't stayed long; Cleaver had sacked Stephenson because of his violence towards Mrs Stephenson.

The handyman had convictions for burglary and theft, assault, and firearms and drug offences. His picture was flashed on TV and appeared in newspapers, and a Midlands car-hire firm reported that he had recently hired a car from them, but that the deposit had been paid by one George Daly who had given an address in Coventry. The Dalys were picked up at home.

When Stephenson saw his picture in the papers he gave himself up, claiming that he had given a lift to two Hell's Angels whom he had told about Burgate House and it must have been them who raided the place. But at his trial he changed his story, saying that he had been at the house, but had remained outside in the car while the Daly brothers went inside.

They replied by blaming Stephenson. John Daly admitted raping Wendy Cleaver, but claimed that he strangled her under instructions from Stephenson. And it was quite clear that Stephenson had planned the burglary in revenge for being sacked and, supposing that he might be recognized, had determined that everybody in the house must die.

They were all convicted, and in passing sentence Mr Justice Hobhouse said that the murders were committed in circumstances of indescribable brutality and cruelty. Stephenson received six life sentences with the recommendation he should serve at least twenty-five years. John Daly received seven life sentences, for rape, robbery and five murders, but George Daly was convicted only of manslaughter and received twenty-two years.

What the killers had not known when they threw the firelighter into the bedroom, was that the whole house would not burn down as they hoped. Burgate House had been converted in the 1940s from a nineteenth-century farm building, many of the old timber beams being replaced with concrete. It might have been cold, but it was virtually fireproof. Only the bedroom in which the bodies were found had been much affected, thus there were plenty of clues left for the police to find.

In another attempt to fleece a wealthy man, Albert T. Patrick, a Texas attorney, managed to persuade Charles Jones, young secretary to the millionaire William Rice, to give the old man chloroform, and Rice eventually died. But when Jones made out various large cheques on Rice's account to the attorney, he managed to misspell Patrick's name. The bank was suspicious and investigated. Jones and Patrick were tried for murder in New York in January 1902. Jones turned state's evidence and was acquitted. The attorney was found guilty of first-degree murder and sentenced to death. But you can't kill a lawyer; first the sentence was commuted to life imprisonment, then in 1912 the state governor granted Patrick a full and unconditional pardon.

Peter Sutcliffe Many newspapers called it the trial of the century, but it nearly didn't take place at all, and in some ways it might have been better if it hadn't.

When Peter Sutcliffe, who lived in Bradford, was picked up by the police in Sheffield on 2 January 1981, in the company of a prostitute, he was taken in for questioning because his car had false number plates. He readily admitted stealing them from a scrapyard, but when a ball-peen hammer and a knife were found near where he had been stopped, the questioning turned towards the Yorkshire Ripper enquiry. Sutcliffe soon admitted that he was the killer. He gave details of eleven murders, although he was suspected of being involved in thirteen, in a marathon session lasting seventeen hours.

He was interviewed later in Armley jail, Leeds, by a succession of psychiatrists, including one supplied by the prosecution, and they were all convinced that he was a paranoid schizophrenic. The Attorney General, Sir Michael Havers, and Sutcliffe's own counsel, James Chadwin QC, then agreed that if Sutcliffe would plead guilty to the lower charge of manslaughter, on the grounds of diminished responsibility, the murder charges would be dropped. He could still be given a life sentence, but there would be no necessity for a full-scale trial. The victims' relatives would be spared the harrowing details of the attacks on their loved ones and the cost of a trial would be avoided.

But Mr Justice Boreham would not accept the plea bargain and insisted on a jury trial. It was understandable. The case had gone on so long, public interest was enormous and emotions were high. Justice needed to be seen to be done, even if some innocent people might suffer.

The first murder was that of Wilma McCann, a prostitute in Leeds, whose body was found on 30 October 1975. She had been struck terrific blows on the top and back of the head with a hammer, her clothing had been undone exposing her body, which had been stabbed many times. This was more or less the pattern for all Sutcliffe's killings, and up to the time of his arrest there had been thirteen, with seven non-fatal attacks on women. Several hammers had been used together with an assortment of knives and sharpened screwdrivers, and the results of his assaults horrified even hardened police officers. Six of his victims were not prostitutes and it seemed that in the latter stages of the reign of terror in Leeds, Bradford, Huddersfield, Halifax and Manchester, any young woman out late at night was liable to be struck down from behind.

When the trial began in May 1981 at the Old Bailey in London, Sir Michael Havers was forced to present the prose-cution case as if Sutcliffe had pleaded not guilty. He described in detail all the Ripper murders and all his attacks. But the real switch occurred with the psychiatrists, whose findings had pre-viously been accepted by the prosecution, but who now found themselves severely cross-examined, so that many of them felt they were on trial as well.

The most ludicrous part of the defence was supplied by Sutcliffe himself. He claimed that during the time he had worked as a gravedigger in Bingley cemetery, from 1964 to 1967, he had had a vision telling him to go out into the streets and kill prostitutes. Although the psychiatrists seemed to accept this as part of his mental disease, neither they nor Sutcliffe could explain why it had taken him at least eight years from the time when he had his vision to the time when he began his 'mission'.

Neither could they explain why he had killed ordinary women walking alone at night as well as women looking for men, and why many of the injuries he inflicted were to the genitals of his victims, if there was, as he claimed, no sexual element in his attacks. The final point was that when he made his confessions to the police, he made no mention of his mission, and only raised this when he talked to the psychiatrists.

The jury of six men and six women found him guilty of all

thirteen murders. He was sentenced to life imprisonment by Mr Justice Boreham, with the recommendation that he should serve at least thirty years.

Peter Sutcliffe was transferred to the high security mental hospital Broadmoor in March 1985, where he now remains, and where he would have been detained anyway had his plea of manslaughter been accepted.

Arthur Thomas Harvey and Jeannette Crewe disappeared from their farm near the village of Pukekawa, twenty-five miles south of Auckland in the North Island of New Zealand, on or about 17 June 1970. After five days Jeannette's father went to the farmhouse and found the couple's eighteen-month-old baby, still alive in her cot, but there were bloodstains in the living-room.

A massive police search was launched and local people were interviewed. The baby seemed well fed after her five days alone in the house and one witness said he had seen a woman near the Crewes' farmhouse during that time.

A month later Jeannette's body was discovered in the nearby Waikato River. She had been shot through the head with a 0.22 rifle. After another month Harvey's body was also found in the river. He too had been shot in the head and his body weighed down with an old car axle.

An examination of all 0.22 rifles in the area turned up two which could have fired the fatal bullets, pieces of which had been extracted from the bodies. One of the rifles was owned by a young farmer, Arthur Thomas, who farmed nine miles from the Crewes, had been to school with Jeannette and had at one time courted her. He had no alibi for the time of the family's disappearance and was arrested.

Thomas was brought to trial at the Supreme Court in Auckland in February 1971. The prosecution said that the car axle had at one time formed part of a trailer owned by Thomas's father, and indeed two stub axles which fitted it were found on a dump on the farm Thomas rented. Wire similar to a type used to bind the bodies was also found on Thomas's farm, and a cartridge case from his rifle was found in the Crewes' garden. The police had reconstructed the shooting and said that Thomas fired the first shot from outside the farmhouse, through the window.

He was convicted of both murders and sentenced to life imprisonment, but his family immediately set about appealing for a retrial and the case became a national issue with a great many people becoming interested.

At length a retrial took place in March 1973. During this a friend of Harvey's who had helped the police with searches claimed that the area where the cartridge case had been found had already been thoroughly searched by the police previously, and it was pointed out that the police had twice had Thomas's rifle in their possession. It would have been quite easy to rig the evidence of the cartridges.

Dr James Sprott, a leading forensic scientist, after examining the cartridges put forward the theory that Thomas's ammunition could not be connected with the bullets which killed the Crewes. In spite of all this, the jury again convicted Thomas and he went back to prison.

The efforts of the convicted man's supporters, however, were not exhausted. Dr Sprott continued his investigations and in all tested some 25,000 cartridge cases to support his theory. David Yallop investigated the case and, in his book *Beyond Reasonable Doubt?* published in 1978, argued for Thomas's innocence. He claimed that he knew the name of the woman who fed the baby during the five days she was on her own and sent her name to the New Zealand prime minister.

Eventually a royal commission of enquiry was instituted and this found that the cartridge case found in the garden had indeed been planted by the police and that another had been substituted by them. The commission also found that there had been excessive police scrutiny of the jury during the second trial.

Arthur Thomas was given a free pardon and released on 17 December 1979. He was also awarded NZ$950,000 in compensation. But he had already served nine years in prison.

The police refused to accept the findings of the royal commission and have never reopened the case, but several people claim that they know who the real murderer was.

Richard Brinkley persuaded an elderly lady in Fulham to sign a folded sheet of paper, telling her it was a list for an outing. He obtained two more signatures in the same way, then, when the old lady conveniently died two days later, produced a will signed by her, with two witness signatures, which left her house and money to him. When her granddaughter contested the will he realized that the witnesses would comprehend his deception and would have to be eliminated. He went to the lodgings of one, Reginald Parker, in Croydon and left a bottle of beer laced with cyanide on the table. But Parker's landlord and landlord's wife drank some of it and died. Brinkley was tried for murder at Lewes Assizes in 1907, convicted and hanged at Wandsworth prison.

Edith Thompson and Frederick Bywaters   Late in the evening of 3 October 1922, a young couple were walking in a quiet street in Ilford, north-east London. They were on their way home after an evening at a theatre in the West End. Suddenly a man rushed up, pushed the woman aside and began striking out at her husband. She ran to a nearby house for assistance, but when her husband, whose name was Percy Thompson, arrived at hospital he was found to have died from stab wounds.

The police became suspicious when Mrs Thompson made no mention of an attacker, saying merely that her husband had collapsed in the street. Investigations soon showed that she had a lover, a young steward on the P & O shipping lines called Frederick Bywaters.

They were interviewed separately at a police station, but at one stage Edith Thompson was conducted along a corridor and saw through an open door Bywaters being questioned.

She cried out: 'Oh, God! What can I do? Why did he do it? I did not want him to do it!'

She then made a statement naming Bywaters as the man who had fought with her husband. When shown this, he confessed that he had attacked Thompson, but hadn't intended to kill him. He also said that Edith had had no idea what he was going to do that night.

When the police searched Bywaters's cabin, however, they came across sixty-five letters which Edith Thompson had written to her lover, covering the period from August 1921 to the death of Percy in October 1922. On the basis of these letters she and Bywaters were jointly charged with murder and conspiracy to murder.

Their trial opened at the Old Bailey in December 1922 before Mr Justice Shearman, after a failure to get them separate trials. Frederick Bywaters had little defence, since he had deliberately assaulted Percy Thompson with a knife, but there was not much against Edith except for the letters.

The vast majority of these contained just the usual things lovers write to each other, but Edith possessed a strong imagination and was an avid reader of romantic novels which she frequently wrote about, and the letters contained passages which, taken out of context and read out by the prosecution in court, showed her in a very bad light.

'I'm not going to try any more until you come back,' she wrote in one. 'He puts great stress on the fact that the tea tasted bitter . . . Now I think that whatever else I try it will still taste bitter, he will recognise it and be more suspicious still . . . I'm going to try the glass again. I've got an electric light globe this time.'

In another she said: 'I've used the light bulb three times, but the third time he found a piece so I have given up till you come home.'

She also sent him cuttings from newspapers about poison cases, and wrote about digitalis, quoting a book which said that it is a cumulative poison. 'Is it any use?' she asked.

After the discovery of the letters Percy Thompson's body was exhumed and a post mortem conducted by Bernard Spilsbury. He found no evidence that Thompson had been poisoned or had eaten broken glass, and Edith denied in court that she had ever tried to harm her husband.

But her performance in the witness box was little short of disastrous. Alternately flirtatious and hysterical, she was often caught telling lies and she completely failed to convince the jury that her letters were the outpourings of an overwrought imagination and not to be taken as literally true.

Whether or not they influenced the young Bywaters it is difficult to say. Certainly the judge hinted strongly to the jury that they did, and this, coupled with the fact that she was an admitted adulterer, swayed the jury of eleven men and one woman against her. She and Bywaters were convicted of murdering Percy Thompson and condemned to death. They were hanged on the same day, 9 January 1923, he at Pentonville, she at Holloway.

Many writers have commented on this trial, most condemning the verdict against her. There seems little doubt that though she was a vain and thoughtless woman, she was not a murderess.

Another lady who was hanged at Holloway for murder, with rather more justification this time, was Styllou Christofi, a fifty-three-year-old Cypriot. Intensely jealous of her daughter-in-law she strangled the girl and tried to burn her body in the garden of the house Christofi shared with her son in Hampstead. She was tried and convicted at the Old Bailey in October 1954.

Robert Thompson and Jon Venables　When Robert Thompson and Jon Venables went for trial on 1 November 1993, at

Preston Crown Court, they were both eleven years old, the youngest children ever to stand trial for murder in Britain this century. And not only was the trial horrifying because of the age of the defendants, it contained details which sickened the jury and everyone who heard them.

At 2.30 that afternoon Mr Richard Henriques QC rose to give the bald facts of the prosecution case. On Friday 12 February, 1993, James Bulger was two years and eleven months old, the only child of Denise and Ralph Bulger who lived in Kirkby, a satellite town on the outskirts of Liverpool. That afternoon Denise decided to go shopping in nearby Bootle with Nicola Bailey, her brother's fiancée. Denise took James and Nicola brought the three-year-old daughter of another of Denise's brothers.

They went into the Strand Shopping Centre and after some time the children began to get fractious, running about in the aisles of shops, and had to be called back by Denise and Nicola. The two women finally entered a butcher's shop. Nicola went to the cooked meat counter and Denise walked across to get some chops for tea. James was standing with his mother while she ordered the chops. Then Nicola looked up and saw the boy standing by the shop door. Denise was about to pay when she looked round. He had gone.

The other child reported that James had gone out of the door and both women rushed out looking for him, but he was nowhere to be found. Eventually they went to the precinct security services and the police were called.

The search continued all that night and all the next day. What made the police very worried was that a security camera in the precinct showed the image of a child being led away by a young boy, with another walking along in front. The small child was identified by Denise as her son.

On Sunday afternoon James's body was discovered on a railway embankment some two-and-a-half miles from where he had been abducted. The body was very close to the tracks and had been cut in half by a train. When the pitiful remains were examined it was thought that the baby had probably died from many severe blows to the head, before being placed on the line beneath a pile of bricks. Bloodstained bricks nearby looked as if they might have been thrown at the child and there was blue paint on his face and hand from a small tin of paint which had also been thrown at him.

The whole country was shocked by the tragedy. The case received massive publicity and pictures of the child being led away were shown on television and published in the newspapers. It soon brought results.

On the following Wednesday a woman went to a police station in Liverpool to report that a young boy she knew, Jon Venables, and his friend Robert Thompson, had been playing truant from school on the Friday, and Jon had come home with blue paint on his jacket. She thought she could also recognize him as being one of the boys in the video pictures.

At the house of ten-and-a-half-year-old Jon Venables the police discovered a pair of his shoes with blood on them, which DNA examination identified as the blood of James Bulger. Paint on Venables's jacket was identical to that on the baby. After a series of very short interviews, conducted with specially trained police officers used to interviewing child victims of sex abuse, Venables admitted that he and Thompson had killed the little boy.

Robert Thompson, also ten-and-a-half, never confessed. Obviously the more 'streetwise' of the two, all he would admit was that they had taken the boy, but he blamed it all on Venables, saying that he had thrown bricks at the baby and hit him with an iron bar. Forensic evidence, however, showed that Thompson was involved: marks on the little boy's face fitted the side of the sole and part of the upper on one of his shoes.

Mr Henriques claimed in court that the boys, in spite of

their young age, had the intention of killing or doing major harm to James. He said that they had already made an attempt that day to abduct a child in the shopping mall, but gave up when the child's mother appeared. He played the tapes of their interviews to the jury and Venables could be heard saying that Thompson had suggested enticing a child to follow them so he could be led out into the street and knocked down by a car. Thompson, said Venables, wanted to push the boy into a canal, was annoyed when he wouldn't look down into the water and threw him down on the ground instead, bumping his head.

A succession of witnesses described how they had seen the boys walking with the toddler between them and, seeing the dishevelled state of the child, many had stopped, but the two boys said they were taking him home, or to the police station, and as they seemed quite nice lads, they were believed.

There were no defence witnesses. Mr David Turner QC, Thompson's counsel, dismissed the suggestion that the boys deliberately set out to cause James harm, saying the idea was diabolical. And he claimed that any attack on the child was done by Venables. Mr Brian Walsh QC, defending Venables, was equally partisan, saying that Thompson was a practised and sophisticated liar, who tried to put the blame for his own actions on Venables.

The jury of nine men and three women thought the two boys equally guilty of the abduction and murder of James Bulger. They were sentenced to be detained at Her Majesty's pleasure.

Baron von Bülow Claus von Bülow was not tried for murder, only attempted murder, but the trials were among the most sensational in the American history of this century and certainly the most expensive.

Martha von Bülow, or 'Sunny' as she is usually known, lived with Claus in a twenty-room mansion she owned near Newport in the State of Rhode Island, some sixty miles south-west of Boston. Reputed to be worth more than $150 million, she had married Baron von Bülow in 1966 and had one daughter by him, Cosima, having already had a girl and a boy – Annie Laurie, known as 'Ala', and Alex – by a previous marriage. Sunny and Claus's marriage was far from happy and at the time of the first incident he was having an affair with a star of a television soap.

On 27 December 1979, Sunny's maid Maria Schrallhammer became worried about her mistress, who seemed to be unconscious in bed, although Claus didn't seem very concerned. When he was eventually persuaded to call a doctor, Sunny was found to be in a coma and near death. However, resuscitation brought her round and she regained consciousness the following day.

One Saturday night the following December, after dinner Sunny's speech became slurred and Claus took her off to bed. The next morning she was discovered unconscious on the floor of her bathroom. She was still alive, but in a coma; this time she never regained consciousness, and remains to this day in what is called a 'persistent vegetative state'.

Claus was indicted on two counts of assault with intent to commit murder, respecting the two comas that Sunny had suffered. The trial began in Newport in February 1982. Dr George Cahill, a leading expert on levels of blood sugar, gave evidence that Sunny had been admitted to hospital on both occasions with very low blood sugar, due, he said, to suspected injections of insulin. This is a drug which occurs naturally in the body – and therefore its presence would not be regarded as suspicious – but high doses of it can be fatal.

Maria said that she had been suspicious of Claus after the first incident and had discovered in his suitcase a black bag containing various drugs. After the second coma she again found the bag and in it saw a phial of insulin.

Twenty-three-year-old Ala, and Alex, twenty-one, had also been suspicious after the first episode and when the second occurred they commissioned a criminal lawyer, Richard Kuh, to begin a private investigation. He employed a private detective who went with Alex to the Newport home and again unearthed the black bag. It contained phials and pills and three hypodermic syringe needles, one of which had an incrustation on the outside which proved to be insulin.

Claus had a good motive to murder Sunny, since he stood to inherit most of her huge fortune should she die.

The jury took six days to make up their minds, but eventually they found von Bülow guilty on both counts of attempted murder, and he was sentenced to thirty years. But he was given thirty days to appeal and bail was set at $1 million.

The appeal was handled by a team led by Harvard law professor Alan Dershowitz and was virtually an attack on the whole prosecution case. After the appeal had been allowed and a new trial ordered, Dershowitz conducted the defence.

At the second trial he brought in other medical experts to show that the tests which had been done to measure the level of insulin in Sunny's bloodstream were unreliable. Truman Capote, the famous writer, who had known Sunny for many years, testified that he had seen her inject herself with a variety of drugs, which she kept in a black bag. Claus himself claimed that although the black bag had originally been his, Sunny had appropriated it to keep her drugs in.

Maria's evidence, that she had seen insulin in the bag, was shaken when Dershowitz was able to subpoena the notes taken by Kuh at his meetings with Maria, Alex and Ala. These showed that Maria had not originally mentioned finding insulin in the bag. The presence of insulin had only been discussed after the results of the medical tests were known.

The final blow to the prosecution case came when Dershowitz was able to show that a syringe needle used to inject insulin would never have the dried drug left on the outside, since the skin would wipe it clean as the needle was withdrawn. The only way insulin would remain on the outside was if the needle was dipped into a solution of the drug and allowed to dry. As Dershowitz pointed out, this could have been a deliberate attempt to manufacture evidence against Claus. And if that were the case it pointed to the innocence of the Baron.

The jury, after deliberating over the weekend, acquitted Claus of all charges and, because there is no appeal against an acquittal, on Monday morning 7 June, 1985, Claus von Bülow walked out of court a free man.

G. Daniel Walker Hope awoke to the feeling of something cold and hard in her mouth. Instinctively she knew it was a gun. There was a man leaning over her. She rolled off the bed, rushed out of the bedroom and into the living-room, to the still figure sitting upright on the settee. 'Help me, Bill!' she screamed.

'He can't help you,' came a voice behind her. 'Bill's dead.'

The man hustled her back into the bedroom, tore off her clothes and raped her several times. Then he tied her up and left her.

Hope Masters was thirty-one. Known as a Beverly Hills socialite, she had been married twice, had three children, but could still wear her twelve-year-old son's jeans. She and her fiancé Bill Ashlock, an advertising writer, had gone for the weekend to the ranch which her mother and stepfather partially owned at Springfield, 150 miles north of Los Angeles. They had been joined there by a tall handsome man who said his name was Taylor Wright and he wanted to interview Bill for the *Los Angeles Times*, though when he got there he seemed more interested in the beautiful Hope Masters than in Bill. It was Saturday 24 February, 1973.

Later, the shadowy intruder returned and untied Hope and she recognized him as Taylor Wright. He told her he was a hitman and that he had shot Bill. He said that he had been hired to kill them both by her estranged husband because she was suing for divorce, but he didn't really want to kill her. He began behaving more like a lover than a hitman and though she was frightened and distraught she started to fall under his spell. He told her that he'd been working for the Mafia and that they would soon come after her and the children, but he would protect her.

He took her back to her apartment in Beverly Hills, leaving the body of Ashlock in the ranch house, and for three days lived there with her, helping to look after the children, but not allowing her to communicate with anyone. Eventually she persuaded him to let her visit her mother and he went with her. Her mother was partially convinced by their story of someone shooting Bill and Hope being afterwards rescued by Taylor, but her stepfather, a prominent Los Angeles lawyer, would have none of it and went straight to the police. Wright said he would also go to the police, then disappeared.

The police didn't believe Hope's story and she was charged with the first-degree murder of Bill Ashlock.

Meanwhile, the Chicago police were on the track of Taylor Wright, whose real name was G. Daniel Walker. A thief and a conman – he was said to have ninety aliases – he had violent habits. He had been in prison for the attempted murder of a policeman, but had wormed his way into the affections of a lady lawyer from the legal services department and subsequently made his escape from the prison hospital. It was from letters he wrote to the lady lawyer that the Illinois state police realized he was in California and involved in the Ashlock shooting. In a combined operation by the Illinois police, the FBI, the Los Angeles police and the Tulare County police, where the murder had taken place, Walker was finally captured in Los Angeles.

The district attorney for Tulare County then indicted both G. Daniel Walker and Hope Masters for the murder of Bill Ashlock.

Walker then sprang a surprise. In conjunction with his lawyer, he had been working on his case, and was able to show that the interception of his letter to the lady lawyer in Chicago was illegal. Thus, everything which stemmed from it, everything linking him to the Ashlock murder, was also illegally obtained by the authorities and could not be used in evidence against him. Judge Ballantine agreed and suddenly District Attorney Joe Haley found himself without much of a case against Walker at all.

Hope Masters's attorney, Tom Breslin, then offered a deal. Drop all charges against her and she would testify against Walker. The district attorney accepted. But Hope could not make up her mind; her feelings for Walker were still ambivalent. Eventually she consulted a priest who told her the only way out was to tell the truth.

She went into the witness box and told the whole story. On Friday 11 January, 1974, the jury convicted G. Daniel Walker of first-degree murder and he was sentenced to life imprisonment.

Later Hope wrote to Walker in prison and has since been to see him.

Jean-Pierre Vaquier was a forty-five-year-old Frenchman who poisoned his mistress's husband with strychnine at the Blue Anchor Hotel, Byfleet, in Surrey. But his vanity led him to talk to newspaper reporters. His photograph was published and recognized by the chemist from whom he had bought the poison. He was tried for murder at Guildford Assizes in July 1924, convicted, and hanged at Wandsworth prison on 12 August.

William Herbert Wallace   This was one of the strangest murder cases ever. The murder reads like a detective story and there have been some twenty books written about it. Raymond Chandler, one of the American 'hard-boiled' school of crime fiction writers, called it the 'Impossible Murder'. There was an incredible trial and an aftermath which made legal history.

The story began on 19 January 1931, when William Wallace, a fifty-two-year-old Prudential Insurance agent, was playing at the Central Chess Club in Liverpool. He received a message, which had been telephoned earlier, to go to an address in Menlove Gardens East at 7.30 the following night to conduct some insurance business.

Wallace made the journey the following evening, but found the address was a false one and returned home to find his wife, Julia, battered to death in the front room of their small terraced house and some money missing from a cash box.

He was arrested by the police and went for trial in April 1931 in Liverpool Crown Court. The prosecution case, put by Edward Hemmerde KC, was that Wallace had set up the trip to Menlove Gardens as an alibi and had killed his wife first. To explain why he wasn't drenched in blood afterwards Hemmerde suggested that he had first undressed, but worn his mackintosh, which was subsequently found beneath the body.

The timings were crucial. Wallace had boarded a tram at just after seven o'clock and was seen by the conductor and an inspector. He claimed to have left home at 6.45. A milk boy who had called at the house reported that he had seen Mrs Wallace at 6.45, but afterwards said it had been 6.30 when he had seen her. This would have left just enough time for the insurance agent to have killed his wife before departing.

Mr Justice Wright summed up in Wallace's favour, pointing out that there was as much evidence for him as against him, but the insurance man made a poor impression in the witness box, coming across as cold and unemotional and just the sort of man to set up an intricate murder plot. The jury took only an hour to bring in a verdict of guilty. Wallace was sentenced to death.

But the appeal hearing before the Lord Chief Justice provided a surprise. The judges were of the opinion, in a decision which had never before been reached by appeal judges, that the case against Wallace 'was not proved with that certainty which is necessary in order to justify a verdict of guilty'. The conviction was therefore quashed. William Wallace was released, but he was a broken man and died soon after, in February 1932.

In 1966 Jonathan Goodman published a book, *The Killing*

of Julia Wallace, in which he reinvestigated the case and made a suggestion that another man had killed Mrs Wallace. However, he couldn't name him because the man was still alive.

On the fiftieth anniversary of the murder, in 1981, Liverpool's independent radio station decided to make a programme about it, and the producer, Roger Wilkes, appealed for anyone who remembered the case to get in touch with him. John Parkes came forward to say that late on the night of the murder he had been working at a local garage when a motorist came in, whom Parkes knew quite well, and asked him to wash his car inside and out. Inside he found a bloodstained glove. The man snatched it away saying that if the police found it he would hang. Parkes said that the motorist's name was Gordon Parry – the same man that Goodman would have named in his book. Parry was so named by Goodman and Wilkes in 1981, for he had died in 1980.

When William Wallace was first interviewed by the police after the murder they asked him if he could think of any enemy his wife might have had or anyone who might have known about him keeping insurance takings at the house. He thought long and hard and came up with a young man who had worked for him at the Prudential, but had been asked to resign for not handing in insurance premiums he had collected. The young man's name was Gordon Parry.

Simone Weber Simone Weber's trial for double murder opened in Nancy, north-east France, in January 1991. The sixty-year-old woman looked like everybody's favourite aunt; buxom, warm and cuddly. Yet she was accused of poisoning an old man for his house and savings, murdering her lover and cutting up his body with a power saw.

When Bernard Hettier disappeared in June 1985, his family and his current mistress immediately suspected Simone Weber. The two had had a stormy relationship for nearly four years, living together part of the time, but having many rows because of Bernard's associations with other women. They still met frequently, Weber often waiting outside the factory where he worked. But Hettier had told various people that he thought she was trying to poison him.

The police found that his car and some personal papers were missing and someone – it turned out to be Weber's son-in-law – phoned Hettier's mistress to say that he would not be able to meet her the next day. Simone Weber's phone was tapped and eventually a garage she was renting under a false name was broken into and the police discovered Hettier's car. In Weber's apartment were found his identity card and car keys and in another apartment belonging to her sister the police uncovered an assortment of guns. In one of her cars was a high-powered circular saw which she had rented the day before Hettier disappeared and which she had since reported stolen.

Simone was arrested in November 1985 and charged with voluntary homicide, theft and illegal possession of firearms. In February of the following year, with Simone still in custody and the examining magistrate desperately seeking evidence to hold her, he ordered the exhumation of the body of Marcel Fixard, an eighty-year-old ex-army officer with whom Weber had had an affair some years before. Subsequently, it was discovered that she had hired a retired actor to impersonate Fixard and they had been married in Strasbourg in April 1980. They had also put false signatures on a deed of sale for Fixard's house and a will making Weber sole beneficiary. Nine days after this she used a forged prescription to purchase digitalis, a drug which in large doses can simulate a heart attack. Fixard duly had a heart attack and died three weeks after the 'wedding'. But the autopsy on Fixard's exhumed body proved nothing, because digitalis very soon becomes undetectable in the body.

Soon after the exhumation, a suitcase which was proved to have belonged to Hettier was found in the River Marne. It contained a torso from which the arms, legs and head had been removed, so that the body could not be proved conclusively to be Hettier's.

It took the examining magistrate five years to bring Simone Weber to trial and all this time she was held in custody, each of her twenty-one applications for release being turned down. It was the longest anyone had been held in France before trial in modern times.

The case against Simone Weber rested on circumstantial evidence and the trial was one of the most bitter in living memory. Weber's estranged husband testified to her jealousy and possessiveness and said she was an adept liar, as did one of her sisters. She replied by roundly abusing them.

Although the circular saw had been scrupulously cleaned, and the blade was never found, forensic examination showed traces of human tissue upon it. But probably the most crucial evidence came from an elderly lady and her husband who had the downstairs flat, below the one Weber occupied. They said that on the night Hettier disappeared they heard a continuous droning noise from above, like a vacuum cleaner. Early the next morning Weber was seen carrying a great many plastic bags down to her car. She spent the next few days thoroughly cleaning the flat, but one day the neighbour saw a plastic bag in the garden and inside was a collection of bloodstained towelling.

The jury judged her not guilty of the murder of Marcel Fixard, but guilty of the murder of Bernard Hettier, although the jury found extenuating circumstances. She was sentenced to twenty years imprisonment.

Another Frenchwoman who killed her lover was twenty-six-year-old Pauline Dubuisson, a Parisian medical student who, in March 1951, shot Félix Bailly because he had thrown her over for another. The jury had difficulty accepting it as a *crime passionel*, since eighteen months had elapsed between when they parted and when she shot him. They found her guilty of murder without premeditation and she was given penal servitude for life.

Ruth Ellis was not so lucky. The twenty-eight-year-old nightclub manageress shot her lover, racing driver David Blakely, outside the Magdala Tavern in North London in April 1955. English juries at the time were not asked to consider the possibility of a crime of passion and Ruth Ellis was convicted of murder and sentenced to death. She was the last woman to be hanged in Britain.

Tracey Wigginton, Lisa Ptaschinski, Kim Jervis and Tracey Waugh   On the night of 18 October 1989, four young women met at a flat belonging to one of them in a suburb of Brisbane, Queensland, Australia, to plan a murder.

Tracey Wigginton was the leader. At twenty-four she was a tall, muscular woman and weighed seventeen stones. A committed lesbian, she was heavily into occultism and devil worship. Lisa Ptaschinski, the same age, was almost as big, but she was a very disturbed woman who had been in Brisbane Hospital eighty-two times in five years for conditions ranging from heroin overdose to eating razorblades and other suicide attempts. She was very much in love with Tracey Wigginton.

Kim Jervis, whose flat they were in, was also interested in the occult; her walls were hung with magic symbols and in her fireplace was a gravestone she had stolen from a cemetery. Tracey Waugh, perhaps the most conventional of the four, was Kim's lover, but was heavily influenced by Wigginton as were they all.

At about 11.30 on Friday night, 20 October, they began cruising in Wigginton's car looking for a suitable victim. They came across forty-seven-year-old Edward Baldock, who had been drinking all day and was clinging to a lamp-post. Tracey Wigginton asked him if he wanted a lift home. He readily entered the car.

They drove to Orleigh Park and stopped near the now

deserted South Brisbane Sailing Clubhouse, close to the Brisbane River. Wigginton-asked Baldock if he wanted sex, and she and he walked down to the riverbank and undressed. She had previously told the others that she would kill with her bare hands if necessary, but a short time later she came back to the car saying that Baldock was too strong.

Ptaschinski said she would help and Jervis gave her a knife. Wigginton and Ptaschinski went back to the river, where the man was sitting naked apart from his socks. Ptaschinski said afterwards that she couldn't do anything, but Wigginton grabbed the knife from her and stabbed him repeatedly in the neck until he was dead. They all drove away thinking they had committed the perfect crime.

But when Wigginton had gone back to the others, Baldock, perhaps fearing being robbed, had pushed his wallet out of sight behind one of the doors of the sailing club. He had also found a bank card belonging to Wigginton which had fallen out of her clothes when she undressed and had placed it in one of his shoes.

When his body was discovered the next morning the police quickly located both wallet and bank card, and Tracey Wigginton was soon in custody. She eventually told the whole story and the three other girls were arrested.

In prison Wigginton underwent extensive psychoanalysis, including hypnosis, and two psychiatrists believed that she was suffering from a multiple personality disorder. But the Queensland Mental Health Tribunal ruled that she was legally sane. In January 1991 she went on trial. She pleaded guilty to murder and was sentenced to life imprisonment.

Later the same month Ptaschinski, Jervis and Waugh went on trial together, charged with murder. They had a strange story to tell. After claiming that they were completely under the spell of Wigginton, they said that she was a vampire. She couldn't eat ordinary solid food and could only live by drinking blood she collected from butchers' shops. They testified that the murder had been her idea and that she had stayed behind with the body in order to drink his blood while the others went back to the car.

Tracey Wigginton, curiously, had made no mention of this during her psychiatric examination even though she had admitted to the murder.

It didn't make a great deal of difference to the others. Lisa Ptaschinski was convicted of murder and received a life sentence. Kim Jervis was convicted of the lesser crime of manslaughter and received eighteen years. Tracey Waugh, against whom there was no real evidence, was acquitted.

Another lethal lady was Louisa Merrifield, forty-six, who moved in with her third husband, seventy-one-year-old Alfred, as housekeeper/companion to old Mrs Ricketts in March 1953. She told a friend that she had worked for an old lady who had died and left her a bungalow. When asked who this was she said: 'Well, she's not dead yet, but she soon will be.' Not unnaturally, when Mrs Ricketts did die soon after, suspicions were aroused. An autopsy showed the old lady had died from phosphorus poisoning. The Merrifields, who inherited under the will, were tried for murder. Alfred, who hardly seemed to know what was going on, was acquitted. Louisa was convicted and hanged at Strangeways prison, Manchester, on 18 September 1953.

Wayne B. Williams   This was a controversial trial; some witnesses, it was said, were more interested in the reward money than in justice for the defendant.

In July 1979 two bodies were found by the side of Niskey Lake, near Atlanta, Georgia. They were of boys aged thirteen and fourteen who had disappeared from their homes in predominantly black areas of the city. One had been shot, the other strangled.

By the following July the number of murders had risen to twelve and it seemed as if the serial killer was preying on black children between the ages of seven and fourteen. They were all male, except for one girl who had been tied to a tree, raped and murdered, and her panties stuffed in her mouth.

The black community was in an uproar, convinced that the murders were racially motivated and committed by a white supremacist. The police replied that this was unlikely since a white man would stand out conspicuously in the areas where the children lived. A task force was put together which eventually reached twenty-five police officers. A $100,000 reward was offered and other cash incentives were put up by recording companies and sports and entertainment celebrities.

The killing continued. By March 1981 the death toll had risen to twenty, with older victims now being included. One man of twenty-three was found floating in the Chattahoochee River in April 1981.

On 22 May a police officer stationed near a bridge over the river heard a loud splash, then saw a young man getting into a station wagon. The vehicle was stopped on the other side of the bridge and the driver detained.

He was twenty-three-year-old Wayne B. Williams, a black man who lived with his parents in Atlanta. In the car the police found nylon rope, a pair of gloves and what looked like a bloodstain on the front seat, but they had nothing further with which to hold him and had to let him go.

Two days later the remains of Nathanial Cater, a twenty-seven-year-old homosexual and the twenty-eighth victim, were removed from the river. Williams was arrested and indicted for the murder.

At his trial in January 1982 at Fulton County courthouse, because of the highly controversial nature of the case, Superior Court Judge Clarence Cooper refused to allow the district attorney and the defence attorneys to discuss the proceedings with the press.

The prosecution's submission was highly circumstantial. Witnesses claimed to have seen Williams and Cater leaving a cinema hand-in-hand just before Cater disappeared, and a witness reported that Williams had been friendly with another victim, Jimmy Ray Payne, who was also found in the river. Williams was only charged with the murder of these two.

The bloodstain on the front seat of his vehicle was of the same blood group as Cater, and dog hairs found on the body were said to be identical to those of Williams's dog, a German Shepherd.

Williams was the only child of an elderly couple who were both teachers; they doted on the boy, supplying him with money to start his own radio station, which failed. He was described as a 'media junkie' and a frustrated dreamer and he dabbled in photography and the music business, publishing leaflets offering young black men the opportunity to have a successful musical career under his influence. One who applied was Patrick Rogers, who became another of the killer's victims.

The jury of eight blacks and four whites took under twelve hours to convict Williams of both murders and he was sentenced to two consecutive life terms.

There have been many doubts raised about the verdict, although it was upheld by the Georgia Supreme Court on appeal. But police officers point to the fact that the killings stopped after Wayne Williams was taken into custody and have not resumed since.

Klaus Grabowski was a German child-molester who had been in prison for his offences and had voluntarily accepted castration. However, it seemed to make little difference to his activities and in May 1980, when seven-year-old Anna Bachmeier disappeared, Grabowski was questioned. He confessed that he had strangled her with her tights, but only after she had tried to blackmail him. At his trial in March 1981 it looked as if he might get a light prison sentence, but Anna's mother Marie stood up in court, walked over to the dock and shot him dead with a 5.6mm Beretta pistol. She was sentenced to six years for manslaughter.

Aileen Wuornos On 13 December 1989, a man's body was found in thick woods to the north-west of Daytona Beach, Florida. He had been shot several times with a 0.22 weapon and was subsequently identified as Richard Mallory, a fifty-two-year-old video-shop owner from Clearwater. His car was missing and there were no clues to his death.

The following May two more bodies of white males were found hidden in woods in the northern area of Florida. It was surmised that all three had been murdered during car journeys and their bodies dumped off the roads. This seemed to be confirmed when the driver of a sausage truck disappeared near Ocala and his body was found not far from his abandoned vehicle.

In July a witness near Ocala saw a car take a bend too fast and career off the road into the brush. Two women got out, shouting and swearing, and ran off. The car proved to belong to a white male Christian missionary who had been reported missing. By September, with bodies continuing to be found, the police of several Florida counties held a conference and concluded that a serial killer, or killers, was on the loose, possibly involving two women.

The police had drawings of the women's faces made from eyewitness reports. These were issued to the press and shown on television. Almost immediately suggestions began to come in, and the women were eventually identified as twenty-eight-year-old Tyria Moore and Aileen Wuornos, thirty-three.

Wuornos had a long criminal record, with offences ranging from disorderly conduct, through simple assault, to armed robbery, but Moore had only been arrested once and then the charge had been dropped. Tyria's family lived in Pennsylvania; investigators interviewed them and soon located her.

She claimed to know nothing of the suspected seven murders,

but said that she thought her lesbian lover Aileen might be involved. When it was pointed out that she could be charged with being an accessory in at least one of the crimes she agreed to cooperate.

By this time Wuornos had been arrested near Daytona Beach and lodged in jail. Moore was flown to Daytona, put up in a motel room, and the police tapped phone calls between the two girls, hoping to get incriminating admissions from Wuornos. Being an experienced criminal, she guessed that the police might be listening and made no mistakes. Eventually, realizing that the police could make it difficult for her lover, she confessed, absolving Tyria.

She was tried in January 1992, only for the murder of Richard Mallory, although Judge Blount allowed evidence of the others to be presented. Her video-taped confessions were played to the jury, but her admissions were only partial. She claimed that she'd only killed to avoid being raped, but could not satisfactorily explain why it had been necessary to pump so many bullets into the victims or to steal their belongings.

The jury of seven women and five men took only an hour and a half to bring in a verdict of guilty of first-degree murder, and after the penalty phase of the trial, the same jury took only two hours to recommend death. Judge Blount condemned her to the electric chair. Appeals are pending; and it took the State of Florida ten years to carry out the death penalty on Ted Bundy (*see* p. 41)

BIBLIOGRAPHY

Notable British Trials Series (eighty-three titles), William Hodge & Co Ltd

Famous Trials (sixteen titles), Penguin Books

Old Bailey Trials (seven titles), Jarrolds

Celebrated Trials (six titles), David & Charles

Andrews, Allen, *Intensive Inquiries* (Harrap, 1973)

Bailey, F. Lee, *The Defense Never Rests* (Stein & Day, 1971)

Barthel, Joan, *A Death in California* (Allen Lane, 1982)

Bechhofer Roberts, C. E., *Famous American Trials* (Jarrolds, 1947)

Bennett, Benjamin, *Was Justice Done?* (Howard Timmins, 1975)

Bishop, George, *Witness to Evil* (Nash Publishing, 1971)

Bishop, Jim, *The Murder Trial of Judge Peel* (Simon & Schuster, 1962)

Bisset, Ian, *Trial at Arms* (MacGibbon & Kee, 1957)

Black, David, *Murder At The Met* (Doubleday, 1984)

Bresler, Fenton, *Scales of Justice* (Weidenfeld & Nicolson, 1973)

Brown, Wenzell, *Introduction to Murder* (Andrew Dakers, 1953)

Browne, Douglas G., *Sir Travers Humphreys* (Harrap, 1960)

Browne, Douglas G., and Tullett, E. V., *Bernard Spilsbury* (Harrap, 1951)

Bryson, John, *Evil Angels* (Viking, 1985)

Burn, Gordon, ' . . . *somebody's husband, somebody's son*' (Heinemann, 1984)

Busch, Francis X., *They Escaped the Hangman* (Bobbs-Merrill, 1953)

Casswell, J. D., *A Lance for Liberty* (Harrap, 1961)
  Only Five Were Hanged (Corgi, 1964)
Chaytor, Rod, *Murder with Menaces* (Headline, 1993)
Church, Robert, *More Murder in East Anglia* (Robert Hale, 1990)
Clegg, Eric, *Return Your Verdict* (Angus & Robertson, 1965)
Cole, Peter, and Pringle, Peter, *Can you positively identify this man?* (André Deutsch, 1974)
Conradi, Peter, *The Red Ripper* (True Crime, 1992)
Cooper, William, *Shall We Ever Know?* (Hutchinson, 1971)
Copeland, James, *The Butler* (Granada, 1981)
Davies, Nick, *Murder on Ward Four* (Chatto & Windus, 1993)
deFord, Miriam, *Murderers Sane & Mad* (Abelard-Schuman, 1965)
Devlin, Patrick, *Easing the Passing* (Bodley Head, 1985)
Dillmann, John, *Blood Warning* (G. P. Putnam's Sons, 1989)
Eddowes, Michael, *The Man on Your Conscience* (Cassell, 1955)
Eddy, J. P., *Scarlet and Ermine* (William Kimber, 1960)
Ellis, Anthony, *Prisoner at the Bar* (Heath Cranton, 1934)
Englade, Ken, *Cellar of Horror* (Angus & Robertson, 1989)
  Deadly Lessons (Grafton, 1993)
Evans, Colin, *Killer Doctors* (Michael O'Mara, 1993)
Fido, Martin, *Deadly Jealousy* (Headline, 1993)
  and Skinner, Keith, *The Peasenhall Murder* (Alan Sutton, 1990)
Fox, James, *White Mischief* (Cape, 1982)
Furneaux, Rupert, *Famous Criminal Cases 1* (Allan Wingate, 1954); *3* (Allan Wingate, 1956); *6* (Odhams, 1960)
  Robert Hoolhouse (Stevens, 1960)
  The Medical Murderer (Elek, 1957)
  They Died by a Gun (Herbert Jenkins, 1962)
Ginsburg, Philip, *Poisoned Blood* (Michael O'Mara, 1992)
Goodman, Jonathan, *Murder in High Places* (Headline, 1986)
  The Christmas Murders (Allison & Busby, 1986)

The Country House Murders (Allison & Busby, 1987)

The Killing of Julia Wallace (Harrap, 1969)

The Lady Killers (Piatkus, 1990)

The Pleasures of Murder (Allison & Busby, 1983)

Gratus, Jack, *The Victims* (Hutchinson, 1969)

Greeno, Edward, *War on the Underworld* (John Long, 1960)

Grex, Leo, *Mystery Stranger Than Fiction* (Robert Hale, 1979)

Gribble, Leonard, *Great Manhunters of the Yard* (John Long, 1966)

Murders Most Strange (John Long, 1955)

Stories of Famous Modern Trials (Arthur Barker, 1970)

When Killers Err (John Long, 1962)

Harris, Jean, *Stranger in Two Worlds* (Macdonald, 1986)

Hastings, Macdonald, *The Other Mr Churchill* (Harrap, 1963)

Hatherill, George, *A Detective's Story* (André Deutsch, 1971)

Helpern, Milton, *Autopsy* (Harrap, 1979)

Henderson, Bruce, and Summerlin, Sam, *The Super Sleuths* (Cassell, 1976)

Holden, Anthony, *The St Albans Poisoner* (Panther, 1974)

Holmes, Paul, *The Trials of Dr Coppolino* (New American Library, 1968)

Honeycombe, Gordon, *More Murders of the Black Museum* (Hutchinson, 1993)

House, Jack, *Square Mile of Murder* (Richard Drew, 1984)

Huggett, Renée, and Berry, Paul, *Daughters of Cain* (Allen & Unwin, 1956)

Hyde, H. Montgomery, *Norman Birkett* (Hamish Hamilton, 1964)

Jackson, Robert, *Francis Camps* (Granada, 1983)

Jonas, George, *The Scales of Justice* (CBC Enterprises, 1983)

Jones, Elwyn, *On Trial* (Macdonald & Jane's, 1978)

Jones, Frank, *Murderous Innocents* (Headline, 1994)

Jones, Frank, *Murderous Women* (Headline, 1991)

White-Collar Killers (Headline, 1992)

Jones, Walter, *My Own Case* (Angley, 1966)

Kennedy, Ludovic, *Ten Rillington Place* (Gollancz, 1972)
    Wicked Beyond Belief (Granada, 1980)

Kershaw, Alister, *Murder In France* (Constable, 1955)

Keyes, Edward, *The Michigan Murders* (New English Library, 1977)

Leasor, James, *Who Killed Sir Harry Oakes?* (Mandarin, 1989)

Lefebure, Molly, *Evidence for the Crown* (Heinemann, 1955)

Lefkowitz, Bernard, and Gross, Kenneth, *The Sting of Justice* (Arrow, 1971)

Leyton, Elliott, *Sole Survivor* (Penguin, 1991)

Linklater, Eric, *The Corpse on Clapham Common* (Macmillan, 1971)

Lucas, Norman, *The Laboratory Detectives* (Arthur Barker, 1971)
    The Sex Killers (Star, 1988)
    and Davies, Philip, *The Monster Butler* (Weidenfeld & Nicolson, 1990)

Lustgarten, Edgar, *The Murder and the Trial* (Odhams, 1960)
    Verdict in Dispute (Allan Wingate, 1949)

McGinniss, Joe, *Fatal Vision* (Sphere, 1985)

Marjoribanks, Edward, *The Life of Marshall Hall* (Gollancz, 1936)

Marriner, Brian, *Missing Bodies* (Arrow, 1994)

Massie, Allan, *Ill Met by Gaslight* (Futura, 1987)

Masters, Brian, *The Shrine of Jeffrey Dahmer* (Coronet, 1993)

May, Henry John, *Murder by Consent* (Hutchinson, 1968)

Morland, Nigel, *An International Pattern of Murder* (Ian Henry, 1977)
    Background to Murder (Werner Laurie, 1955)
    Hangman's Clutch (Werner Laurie, 1954)

Mortimer, John, *Famous Trials* (Penguin, 1984)

Muncie, William, *The Crime Pond* (Chambers, 1979)

Noguchi, Thomas T., *Coroner At Large* (Pocket Books, 1985)

Oddie, S. Ingleby, *Inquest* (Hutchinson, 1941)

Odell, Robin, *Exhumation of a Murder* (Harrap, 1975)

O'Donnell, Bernard, *Crimes That Made News* (Burke, 1954)

Packer, Edwin, *The Peasenhall Murder* (Yoxford, 1980)

Park, William, *The Truth About Oscar Slater* (Psychic Press, 1927)

Radin, Edward D., *Headline Crimes of the Year* (Little, Brown, 1952)

Reddy, Tom, *Murder Will Out* (Gill & Macmillan, 1990)

Reuben, William A., *The Mark Fein Case* (Dial, 1967)

Reynolds, Michael, *Dead Ends* (Boxtree, 1992)

Roughead, William, *Classic Crimes* (Pan, 1951)
   The Murderer's Companion (The Readers Club, 1941)

Rowland, John, *Criminal Files* (Arco, 1957)
   Unfit to Plead? (John Long, 1965)

Seth, Ronald, *Petiot* (Hutchinson, 1963)

Simpson, Keith, *Forty Years of Murder* (Harrap, 1978)

Smith, Arthur, *Lord Goddard* (Weidenfeld & Nicolson, 1959)

Smith, Sir Sydney, *Mostly Murder* (Harrap, 1959)

Smith-Hughes, Jack, *Eight Studies in Justice* (Cassell, 1953)

Symons, Julian, *A Reasonable Doubt* (Cresset, 1960)

Taylor, Bernard, and Knight, Stephen, *Perfect Murder* (Grafton, 1987)

Tibballs, Geoff, *The Contract Killers* (Boxtree, 1993)

Thomas, Donald, *Dead Giveaway* (Michael O'Mara, 1993)

Thomas, Mark, *Every Mother's Nightmare* (Pan, 1993)

Thompson, Thomas, *Blood and Money* (New English Library, 1978)

Thorwald, Jürgen, *Crime and Science* (Harcourt, Brace & World, 1967)
   Dead Men Tell Tales (Thames and Hudson, 1966)
   Proof of Poison (Thames and Hudson, 1966)
   The Marks of Cain (Thames and Hudson, 1965)

Thurlow, David, *The Norfolk Nightmare* (Robert Hale, 1991)

Tullett, Tom, *Portrait of a Bad Man* (Evans, 1956)

Valentine, Steven, *The Black Panther Story* (New English Library, 1976)

Vincent, Adrian, *Fatal Passions* (Warner, 1992)

Walls, Dr H. J., *Expert Witness* (John Long, 1972)

Wambaugh, Joseph, *Echoes in the Darkness* (Bantam, 1987)

Webb, Duncan, *Dead Line for Crime* (Frederick Muller, 1955)

Wensley, Frederick, *Detective Days* (Cassell, 1931)

Wild, Rowland, *The Jury Retires* (Robert Hale, 1937)

Wilkes, Roger, *Wallace* (Bodley Head, 1984)

Williams, Emlyn, *Beyond Belief* (Hamish Hamilton, 1967)

Williams, John, *Hume: Portrait of a Double Murderer* (Heinemann, 1960)

Wilson, John Gray, *Not Proven* (Secker & Warburg, 1960)

Wilson, Patrick, *Murderess* (Michael Joseph, 1971)

Wilson, Robert, *Devil's Disciples* (Javelin Books, 1986)

Woffinden, Bob, *Miscarriages of Justice* (Hodder & Stoughton, 1987)

Wolf, Marvin J., and Mader, Katherine, *Fallen Angels* (Ballantine Books, 1986)

Wolfe, Sebastian, *Kiss and Kill* (Xanadu, 1990)

Wright, William, *The Von Bülow Affair* (Arlington Books, 1983)

Wynn, Douglas, *Blind Justice?* (Robert Hale, 1990)

Yallop, David, *Beyond Reasonable Doubt?* (Hodder & Stoughton, 1978)

Booksellers specializing in second-hand, and occasionally new, true crime books

Clifford Elmer Books, 8 Balmoral Avenue, Cheadle Hulme, Cheadle, Cheshire SK8 5EQ, 0161 485 7064

Grey House Books, 60 Portobello Road, London W11 3DL, 0171 221 0269

Jeremy J. Kirker, 7 Allingham Court, Haverstock Hill, Hampstead, London NW3 2AH, 0171 794 6803

Onyx Books, Spring Cottage, The Batch, Hill Road, Sandford, Bristol BS19 5RH, 01934 822781

INDEX

All Pan Books are available at your local bookshop or newsagent, or can be ordered direct from the publisher. Indicate the number of copies required and fill in the form below.

Send to: Macmillan General Books C.S.
             Book Service By Post
             PO Box 29, Douglas I-O-M
             IM99 1BQ

or phone: 01624 675137, quoting title, author and credit card number.

or fax: 01624 670923, quoting title, author, and credit card number.

or Internet: http://www.bookpost.co.uk

Please enclose a remittance* to the value of the cover price plus 75 pence per book for post and packing. Overseas customers please allow £1.00 per copy for post and packing.

*Payment may be made in sterling by UK personal cheque, Eurocheque, postal order, sterling draft or international money order, made payable to Book Service By Post.

Alternatively by Access/Visa/MasterCard

Card No.   ☐☐☐☐☐☐☐☐☐☐☐☐☐☐☐☐☐☐☐☐

Expiry Date ☐☐☐☐☐☐☐☐☐☐☐☐☐☐☐☐.☐☐

Signature _____

Applicable only in the UK and BFPO addresses.

While every effort is made to keep prices low, it is sometimes necessary to increase prices at short notice. Pan Books reserve the right to show on covers and charge new retail prices which may differ from those advertised in the text or elsewhere.

NAME AND ADDRESS IN BLOCK CAPITAL LETTERS PLEASE

Name _____

Address _____

_____

_____

_____

8/95

Please allow 28 days for delivery.
Please tick box if you do not wish to receive any additional information. ☐